From Promise to Performance

From Promise to Performance

A Journey of Transformation
at SmithKline Beecham

ROBERT P. BAUMAN
PETER JACKSON
JOANNE T. LAWRENCE

HARVARD BUSINESS SCHOOL PRESS

BOSTON, MASSACHUSETTS

Copyright © 1997 by the President and Fellows of Harvard College
All rights reserved
Printed in the United States of America
01 00 99 98 97 5 4 3 2

Library of Congress Cataloging-in-Publication Data

Bauman, Robert P. (Robert Patten)
    From promise to performance : a journey of transformation at
SmithKline Beecham / Robert P. Bauman, Peter Jackson, and
Joanne T. Lawrence.
        p.   cm.
    Includes index.
    References: SmithKline Beecham Pharmaceuticals Management.
    ISBN 0-87584-634-3 (alk. paper)
    1. Pharmaceutical industry—Great Britain—Management.
    2. Pharmaceutical industry—United States—Management.
    I. Jackson, Peter   II. Lawrence, Joanne T.   III. Title.
    HD9667.9.S64B38   1997
    338.7'616151'0973—dc20   96-10892
                                                          CIP

The paper used in this publication meets the requirements of the
American National Standard for Permanence of Paper for Printed
Library Materials Z39.49-1984

Note: Throughout this book, financial figures are provided in both
pounds sterling and U.S. dollars. As a U.K. company, SmithKline
Beecham reports its accounts in pounds sterling but also translates
these amounts into U.S. dollars for the convenience of its U.S. shareholders. The dollar amounts throughout this book have been translated at the exchange rate used by SB for that particular year.

We must recognize that change is a continuous journey and not a destination . . . no decision is perpetual and there is no "right" way of doing things that cannot be improved.

—Excerpt from the operating philosophy of
Beecham
April 1988

Contents

Acknowledgments

THIS IS A STORY THAT HAS literally involved thousands of people, each of whom has had a role in developing its plot and influencing the outcome. But in the interest of making a complex story simple, we have had to keep references in the text to a minimum. Therefore, we take this opportunity to recognize the contribution of all these individuals, as well as a few in particular, some of whom are external to the company.

The single greatest acknowledgment must first be given to the chairman and cofounder of SmithKline Beecham (SB), Henry Wendt. Henry first encouraged SmithKline Beckman (SKB) to endorse the merger and then, throughout the entire period, led the SmithKline Beecham board to support the executive management with vision, dedication, and enthusiasm. From the very beginning, and especially during the critical early phases, Henry demonstrated an unswerving commitment to building SB as a "new and better" company. No one worked harder than he in pursuit of that aspiration.

Much of what was achieved also would not have been possible without the ongoing support and encouragement of the nonexecutive members of the board. The board members today epitomize in experience, attitude, and approach the highest possible standards in the company and the global, world-class aspirations of SB.

Because this is a management book, it is written from the perspective of those at the top of the organization. In referring to the Executive Management Committee (EMC) as a collective group, the term fails to capture the contributions made by each individual as a result of his unique personality, highly professional experience, and keen intellect. Furthermore, it does not reflect the fact that between 1986 and 1993 there were actually three EMCs: the Beecham Group EMC, the merger-created EMC, and the EMC that has evolved into today's Corporate Management Team (CMT), led by chief executive Jan Leschly. From the time that Jan joined SB in 1990, he actively participated in shaping the concepts that defined SB's new culture and worked energetically to develop and implement the management system that became the *Simply Better Way*. Under his leadership, the CMT has raised SB to a higher standard of excellence and level of performance than many would have believed possible in 1989.

The EMC alone, however, could never have reached 52,000 people. So we especially honor all the managers who played such a pivotal role in helping this story unfold. Despite times of enormous uncertainty and personal feelings of substantial skepticism (sometimes bordering on absolute disbelief), their willingness to give new management ideas a try helped break new ground. It was their collective energy and effort that sustained the momentum needed to build SB. Without the strong foundation they established, SB would not be the viable global competitor it is today.

Of this management, there were a number of corporate staff who deserve special mention for their leadership efforts throughout the journey. Too many to mention, these individuals devoted their full-time energy to the development and management of the human resource, communication, and finance systems that were essential to supporting and progressing this change effort.

In the end, realizing the Promise of SmithKline Beecham depends on every employee, all working together in pursuit of a common goal. And so we especially want to recognize the 52,000 employees of SmithKline Beecham all around the world, those past and those present, who every day, in everything they do, are striving to make SB a consistently high-performing winner.

Complementing these very strong internal heroes were a number of advisers from ouside SB. Selected soon after the merger decision, Simon Robertson (now chairman, Kleinwort Benson) and Robert Norbury (chairman, Investment Banking, NatWest Markets) were each hired on behalf of Beecham. Both were essential in helping to structure and sell the complex transatlantic merger of equals to the critical financial communities, particularly in the United Kingdom.

As the tranformation continued, there were several consultants with whom we worked side by side, and whose efforts on SB's behalf we acknowledge with thanks. The first was McKinsey & Co., led by then-partner Chuck Farr (now vice chairman, American Express Company). Chuck, with Jon Duane (formerly of McKinsey's London office, now of San Francisco) and others from McKinsey's global network were very influential in helping first to integrate the two former companies and then to move SB forward toward becoming The *Simply Better* Healthcare Company.

Our search for a tested model for cultural change led us to Professor W. Warner Burke of Columbia University, New York. Throughout the entire period, whenever the EMC found itself distracted by obstacles that were preventing the team from working as a team, it was Warner who would help to facilitate our differences, enabling the group to continue to move forward. Finally, as the executive team tried to define the characteristics of a world-class company, it was Colin Fox and Thom McDade, managing directors of Deltapoint Consulting Group, who offered great insights and assistance in the company's learning about continuous improvement and managing by process.

Each of these individuals, together with their own teams of excellent support people, deserve much greater credit than the text illustrates.

We owe our thanks to Dana Hyde, whose careful and diligent research efforts are reflected in the SB Case Study at INSEAD. We also thank Marjorie Williams at Harvard Business School Press, who so skillfully saw us through publication, and express our deepest appreciation to Professor Chris Argyris (James Bryant Conant Professor of Education and Organizational Behavior, Harvard University), whose willingness to constantly review our work with both open and honest feedback as his only priority we came to value greatly.

Finally, we would like to thank our families and friends, all of whom have exhibited enormous patience with us. Not only did they live once through all the events described herein; they had to live through them all again as we tried to recapture on paper what professionally was such an extraordinary experience.

From Promise to Performance

Why This Book?

WE LIVE IN PARADOXICAL times. We have expanding markets, but shrinking industries; on-line information networks, but communication failures; growing developmental needs, but limited resources. The result is a world fraught with competition, where innovation, speed, productivity, and quality are simultaneously important. Those who study business say this is a revolution of major proportions, that business and management are being redefined for the next century. Different alternatives—from the virtual corporation, to the network of alliances, to federations over corporations—have all been suggested.

Clearly, not every company will make the transition successfully. Those that do will be those that recognize how, as the environment has evolved, so too have the goalposts for defining success. They will be the ones that consistently strive to be the best in their industries—for only by being their industry's best can they be assured of the customers, employees, and resources necessary for continued growth. By definition, there can be only one "best" in a given industry or market. The race to be that one is relentless.

As companies strive to move from the middle of the pack to their industry's top tier, many will have to undergo major change in the search for true competitive advantage. This is change defined in its very broadest context: the complete transformation of a company into one that is different in order to pursue a newly defined strategic direction. It is all-encompassing change, addressing every aspect of the organization: business strategy, organizational structure, employee behavior, and management systems. Furthermore, our definition does not limit transformation to that of a one-time change; it includes evoking within a company the ability to keep on changing—to *sustain* change.

In 1986 one of the United Kingdom's major diversified consumer-oriented companies, Beecham Group, identified the need for change. First it changed its leadership, then it changed its business strategy. Those two decisions led Beecham—then ranked twenty-third in world pharmaceuticals—to U.S.-based SmithKline Beckman (SKB), which at the time ranked ninth in world pharmaceuticals. The two came together in 1989 to create SmithKline Beecham (SB), an integrated healthcare company.

The rationale for the initiative was strategic and some would say visionary, as both companies sought to prepare themselves for what they viewed as inevitable changes in the global healthcare industry. Merging their resources, particularly in the hallowed areas of research and development and sales and marketing, was to achieve a competitive advantage in an increasingly global market with growing price consciousness and regulatory control.

There were a number of unique characteristics about the SKB/Beecham merger at the time. It was:

- ❖ the first of what later became a string of consolidations in the pharmaceuticals industry in the 1990s
- ❖ the first to deliberately come together around a vision of "integrated healthcare"
- ❖ at the time the largest transatlantic equity swap in business history
- ❖ a hitch-free approval process, despite the financial and legal regulatory systems of two countries
- ❖ one of the few transactions to be promoted and, more important, actually executed as a true "merger of equals"

In 1989 comments by the press and analysts could be summarized in one analyst's comment: "We question . . . whether the enlarged group will be able to match the growth rates of its leading industry competitors."[1]

By 1994 SmithKline Beecham ranked fifth in pharmaceuticals and second in healthcare. In less than five years, its revenues from continuing operations had grown more than 40 percent, from £4.3/$6.9 billion to £6.1/$9.3 billion, and pre-tax profits had increased by more than 75 percent, from £724 million/$1.17 billion to £1.3/$1.9 billion. Market capitalization had risen more than 70 percent, and totaled £12/$17 billion by December 31, 1994. Under its new management team, it was well on its way on to achieving even greater success.

In 1995, commenting on the 1994 results, the *Financial Times* stated:

> SmithKline Beecham should be pleased with itself. Few drug companies are capable of generating any sales growth in the year their top-selling product loses US patent protection. Yet SB's underlying pharmaceuticals sales expanded 5 per cent. . . . That is partly thanks to SB's marketing skills. . . . SB's skinflint grip on costs is also impressive: selling, general and administrative expenses were static, even though group turnover rose 8 per cent . . . prospects for this refocused organization are excellent, given the strong pipeline of new products and the absence of any significant patent expiries for the rest of the decade. . . .[2]

By most counts, the transformation of SmithKline Beckman and Beecham into SmithKline Beecham, a global healthcare leader, is considered a success. But how did it happen? Conventional wisdom at the time said "mergers never work."[3] A look at the historical performance of previous mergers tended to confirm this.

The reasons mergers don't work are multiple. First is the difficulty coming to terms around shareholder value; it is often very difficult to make assets equal. Then comes the difficulty selling it: why would shareholders accept equal value if they could realize a premium by allowing either company to be acquired?

Next is the problem of delivering the near-term financial and business promises. Frequently during integration one company ends up taking over the other: part of the organization becomes demotivated, and the goals set for the newly combined entity are never achieved.

Most important, many mergers don't work because completion of the merger and structural integration is seen as an end, rather than a beginning. Managers fail to see the merger as simply the first step in a long journey toward building for the future. When one company culture is allowed to take over, it often means that the very culture that led to the need for change is allowed to perpetuate. Without change in the culture or in the way the company works, the problems that sparked the merger remain. Nothing has really changed; just the size of the company.

By addressing each of these issues, SB avoided many of the common pitfalls and came up with positive results. There is no doubt that today's SmithKline Beecham is a company different from either of its predecessors.

As more companies attempt to transform themselves to compete in an ever changing global environment, interest has grown in the story of SmithKline Beecham and what began as a cross-border merger of equals but became a complete transformation.

STRATEGY-DRIVEN CHANGE VERSUS CHANGE-ORIENTED STRATEGY

In most cases companies start with business strategy, then decide how and what they need to do or change to achieve it. The strategy is the goal, the change the means. We have a different premise: for a company to continuously win, we believe it must see change itself as an end: that is, an organization must see the ability for continuous self-renewal as integral to its primary strategy.

This means creating an organization where employee behavior not only serves as one of the key drivers of today's business strategy, but also continuously shapes and redefines that strategy in ways that allow the organization to meet today's challenges and anticipate tomorrow's changes.

It is this premise that lies at the heart of the book:

❖ Integral to becoming and staying the best is having the ability within the organization to sustain change around a core set of values.
❖ The capacity to change is not a singular means to success; business strategy must be logical and sound, and products and services must be of value. Having the ability to change but lacking the right business components will not guarantee success.
❖ It is our belief, however, that no matter how sound the strategy and product offering, an organization that lacks the capacity for change *cannot* become and remain the best over the long term.

This book describes how, having defined a logical business strategy, a company can create an organizational culture that supports that strategy's realization. It illustrates the processes and systems by which an organization can sustain an environment that embraces change. Only by creating and integrating this capability to change will an organization achieve its ultimate goal: that of becoming and remaining the best.

BECOMING THE BEST

The phrase "to be the best" is expressed easily and altogether too often. Not until they start to consider the dimensions of "best" do members of an organization realize how difficult and demanding the challenge is. According to various investor and media surveys, including *Fortune* magazine's annual ranking of most admired companies, the "best" organizations are better than their competitors in ten key areas:

- ❖ Ability to add value
- ❖ Quality of management
- ❖ Ability to attract and keep top talent
- ❖ Quality of products, services, client relationships
- ❖ Record of innovation
- ❖ Sound financial performance
- ❖ Effective use of assets
- ❖ Anticipatory competitive strategy
- ❖ Leading market share
- ❖ Corporate citizenship

Many have embarked on the journey toward excellence only to abandon it. Statistics suggest that seven out of ten organizational efforts to implement change programs aimed at becoming the "best" fail. Among numerous reasons cited are the following:

- ❖ Inconsistent senior management
- ❖ Unclear vision; inarticulate, unrealistic goals
- ❖ Unaligned management and reward systems
- ❖ Little if any integration with the ongoing businesses
- ❖ Lack of widespread involvement
- ❖ Unsustainable momentum

Firms that have been successful at introducing and sustaining change and continuously maintaining a rating as their industry's best are few. To just a handful around the world would we give this accolade. Whereas many companies can copy successful strategies, few can emulate an organization's internal capacity for change. Think about those that are capable of reinventing themselves, defining whole new industries, or delivering year after year of increased performance. Companies such as 3M, Procter & Gamble, Motorola, and General Electric stand out as unique as much for their business achievements as for their organizational culture. As their performance shows, they have achieved this capacity for change, making it a truly sustainable competitive advantage.[4]

Why do more companies not come to mind? We think it is because achieving this culture of continuous renewal takes time, planning, and hard work—far more than most managers realize when they begin.

HINDSIGHT

Before we begin the story of SmithKline Beecham, we want to share with you the way we have thought about the events that occurred during the seven-year period this book covers. As this is a management book, the story it tells is meant to illustrate how to implement change, rather than to relate the history of a business. Events and individuals included have been selected based on how well they support some key managerial concepts (outlined in the next chapter) and are focused very much on the leadership and organizational issues that lie at the heart of any transformation effort. Where business issues are raised, they serve more to remind the reader that transformation occurs against backgrounds of enormous complexity; not only is management implementing change initiatives, they are also continuing to run the business.

We begin by assuming there exists a sound business strategy and product; the organizational culture is developed to support the business, not replace it. In fact, this is what makes successful change so difficult. It must be managed in parallel with the demanding day-to-day decision taking required to run the business effectively.

The story begins with Beecham's need to define a logical, effective new business strategy. But the effort to realize that strategy's full potential came to depend not just on the traditional functions of strategic planning and finance, but more on the alliance of those functions with human resources and communications. It was this unique combination of functions not normally considered in the mainstream that played a crucial role in helping to redefine the former two companies into a single viable global competitor.

The SmithKline Beecham transformation story is about strategic leadership—the ability of leaders throughout the organization to tap every human and capital resource and system available in the near term, consciously and systematically reshaping and redefining the resources to align them with winning for the long term. It reflects the personal perspective of the then chief executive and two managers in functions they believed were critical to support the company's goals: human resources and communications.

The authors do not pretend to provide definitive answers to what is an enormously complex management issue. This book is not a prescriptive "how to," nor is it meant to debunk or to reinforce any of the literature that came before or will come after it. It is more the product of remembering how difficult we found our task and how much we wished for a picture of what to expect. Through telling the story and sharing our first-hand learnings, we hope to help those facing a similar challenge: to create something brand new that can compete effectively and succeed over a sustained period of time.

That is the spirit in which this book is written. We offer our learnings as a guidepost, encouraging others to do as we did. Please take these ideas, augment them, adapt them, and move them forward, defining a new best way—the one that is right for your organization. For in the end, to be true to itself, while the principles of change may remain constant, the process of *how* to change should keep evolving, reaching a new and higher level of attainment each time.

CHAPTER ONE

Introducing the Five Requisites

WHEN INDIVIDUALS SEEK personal change in pursuit of a higher goal, it often means they must change a particular mindset, learn from others about how they succeeded, or acquire some new skills. We believe that organizations, like individuals, need certain attitudes and skills in place if they are to succeed.

As we reflected on our own professional experience and learnings through the years against the background of our experience first at Beecham, then at SmithKline Beecham, we identified five characteristics that we believe are essential for instilling the capacity for change within an organization.

Having christened them the "Five Requisites," we believe they are essential to a company becoming and staying the best and that any organization capable of sustaining change will have, at a minimum, these five characteristics embedded in its culture. We offer them not as "one best way," but as guidelines based on practical experience:

❖ A winning attitude
❖ The organization as hero
❖ Cumulative learning
❖ Strategic communication
❖ Aligned behavior and strategy

In this chapter, we describe the Five Requisites and explain why they are important. They will be illustrated throughout the story that follows and summarized at the end of each chapter. We introduce them now because we believe that our story, however interesting in itself, will be more meaningful when the reader sees these principles in action.

A WINNING ATTITUDE

At the heart of every successful organization must be a vision of "winning" and an unquenchable desire to keep on winning. To create a winning attitude, an organization must first identify its ultimate purpose (*why* does it want to win?) and the values through which it will achieve this purpose (*how* does it want to win?).

Purpose and values are meaningless without quantification: what would it look like if we achieved that vision or behaved according to those values? Purpose is inspirational, self-motivating, and, most important, self-sustaining. Having a clearly defined purpose provides meaning, a reason to succeed that makes the organization want to undertake the task.

Purpose is inspirational and long lasting. It differs from strategic intent, a more quantifiable and aspirational goal that usually has a defined timeframe. Strategic intent is a "sizeable stretch goal."[1] It must be credible and realistic, yet at the same time it must stretch the organization's capabilities and imagination. If the balance is not struck correctly, strategic intent will be viewed either with frustration (too big a leap) or with ridicule ("who are they kidding?"). Ideally, an organization has both: purpose to provide long-term direction, strategic intent to assess its progress along the way.

Both purpose and strategic intent are important, direction setting phrases that help to focus an organization's attention. But in and of themselves, they are not enough to create a winning attitude. A winning attitude is created through the collective way employees behave, and is imbedded within the values which underlie and shape an organization's environment.

Whereas many companies may have similar statements of purpose, or may articulate the same values, how these values influence employee behavior can become *the* characteristic that distinguishes a company from its competition.

The values organizations choose to emphasize should be directly derived from their strategy, not from a separate exercise. The link between what an organization plans to do to reach its goal and the behaviors it requires on a day-to-day basis should be clearly stated in a way which allows for ongoing measurement. Employees need to understand what is expected of them, and how their daily behavior will actually contribute to their collective success.

The identification and implementation of these values becomes all important: they provide organizational focus. If the values do not lead to the behavior required to deliver the strategic goals, they may be self-defeating by dissipating organizational energy.

To influence corporatewide behavior, it is necessary to drive the values deep into the organization, where their pursuit and practice by every employee will ultimately determine whether or not the company develops the will to win.

Together with purpose, values establish a single-mindedness that focuses and aligns an organization's efforts. The pursuit of purpose and values becomes a self-motivating force for continuous growth.

Those who have a winning attitude are constantly dissatisfied with current performance. This dissatisfaction forces continual change: for every target met, a new and higher one is set. A winning attitude imbues the organization with a sense of urgency and competitive spirit that is ongoing. The targets set are against its own performance as well as the performance of others outside.

An organization knows it has won when it has achieved the tangible signs/goals it has set—be they internal or external—and that achievement is recognized for taking the organization one step further along the journey. But it cannot rest or grow too complacent; the challenge then becomes retaining its position as "the best."

Most important, the organization dedicated to winning consists of individuals who seek to succeed as part of something bigger than themselves; the whole becomes more important than its parts. Like all true champions, the star performer knows when to pass to another player if it means the team can score.

This commitment to winning is radically different from responding to a crisis, which often is the driving force behind strategic initiatives and transformation efforts. Responding to a crisis may mean winning in the short term, but developing a winning mentality means ensuring growth over the long term.

Along the journey there is a need for small wins, some way of knowing whether the organization is on the right road. *Milestones* mark progress against achievement of the purpose and provide a point of focus for getting things done. We define milestones as significant events or key targets intended to keep driving everyone forward, a means of helping an organization keep score as it pursues its goal to be industry leader. Within transformation, milestones help progress the change effort and at the same time provide a means to pace the activities and sustain momentum. Milestones can be key events as big as a merger approval or as small as the date of a management conference. They can be the specific targets set to measure business and financial progress and monitor whether the strategy is on track.

Reaching a milestone provides an opportunity to celebrate and helps reinforce a sense of winning, as the organization sees it is making steady, logical progress in the near term against its ultimate goal. Milestones are important because they can serve to shape the aspiration of the organization at large. They help to define what winning looks and feels like.

The process by which milestones are set can become a critical part of accomplishing them. When the ultimate goal and major milestones are established centrally, but each area is allowed to translate them locally, there will be organizational alignment as well as personal commitment to achieving the common goal. As each milestone is met, individuals and business units see their progress and celebrate their victory, which propels them forward to achieve the next one. Well-defined milestones provide individual motivation even as they sustain organizational momentum, constantly moving the team to a higher playing standard. Time frames become shorter and targets set higher as their confidence to win grows.

To be effective, companywide milestones should be defined in such a way that they are seen as:

❖ worthy of achievement—that is, integral to the ultimate purpose
❖ measurable in quantity and in time
❖ easy to understand and communicate
❖ aspirational but achievable

Without milestones that employees can relate to and influence, an organization can drift off course, never realizing its aspiration, never really winning.

THE ORGANIZATION AS HERO

The best leaders, research shows, are those whose organizations have a collective "we did it ourselves" spirit. Sustainable success cannot be achieved by a single leader; it needs critical mass.

In a winning organization, everyone works together—heart and mind—in pursuit of a higher purpose. Much like heroes who work with both soul and intellect, they commit to a task often beyond themselves to achieve a greater good.

In those companies where the organization is the hero, employees see success as a direct result of their individual and cumulative efforts. Because they help set the goals and define the means of reaching them, they are absolutely committed to achieving those goals. They see the organization's success as a reflection of their personal accomplishment, and the recognition they receive reinforces that belief.

This is not a revolutionary concept: it sounds very much like empowerment. But there is a difference in how we believe the concept should be executed. The organization as hero doesn't mean free fall, with groups of teams doing their own thing. It actually means the opposite: creating a highly disciplined environment in which all major activities are aligned and linked toward achievement of a single purpose. Through a rigorous process, employees are able to contribute significantly to the activities that will accomplish that purpose.

To create this management system, senior management accepts a role different from the one it has played previously, and employees are considered differently from the way they have been in the past.

For example, where senior management has often been viewed as the hero and directly responsible for an organization's success, in our model its principal role is to create the environment in which others can be successful—that is, to ensure that employees do not fail. Where leaders have previously assigned job tasks and responsibilities, now they must create the strategic framework, support systems, and processes that allow employees to use their full emotional and intellectual capabilities to become accountable for winning. The guidelines management provides involve the entire organization from the very beginning. Senior management sets the criteria through which each team can define its strategy, identify its goals, determine milestones and measures, and implement the plan. In short, leaders create a disciplined process aligned with the long-term goal, but those employees on the teams are responsible and accountable for determining all the content. In this way senior management guarantees that the process is consistent with the culture it is trying to create and that the organization's output is aligned with the overall corporate goals, but the implementation plans are the direct result of what individual employees can influence. Senior leadership is all directed toward making sure that the organization is—and, most important, sees itself as being—the hero of its own achievement.

When the organization is the hero, employees are viewed as having a real contribution to make; everyone feels his or her contribution counts and has a direct impact on whether the organization fails or succeeds. All are involved, and each is responsible and accountable for what happens. Their reward and recognition is based on individual performance and collective achievement. There is no "them" and "us"—just "we"—as everyone works together toward achievement of the heroic goal. Based on steady, consistent accomplishment of preset goals, a sense of pride builds within the organization.

Along the way there are heroes of battles, and there are heroes of wars. Each is critical to overall success, and each must be recognized for his or her contribution.

CUMULATIVE LEARNING

Much has been said in recent literature about the importance of ongoing learning in successful organizations. Continuous growth requires continuous learning—at a personal and at an organizational level.

We have adapted this concept slightly: in our view, companies that sustain success have "cumulative learning." They constantly seek new ideas that they augment, adopt, adapt, and integrate into their own existing knowledge bank. They are not trying constantly to replace old with new, but instead are more focused on learning how new concepts can be used to add value to their own ideas. These companies interpret, reshape, and share these new learnings to enrich their own model and in the process make that learning uniquely theirs. Leaders are careful to place these learnings within a consistent framework so that employees don't view new management ideas as one-off programs but as enhancements within their own ever-evolving management system.

These enhancements reflect the successful organization's obsession with continually improving its performance in pursuit of winning. It tries to analyze and understand how it does everything in order to constantly do better. It understands what it knows, as well as what it doesn't, and seeks new ideas to fill the knowledge void. In the winning organization, growth in specialized knowledge and skills is not only encouraged, but actively supported through massive investment in well-defined and carefully directed training and development programs. Skills are not randomly selected but are consistent with what the company has defined as the key behaviors and capabilities required for competitive advantage. Training and development are an integral part of how the company is managed.

In an organization where cumulative learning exists, investment in people to learn relevant skills is seen as a major priority. Employees are urged to use data and analysis in their day-to-day work and to constantly challenge what they do in order to continually improve. Common methods and tools are used to encourage consistent standards and teamwork. They share information as a way of life, are not afraid to test or pilot, and are open to learning in different ways: on the job, from each other, from outsiders, from customers, and from suppliers. Lateral promotions to build breadth and understanding are valued as much as upward ones. Learning actually occurs by **everyone** doing, thereby accelerating movement along the entire organization's experience curve.

STRATEGIC COMMUNICATION

Strategic communication is both content and process. As content, it is about translating and interpreting company strategy into a few clearly stated ideas that are used to create the strategic context or framework for communicating to all stakeholders. This framework creates focus and reduces the danger of meaningless communication, information overload, and diffused organizational energy.

At another level, strategic communication is a well-designed, structured management process that is systematically implemented. It defines a common language and a single voice (with local accents) that is clear and credible to all stakeholders. As a process, it provides a means through which ownership of vision and values is transferred and best practices are shared; learning and innovation occur as individuals engage in continuous dialogue where feedback is fundamental. The ideal is to create a risk-free environment where ideas can be tossed back and forth without fear of reprisal and agreements reached on the basis of mutual respect and trust.

Externally, a systematic process for communicating corporate strategy and expectations is one that seeks stakeholder alignment through greater understanding and appreciation of corporate direction. It also provides a means of external assessment: is the company doing what it said it would do?

The company that uses communication strategically views it more as education and marketing than as straight news. It defines the product (in this case the strategy and culture) and its attributes, establishes key objectives, segments the market, and positions the product in a way that is meaningful and appropriate to the customer. Finally, customers are consulted: Did they buy what management was offering? What did they think of it? How can it be improved?

Each campaign builds on what has gone before and works within the same defined framework to ensure consistency and continuity—both key to creating management credibility and strategic focus.

Essentially, strategic communication helps to build reputation and shareholder value from the inside out. Employees learn how they are expected to behave against the new vision and values and, as importantly, why. As they deliver against these expectations and improve customer satisfaction, company performance rises, and this is recognized by investors. The triangle becomes a reinforcing one: as the company wins, employees are remotivated to keep winning. Communication becomes the link between strategy and the organization required to deliver it; customer satisfaction and investor perception are driven by an employee-driven reality.

ALIGNED BEHAVIOR AND STRATEGY

It is always intriguing to trace how the transformation process begins in a company. Often the initiative springs from business strategy, yet somehow along the way the effort becomes separated from the business. Employees begin to see behavior and culture in one corner, work in another.

We believe a successful organization is one in which *all* organizational activities have been linked in a way that is dedicated to driving ever-higher performance. We call it "hardwiring the soft stuff."

We define hard elements as those that drive *what* a company does—that is, its business strategy—while elements that are soft are those that drive *how* it does it—that is, the organization's values and behaviors. These hard and soft elements work and support one another; they are integrated, managed, and measured to achieve the same goal. Hardwiring means making all those elements that are critical to success measurable, linking day-to-day actions with long-term strategic goals.

To achieve this integrated model, an organization first must decide which key drivers are important to realizing its strategy. Once self-analysis identifies these core behaviors (or whatever elements are decided), rather than being relegated to lucite cubes they are used to drive everything the company does.

Using the behaviors or values tactically as well as strategically can also help eliminate the complaint that normally arises in any transformation effort: "This is great, but it's so time consuming. When can we get back to our real jobs?" Members of the organization begin to understand that behaving in a certain way *is* their job, and that only by aligning *how* they work with *what* they do will they actually enable the business to implement its strategy. They begin to see their everyday work as part of a longer-term plan.

This consistency leads to greater organizational focus as everything is moving in the same direction. For employees, having an entire management system built around the very same behaviors they are supposed to practice is reinforcing and reassuring and encourages greater accountability and responsibility. They know what they are supposed to do, how they are supposed to do it, and where their work fits into the bigger picture. The simplicity and consistency inherent in the framework creates a sense of stability and security. Employees know what is expected of them and that they will be rewarded on the basis of consistent standards.

There is a fairness and integrity built into the management system: goals and expectations are painstakingly clear to everyone, and the same standards are universally applied, without exception. See table 1-1 for a summary of the Five Requisites.

MAPPING OUT THE JOURNEY

In thinking about how the Five Requisites were shaped as the transformation process unfolded, we have organized what occurred into four phases.

Table 1-1. Summary of the Five Requisites

WINNING ATTITUDE
- ❖ Establishes the purpose
- ❖ Identifies the competition
- ❖ Outlines the strategy
- ❖ Determines the milestones

ORGANIZATION AS HERO
- ❖ Employees own and deliver the business outcomes (the what). Management provides support through well-defined processes and systems (the how)
- ❖ Employees see themselves as major contributors to the company's goals
- ❖ Employees work in customer-focused teams, sharing information openly and widely
- ❖ Employees take pride in and celebrate each other's successes

CUMULATIVE LEARNING
- ❖ Continuously studies, evaluates the competition, the industry, and changing business and management trends
- ❖ Learns from each other, previous bests
- ❖ Rather than discarding and replacing existing management practices, adopts, adapts, extrapolates, and reinvents old and new ideas, constantly adding to a personal and organizational knowledge base

STRATEGIC COMMUNICATION
- ❖ Focuses on both content and process and is viewed more as education and marketing than straight news
- ❖ Creates a strategic context through which messages to all stakeholders are aligned with corporate purpose
- ❖ Is viewed as fundamental and integral to realizing strategy, and a key management responsibility
- ❖ Encourages an open environment where new strategies, ideas are shared, building trust and reputation

ALIGNMENT OF BEHAVIOR AND STRATEGY
- ❖ Identifies talents, skills necessary to successfully execute the strategy
- ❖ Designs human resource systems and management processes that develop and link the desired behavior to business achievement
- ❖ Ties day-to-day actions to long-term strategic goals through measures

We present the four phases here to provide the reader with a chronological road map of our journey and a simple way to think about the phases of transformation. (See also figure 1-1.) The chapters provide examples of key milestones which we will share as we go along.

Phase I: Defining a New Strategy

Phase I is all about the changing business environment and redefining strategy, which often establishes the need for change. In Beecham Group's case it meant first changing the management team, then establishing an aspiration to be an integrated healthcare company. That aspiration meant seeking and then selling a "merger of equals."

Phase II: Building a New Structure

Phase II is about defining the structure needed to deliver the strategy and achieve the financial targets. In the new SmithKline Beecham this was the period of combining two businesses and making one company structure from two. Often phase II is the point at which those managing mergers and acquisitions stop, and the full potential of their strategic initiative is never realized.

Phase III: Developing a New Culture

Phase III, defining a new set of values to match the new strategy, is the point at which many would argue that true transformation into a different kind of company begins. In the case of a merger a single structure does not necessarily mean "one company." Structure alone cannot deliver a new strategy: allowing existing cultures to perpetuate can often undermine the new company's success. At SmithKline Beecham this was the time when new Values and Practices intended to deliver the Promise of the new company were defined and introduced to the organization.

Phase IV: Designing an Entire Management System

Phase IV becomes all important, as all the pieces come together to create an entire management system aligned toward achievement of strategic goals. At SmithKline Beecham it was this holistic approach that culminated in the creation of a new management architecture, which became one of the strengths of the new company.

The four phases are not necessarily discrete; some activities from one phase carry over into the next. Neither are the phases complete; they are iterative. We believe that in true transformation the four phases are repeated, and that each is but one loop in an ever-rising spiral toward excellence.

THE STORY

As the story of SB unfolds against the four phases, we will share with the reader how each of the Five Requisites developed during each phase. In explaining how we thought about them, as well as how they were enacted, our hope is that readers will make the Five Requisites part of their own cumulative learning.

To make reference to these lessons as simple as possible, we have summarized them at the end of each chapter according to the Five Requisites. When we reach the final chapter, we will share with those who have joined us on our journey some of our overall learnings about implementing change. We hope that readers will find this first-hand account helpful. Our Epilogue will put the experience in perspective as we reveal how SmithKline Beecham is doing in 1996, ten years after this book begins.

And now to begin the journey . . .

There are four phases to the SmithKline Beecham transformation story. Throughout each phase the Five Requisites are present but emphasis varies.

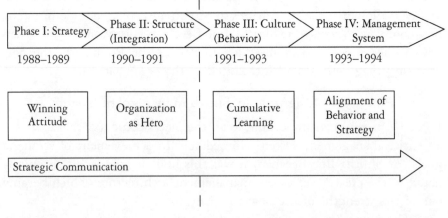

Figure 1-1 *Relating the Four Phases to the Five Requisites*

The Story of Beecham

THE EXCESSIVE 1980S, THEY would call it later: a time of great optimism and exuberance, if not overindulgence. Ronald Reagan and Margaret Thatcher dominated the political scene, privatizations and take-overs were driving the financial markets, and the personal computer was leading to major changes in the workplace. The bulk of the population seemed to be aged thirty-something, and the more affluent ones had been labeled "Yuppies" for their conspicuous consumption of luxury brand goods. Japanese manufacturers were making major inroads in targeted industries and now dominated the markets for electronics and automobiles.

The $130 billion pharmaceutical industry seemed immune to what was going on around it.[1] Above the fray, or so it believed, it operated pretty much the way it always had. This was an industry that prided itself in scientific excellence as a noble pursuit. Its contribution to society was highly rewarded:

❖ Between 1984 and 1986, growth in annual earnings before interest and taxes for the top fifteen pharmaceutical firms was over 18 percent; growth in sales exceeded 15 percent per year.
❖ In 1985 the average operating margin of the world's ten largest pharmaceutical firms neared 30 percent.[2]

The pharmaceutical industry's major determinants of success were research and development, followed by strong marketing. The more successful companies invested heavily in both.

For example, by the mid-1980s the top five pharmaceutical companies were investing an average $300 million (or 10–15 percent of annual sales) in research and development.[3] While new products were supposedly protected from competition by patent laws for up to twenty years after their initial discovery, the reality was that it usually took ten to twelve years for a new medicine to work its way through development and government approval, leaving only eight to ten years' protection, depending on the country. One of the toughest regulators was in the United States—the Federal Drug Administration (FDA). (However, with approximately $45 billion in sales annually, the United States was also the world's largest market for prescription medicines and one of the least affected by government price controls.) By the mid-1980s U.S. product introductions, which had averaged forty-five per year during the 1950s and 1960s, had dropped to twenty-five per year, reflecting both a more stringent regulatory environment (the Thalidomide tragedy occurred in the 1960s) and the high cost of product development.[4] Competitive urgency was down, as most companies in the industry could afford to bask in the glory (and high margins) of just a few products.

It was every company's goal to discover a compound that offered a new solution to an acute illness (such as flu) or a chronic condition (such as stomach ulcers) and be first to launch that medicine globally, enjoying a virtual monopoly until the patent expired or a second generation of the product was introduced. Through aggressive marketing and direct selling, companies would strive to recoup their enormous R&D investment, hoping the new medicines would achieve blockbuster status (more than $500 million annual sales) before losing their patent protection.

As development time and costs continued to rise, the pressure on marketing had grown enormously, and by the mid-1980s many pharmaceutical companies found they were allocating nearly 30 percent of their sales, or some $600 million annually, to marketing. Of that amount, nearly 80 percent was dedicated to reaching the doctor, primarily through expanding sales forces. In the United States, for example, major firms were employing about 1,500 sales representatives.[5] The marketing style of the industry was more product-push than customer-in.

For all these reasons, a number of pharmaceutical companies had grown up around single products or therapies, and by the late 1980s the highly fragmented pharmaceutical industry contained hundreds of companies. Of the $130 billion in worldwide sales of prescription medicines, the top ten firms generated slightly more than 25 percent. Of those, U.S.-based Merck, the industry leader, accounted for 4 percent, with annual sales of nearly $5 billion. Its pretax operating margins were more than the average 30 percent.[6]

The outlook for growth in the pharmaceuticals market was positive: there remained a number of illnesses and diseases to conquer, and populations were increasing in developing countries and among the elderly. The second factor was two-edged: while it meant the market size was growing, it also meant that governments—in many countries the payers of healthcare—were becoming more and more interested in containing costs. Some countries had effected price regulations in the 1960s, and now further steps were being taken to tighten controls. Germany fixed prices for reimbursement at generic price levels, Japan was requiring significant price cuts, and even the United States, one of the freest markets for prescription medicines, was proposing a best-price system as part of its Medicaid/Medicare programs. The high margins that the industry had experienced and that had ensured its continuing ability to fund further research and development were coming under increasing threat.

These factors were influencing the industry in two ways. Over-the-counter (OTC) medicines were gaining in variety and popularity as more patients were encouraged to self-medicate, and the number of generic drug manufacturers was rising. Generic companies produce unbranded medicines similar to branded products on which patents have expired. They sell the off-patent products at prices as low as 20 percent of the patent-product price. Both industries are carefully regulated to ensure continued product safety.

In 1986 the world's largest selling prescription medicine was the ulcer treatment Zantac, with sales of $2 billion. Zantac belonged to Glaxo.

BEECHAM GROUP

One of Glaxo's main U.K. rivals was Beecham Group. Beecham traced its origins to 1842 and was one of the first to use advertising on an extensive scale for its home remedies.

In its early years Beecham produced OTC medicines and gradually expanded into toiletries and health drinks, primarily through acquisition. In the 1940s, with little fanfare, management established the Beecham Research Laboratories to help fund the company's future. This led to the

1959 launch of the world's first semisynthetic penicillin, and by the 1960s Beecham was one of the world's largest sellers of antibiotics.

In the mid-1980s Beecham was a well-known and highly respected blue-chip company in Britain. Its £2.6 billion in annual sales derived almost equally from two major subgroups: consumer products, and prescription and OTC medicines. Within the two subgroups were six business lines (see table 2.1). Beecham's consumer products portfolio included such leading brands as Lucozade energy drink, Ribena blackcurrant fruit drink, and Aquafresh and Macleans toothpastes. Within its toiletries portfolio were Brylcreem and Silvrikin hair products, while cosmetics consisted of such strong European franchises as Yardley, Lancaster, and Jil Sander. Beecham's most important market was the United Kingdom.

By 1985 Beecham's prescription and OTC medicines represented approximately three quarters of Beecham's £335 million trading profit. It offered a broad range of antibiotics and shared with Eli Lilly the rank of the world's largest producer. Amoxil was the most frequently prescribed medicine in the United States, while Augmentin was quickly becoming its fastest growing oral antibiotic. With leading brands such as Sucrets, Nice, Day/Night Nurse, and Beecham Powders, Beecham was the United Kingdom's largest supplier of OTC cold and flu remedies, while market leaders Tums (antacid tablets) and Oxy (acne treatment), added significantly to its OTC position in the United States.

Beecham's scientists had a reputation for "discovering a helluva lot on a shoestring,"[7] and by 1985, despite its meager £88 million annual investment in research and development, there were a large number of new compounds in the development pipeline. Three had great promise: one to aid heart-attack sufferers, another to treat depression, and a third to reduce the nausea associated with chemotherapy. Still, the difficulty

---

Table 2-1. Beecham's Sales Breakdown, March 31, 1986

Consumer products		Prescription and OTC	
Health drinks	} 30	Ethical pharmaceuticals	} 27
Toiletries		Animal health	
Cosmetics	17	Over-the-counter medicines	6

Source: Beecham, Annual Report, 1986–1987, p. 39.

---

was bringing the products to market, and at this point Beecham was hesitant to make the necessary investment, which would have curtailed its earnings growth. The company was generating about £700 million in overall pharmaceutical sales, ranking it a very distant twenty-third in the world.[8]

Overall, its more than 300 different branded products were sold in 130 countries. While it was geographically spread among the United Kingdom/Europe, United States, and Rest of the World, the U.K./Europe segment accounted for more than 51 percent of all its sales and 80 percent of its trading profit in 1985. Beecham employed close to 41,000 people around the globe, more than half of whom were in consumer products.[9]

In 1973 Beecham attempted to expand its pharmaceuticals business and made an unfriendly bid for Glaxo Holdings. The Mergers and Monopolies Commission, fearing such a merger would limit research and development in the United Kingdom, refused to let it go ahead without a detailed referral. The threat of an exhaustive inquiry halted Beecham's efforts.

Some would say later that this is when Beecham started to lose its way. From 1976 onward the company initiated an aggressive diversification strategy, acquiring more beverages, food, cosmetics, and home improvement products. The cost of these acquisitions meant fewer funds were available for pharmaceuticals research and development. As a result of the non-pharmaceutical acquisitions, the number of new prescription medicines actually launched by Beecham by 1985 had gradually declined, and the trading profits contributed by pharmaceuticals had decreased from 55 percent in 1972 to 44 percent in 1985.[10] The new strategy—if it could really be called that—seemed to be taking the company in a direction that was exactly contrary to what lay behind its bid for Glaxo.

By the mid-1980s this former stock-market high flyer had started to slow down; its shares were trading on the London Stock Exchange between £2.82 and £3.85 in 1985. (This was a 12–16 times' multiple compared to 25 for its major U.K. rival, Glaxo, and 21 for the U.K. pharmaceutical industry.)[11] Despite booming economic conditions and a strong product portfolio, its profit growth—which had been an aggressive 15 percent per annum—plateaued at 1 percent in 1985, to £83.8 million.[12] Its credibility with shareholders and security analysts was dwindling, exacerbated by poor to no communications with "the City" (London's financial community). When analysts were fortunate enough to reach the company, their telephone calls often would be answered with an arrogant click. As far as Beecham was concerned, the plateaued earnings were just a hiccup, a minor blip: management resented the analysts' questions of concern. Yet with close to 80 percent of its 756 million shares held by institutional investors, the financial market was not one Beecham could afford to ignore.[13] Beecham's shining reputation as a blue chip, strong growth stock was beginning to tarnish.

Finally, on November 8, 1985, Beecham Group's vice chairman, Lord Kenneth Keith, led a boardroom coup that resulted in the resignation of the existing executive chairman, Sir Ronald Halstead, who had been in the position slightly over a year. It also led to the retirement of three board members and the personnel director and reassignment of the finance director, all before the annual general meeting the following July. All in all, of the six executive and five nonexecutive board members, more than half had resigned or retired over the course of six to nine months. Lord Keith became the replacement chairman on the same day as the coup.

It was Lord Keith—a well-respected, highly regarded figure in British industry—who refused to accept Beecham's fall from grace and suggested to the board that Beecham consider refocusing its efforts on developing the pharmaceuticals business, which he believed would provide greater shareholder value over the long term. To do so, he told the board, would probably require an executive chairman from outside the company. Such a search could take time. In the interim the chairman of consumer products, John Robb, was asked to step in as group managing director of Beecham Group.

What became a long, exhaustive search for a new executive chairman began in the United Kingdom but soon went global, as it appeared unlikely that any of the small fraternity of top U.K. company heads would move to the troubled Beecham Group. Meanwhile, rumors had started circulating about Beecham becoming a takeover candidate, with ICI and Unilever mentioned most often as possible predators.

A CHANGE IN LEADERSHIP

By Spring 1986 the search led one executive recruiter to contact Robert P. Bauman, then vice-chairman of U.S.-based Textron, an aerospace/financial-services conglomerate located in Providence, Rhode Island.

Bob Bauman had spent twenty-three years with General Foods Inc., a multi-billion dollar consumer products company with a well-known product line that included Maxwell House coffee and Jello. During his career there, he had risen from a "coffee salesman" (as he still described himself) in the U.S. Northeast region to president of General Foods' rapidly expanding international operations. In 1980 he had joined the board of General Foods' corporate neighbor, Avco Corporation, a $4 billion financial services and aerospace conglomerate. One year later, he was elected its chairman and CEO at age 49. In late 1984, after an embattled six months, Avco was acquired by Textron, another conglomerate, as a white knight. Bob moved to Providence, Rhode Island as vice chairman of Textron in 1985.

When he was approached by the executive search firm in early 1986, he knew that his long-term future was not with Textron; he was simply fulfilling his personal commitment to ensure the Avco acquisition was a success. Having been a chief executive, he obviously wanted to be heading a company again.

Beecham appealed to him for a number of reasons, including the opportunity to lead a truly international company. What exhilarated him most, however, was its enormous potential. Yes, it would take a lot to turn Beecham around, but the challenge of realizing that potential excited him.

There were some concerns, though. When Bob did his research, he was advised that his chances of survival at Beecham for more than a few years were fifty-fifty at best. If he failed to deliver the improved performance, he could find himself driven out by an impatient and disillusioned marketplace. Would it be Avco all over again, he wondered, where investor frustration eventually led to its takeover?

He and Lord Keith started to discuss the terms of his appointment. The advisers bantered back and forth on issues such as salary (U.S. salaries were notoriously higher), protection of a pension, and relocation to the United Kingdom. Then it came to the length of tenure and his title. On both points, Bob was adamant. No longer than seven years maximum, with an annual review. If both sides agreed, he would agree to stay as executive chairman until September 15, 1993, which was six months past his sixty-second birthday and coincided with the company's normal retirement age.

His stance reflected his very strong belief that no chief executive should occupy that position in one company for more than seven to ten years. At the point when a new leader came in, he believed, there was usually a clear assignment; thus there should be an agreed-on time frame in which to complete it. After that time the person was likely to become repetitive and less inclined to initiate or be open to new and better ideas. According to Bob, long-term chief executives ran the risk of becoming so predictable in their behavior that other managers in the organization would do and say what they thought the chief executive wanted, rather than what the company needed. He firmly believed that the major issue facing a leader was not to ensure continuity—systems and the organization itself could guarantee that—but to ensure the continuity of change, so the organization would constantly reexamine and renew itself. Given the task—change Beecham—he thought he and Lord Keith should commit to a time frame in which the board should expect that to happen.

Finally, Bob would come in only if he was named executive chairman (the equivalent of chairman and CEO in the United States). John Robb would remain group managing director.

Lord Keith pondered his demands and reconsidered what he was proposing: that Beecham's board appoint an outsider to both the company and the industry, an American unknown to the U.K. investment community, despite the disillusioned analysts and the high profile of Beecham. It was an extremely big risk. Still, he believed that change was crucial for Beecham's survival and that Bob was the outside change agent they needed. He decided to take the risk.

Bob met with the board members briefly in May. A few weeks later, his appointment as the first non-British head of the very British Beecham Group plc was approved and announced. He would join Beecham Inc in June 1986 and work in the United States until the papers necessary for working in the United Kingdom came through in September.

The reaction was not overwhelmingly favorable. The City wondered what Beecham was thinking: not only was Bob an American with a Harvard Business School background (meaning textbook approach, in their view), he had no pharmaceutical experience and they were paying him one of the highest salaries in the United Kingdom.

If the reception was not good externally, it got off to a worse start internally. John Robb, who had been acting as group managing director for the past eleven months, had been under the impression that Bob would be coming in as a titular nonexecutive chairman, not a hands-on executive chairman. What made it even more difficult was that John had actually started to set Beecham in the right direction. Reflecting the desire to focus more on pharmaceuticals, the former head of the consumer products subgroup had arranged the disposal of some of the noncore businesses such as Do-It-Yourself. By Autumn, John had already initiated deals that would result in thirteen disposals for £237 million, generate enough cash to help reduce gearing (leverage) from 33.3 percent to 4.3 percent by year end, and produce £21 million in net profit in the 1986–1987 financial year.[14] (Beecham's financial year ended March 31.) His anger and disappointment was real and well understood, especially by those in the consumer products business, many of whom he had worked with for nearly twenty years.

DEFINING A STRATEGY

Bob's first task was to understand exactly where the company stood strategically, organizationally, and culturally and—given his board assignment—to assess its desire and ability to change. He sought internal and external opinions, visiting informally the top twenty-five managers for two hours each and meeting with outside analysts, advisers, and suppliers.

This activity appeared consistent with sound management theory: all the textbooks advise new management to take time in the first ninety days to listen and from that input set the agenda for the company.

But Bob saw it differently. For him, these meetings were *his* means to define the agenda. It was up to him as the new executive chairman to determine what *he* wanted to convey as well as what he needed to learn to set the tone and direction for the days that would follow. He used the meetings to accomplish several things:

❖ Learn what the top twenty-five understood the *corporate* strategy and objectives to be and whether there was much consensus around them. The aim was to have the managers focus on big corporate issues, playing down their natural tendency to think about their individual areas.

❖ Learn how the managers thought about different issues, particularly change. Did they feel there was a need to change, or were they comfortable with the status quo? If they did think that change was necessary, what change did they recommend? He wanted to understand how much of the existing management recognized the need to do things differently—and to what degree. How far apart were they as a management team in their views on the necessity for change?

❖ Establish a sense of urgency on what the company's problems were and clarify how they would define the corporate agenda.

Through the questions he raised and the discussions they generated, Bob learned about management, but, more important, the Beecham managers learned about Bob. His questions conveyed to them what he felt was important for Beecham: namely, its strategy and its ability to change. When conversation became too specific about an individual business, he would bring it back to Beecham. Everything else at that point was extraneous.

What he heard was complacency, a company grown content, victim of its previous success. "Everything is fine," the managers seemed to say in unison, "This is just a minor blip; why change anything?" was a common answer to Bob's question on strategy, while the response to his query on organizational culture was often a blank look. Although the board professed that it wanted to be a pharmaceutical company, Beecham was being run—and was perceived—more as a diversified consumer products company. There was no clear consensus about which way the company was going and why. Those who did understand what he meant by culture painted a picture of two very different companies, each entrenched firmly behind seemingly impenetrable barriers.

Essentially, consumer products and pharmaceuticals ignored one another, and both ignored the corporate staff. The consumer brands people were lean and mean; very cost conscious and extremely aggressive, always trying to make progress on all fronts at once, always striving to do everything better and cheaper. They were good operators, tracking sales day to day, making deals to acquire new brands. "Build the brands—build the business" was the strategy. They viewed themselves—as did the marketplace—as worthy competitors of companies like Unilever and Procter & Gamble.

The pharmaceutical people were more complacent, with little sense of urgency. They had developed their business from within and were far less worldly in terms of making deals. In an industry where interdependencies to copromote, codevelop, and comarket were the norm, most major companies had an average of 50 or more such agreements. Beecham had less than ten and stood apart for its insularity.[15] The science was good and commercially driven, so pharmaceuticals had a pipeline of potential products that was rapidly filling. But there was little effort to build the capability it would need to market them globally once they were ready.

When it came to Beecham Group, the pharmaceuticals people believed that they generated all the profits and that the consumer products people wasted those profits on marketing. The consumer brands people thought that pharmaceuticals was just throwing money down a big deep R&D well. There was no common meeting ground. The barriers between the two businesses came down to very personal levels: Beecham managers in a given country were told not to talk their counterparts in the other business.

Bob asked the financial community questions similar to those he had asked the management. He especially wanted to know how Beecham compared with its competitors. Whereas the inside team felt there was no need to change, the outside team was saying Beecham *had* to change. Bob learned that the financial people did not know where Beecham was going or how it was going to get there. They felt it was arrogant and sleeping; that it hadn't made the investment required to carry it forward, especially to realize the potential of its prescription medicines pipeline. And no one from inside the company was bothering to tell them anything any different.

It became clearer and clearer why the board had needed someone from outside the company to come in and lead the change: internal managers were just too entrenched in the old ways to move outside the existing framework. While he realized that he must work with the existing managers until he had assessed both their competence and their ability to change, he also knew he would need to bring in some management from outside Beecham if he were to have any real support.

In reconstituting the board earlier that year, Lord Keith had effectively opened up three of Beecham's top corporate management positions. In addition to the executive chairman, two executive (inside) directors had come off the board. One, the head of personnel, planned to retire; the other, the head of finance, was moved into a less critical position. This provided the opportunity to recruit two more outsiders who would bring a fresh and objective perspective to the business and support his efforts to change the company. He began interviewing candidates for the two positions almost immediately.

BUILDING THE TOP TEAM

Bob met Hugh Collum, the finance director for Cadbury Schweppes, in October 1986, soon after his arrival in the United Kingdom. At age 46, he was highly regarded and well connected in British industry. Reserved, hardworking, and detail-oriented, Hugh liked to confront the tough issues—all essential attributes in his role. There was absolutely no reason for him to consider leaving Cadbury, which was growing globally and viewed as a rising star in the City, for the less-than-golden Beecham. But Hugh enjoyed a challenge. Cadbury was a company with excellent prospects, but Beecham had the potential of being a turnaround. Hugh knew there would be a lot to do to get the company on the right path, and he relished the opportunity to help drive the effort.

Bob knew that Beecham needed someone of Hugh's caliber and stature if it was ever to achieve credibility with the City; as an American unfamiliar with Britain's accounting standards, he also needed someone who was absolutely expert in U.K. business practice. But aside from impeccable credentials, the new finance head would have to share his desire for change. Could he convince Hugh of Beecham's promise?

Hugh had professional expertise, was change oriented, and possessed a dry sense of humor—another key characteristic. As managers their **apparent** styles—one very structured, the other much less so—could not have differed more, but as individuals they shared the traits that would be so critical as they drove the changes to come. Hugh was the first hire. He joined the company as head of finance and was named to the board in January 1987.

What Hugh found in place on his arrival were few of the systems that he would have expected for a company of Beecham's stature: there was no formal strategic planning, no treasury function, no internal audit department; information systems were still far behind. The executive chairman breathed a huge sigh of relief as a myriad of finance and systems issues were handed over to Hugh.

With one major position resolved, the focus was now on hiring a personnel head. This role was critical if Bob hoped to build a real team or change the unsupportive culture that he saw blocking Beecham's moving not only forward, but in any direction at all.

In February 1987 Bob met Peter Jackson. Peter had been chief executive, personnel for British Oxygen Company (BOC), a multi-billion dollar chemicals company he joined in 1979. Not only had Peter worked with the one other American currently serving as a chief executive in the United Kingdom, but he had been very influential in the integration of BOC's successful 1979 acquisition of the American chemical company Airco, considered at the time to be the major transatlantic deal.

Peter held a Ph.D. in occupational psychology and had done his post-graduate work in London during the early 1970s, a time of enormous political and social change that culminated in the election of Margaret Thatcher in 1979. His entire orientation was around the collective effect of individual behavior on organizational behavior.

Whereas Bob had focused first on functional expertise for the finance director, for the personnel director he worried less about expertise in human resources systems and more about the candidate's understanding of company culture and how it drove the business. This was the most critical attribute of the head of human resources: someone who could understand the business well enough to know how employee behavior could influence outcomes, and who could coach and counsel the chief executive to ensure that his own behavior was consistent with the desired goals. Beecham could always find someone to help design and administer benefit plans; but as chief executive he must have on board someone he could trust to provide honest feedback.

The two men's accounts of their first interview were similar. Peter, whose reputation for delegating administrative details became legendary, never once mentioned the normal personnel systems like compensation and benefits. The whole conversation focused on the business and how, ultimately, it was people, not management, who implemented strategy. The words "culture" and "change" were not specifically mentioned; it was somehow implicit these were within the role of a human resource director.

But when Peter went to do his research, he found the jury still out on Bob and the long-term prognosis for Beecham not good. Rumors of a takeover loomed ominously. He challenged Bob with two questions: Would he be successful? Did he know what Beecham would look like in five years' time?

Bob's first response that yes, he (ergo Beecham) would be successful, put Peter somewhat at ease. It was hard not to believe him. But when he said no, he did *not* know what Beecham would look like in five years, Peter was taken aback. He was further surprised by the reason. Bob didn't have a clearly drawn vision; to have one would be preemptive, he explained. Vision was something he believed a management team had to shape together.

Peter remained hesitant. He had already been through a major change effort at BOC: that initiative had taken six years, a countless number of seven-day work weeks, immeasurable amounts of energy and thousands of miles of air travel. More than anyone else at that point, Peter knew from his own experience the kinds of challenges that could lie ahead. And he wasn't sure he wanted to go through it all again.

In the end, it was Bob's aspirations and absolute commitment to change that sold Peter. An added benefit: the men shared an almost obsessive love of sports and the same sense of humor. They laughed so much during the course of the interviews that both men knew they could have fun together, no matter how tough it got. In the end, Peter was sure he had joined Bob, but he wasn't sure he had joined Beecham.

That feeling was reflected in his employment contract. Peter agreed to stay with Beecham only as long as Bob did—until the end of their assignment to change Beecham. Both would leave in September 1993.

Peter joined Beecham in July 1987, five months after the initial interview. He was named as a board director in September 1987. What he found for human resource systems was not unlike what Hugh found in finance: in place were few, if any, programs that supported company goals. While the company aspired to have the best managers, executive compensation levels lagged behind those of competitors; there were few management development or training programs and no uniform objective setting or performance appraisal systems; the present employee incentive scheme hadn't changed since 1950. Peter wasn't sure where to begin.

The three new members of management had come from outside the company and been selected for their strong management expertise rather than industry experience. Suddenly, in a company where both the board and the corporate staff had taken a back position to operations, the new appointments created a strong power base at the company center. The only top management positions that remained unchanged were those heading the main operating units (average length of service: twenty-five years) and the Beecham Group secretary, Fergus Balfour. Fergus, a hard-working, unassuming professional, was a rare combination of cautious legal expertise and good business acumen. His strong sense of ethics and fair play, combined with a Scottish wit, made him an important bridge between the old and the new in the days that followed.

The two sides were thus established: the new group deliberately brought in to change the company, versus those who had been directing the business units for years and obviously felt less need to change. Together, the three new corporate executives and five long-standing operating managers formed the executive management committee (EMC)—the body that set policy, allocated resources, and ran Beecham.

During his first ninety days with Beecham, Bob met with more than twenty-five managers, visited all the major sites in the United Kingdom and many abroad, and met with numerous outsiders including major shareholders, analysts, and customers. He was out of his tower office in the 1930s art deco headquarters building more than he was in it, and his visits to some locations marked the first time the Beecham plant managers had ever met their company's executive chairman.

ESTABLISHING THE NEED FOR CHANGE

What Bob learned convinced him that Beecham Group was rapidly losing control of its own destiny.

The industry was ripe for consolidation. It had all the symptoms characteristic of industries that had experienced massive reorganization in previous decades, including high research and development costs, long (over ten years) product development cycles, products with high-risk profiles, and rapidly changing technology. But the infighting between Beecham's two major businesses meant that nothing was moving forward, and failing to move forward meant eventual extinction.

The first step had to be for the EMC to unite as a team working for *Beecham's* goals, rather than as separate business heads focused on their individual responsibilities. Given the inherent conflict between the businesses, exacerbated now by the old-versus-new management mentality, this would be the toughest challenge.

The best way to achieve management alignment was to have the EMC work on a task together. The harder and more important the task, and the more integral its members felt the EMC was in accomplishing that task, the better the chances of them coming together.

Ultimately, because individual success depended on Beecham's success, strategy development was a good vehicle around which to build the team: strategy was bigger than any one group or unit, and everyone on the EMC was critical to its achievement.

As their new executive chairman, of course, Bob was in a position to tell them *his* view of what the strategic goals could and should be. But having the perfect strategy was not as important to him as having the organization involved in its development and therefore really dedicated to its success. He might gain their intellectual acceptance with a plan of his own, but he knew he would not gain their commitment. For genuine commitment, it had to be *their* strategy, and that could evolve only if they developed it together. What he *could* do, however, was to try to build a case for why they had to change and instill a sense of urgency around this need. He had to make them see that standing still just wasn't an option.

Bob tried to stimulate debate, advancing some ideas as to what might be needed, encouraging a discussion of how they might go forward to develop a strategic plan. Enthusiasm was nonexistent, and debate was limited, with each business head looking to the others for comment.

What became very clear at this point was how far apart he and the others on the EMC actually were. All they heard from the executive chairman was theory and rhetoric (they thought), and all they saw was a man in a hurry to do something. Bob had failed to present his case for change convincingly.

Recognizing the importance of their support, yet sensing the growing gap between him and them, Bob determined that bringing in some external resources might help. A highly regarded outsider could provide an objective view of both the industry and the company—something he now knew the management would never accept from him. He proposed—somewhat gingerly—to the EMC that developing a long-term strategy to which they could all agree might not be something that they could resolve themselves. The questions were just too big and too important. He suggested they bring in some consultants to help.

Beecham's was not a consultant-oriented culture, and veteran managers did not think it needed a consulting firm now. They cited the usual reasons companies reject consultants: they knew their own business, they knew what needed to be done, consultants just feed back a company's own ideas and charge high fees for doing so, it would be far better and effective if they worked on it themselves. The consumer brands people, especially John Robb, were absolutely opposed to the idea. Thus ensued a battle as to who was going to run the company, the new corporate management team or the established heads of the major businesses.

At another level it was also about short-termism versus long-term strategy. John Robb had been focusing Beecham Group's efforts on reducing costs and divesting businesses. He believed hiring a consultant would not only be a major expense, but also diffuse their focus and energy.

The issue became so intense it was taken to the board at the next meeting. The nonexecutive directors agreed that defining a long-term strategy for Beecham was a high priority and that a consulting firm should be brought in as a resource.

While Bob may have initiated the idea of hiring consultants, he advised the EMC that selecting this consultancy was to be shared by the entire EMC and not delegated to any one of them. If strategy was to be the EMC's responsibility, then they had to participate in every decision affecting its development. This included deciding who should help them.

He also had a very strong view about how a company, starting with the chief executive, should select, manage, and work with consultants. The first step was to define the assignment clearly in writing. The next step was to identify firms with actual experience in both the task and the industry, looking for those that possessed up-to-date industry information. But collective firm expertise was not enough: it then became important to assess whether the proposed individual consultants personally had been involved in a similar type effort. Of the firms that qualified, the next step was to determine which had the best talent. The EMC wanted to interview the firms' best and brightest and then be assured that these were in fact the consultants who would be working with Beecham.

To make certain all the short-listed firms did present their strongest consultants, Beecham advised each firm that it was up against a number of rivals and identified those in the running. Bob also let them know that he, as chief executive, was behind the assignment. Knowing their work would get a proper hearing at the highest level, most consulting firms would guarantee that Beecham got their best talent.

Beecham then outlined the terms: the consultants placed on the assignment would work alongside the company managers as equal team members. They were not to lead the teams, but to be a resource. They would also be required to transfer their learnings and insights to the company, helping Beecham build its own strategic competence.

Before making a final decision, Beecham checked with the firm's former clients to assess the effectiveness of the consultants as both facilitators and independent thinkers. While they wanted the consultants to be part of the company team, EMC members also wanted to know that they could remain objective. Could they achieve the best solution for the company based on rigorous analysis, avoiding politics and the easy answers that might make them more acceptable to the organization?

Involving the EMC in the time-consuming selection process satisfied another critical criteria in the selection of a consultancy: whichever firm was hired would be credible and acceptable by the organization.

After interviewing three firms, the EMC selected Booz•Allen in December 1986. In its first presentation on pharmaceuticals, Booz•Allen cited the industry's attractive fundamentals, such as the huge number of unmet healthcare needs, the fertile technology, and the prospects afforded by creating the blockbuster medicine. But, they warned, blockbusters often made companies dangerously cyclical, moving company fortunes up and down almost overnight. Companies became victims, in a way, of their own success. They also confirmed Bob's view that the industry was showing all the classic signs of an impending upheaval.

Within this scenario, Beecham was identified as being in the nondescript middle; it was not a niche player like Wellcome nor a big global outfit like Glaxo and Merck. The middle players were the ones who would lose out.

The first assignment was to assess the portfolio of potential products, i.e., those compounds still in development. The Beecham development study was not easy. There was little, if any, natural goodwill between the consultants and the Beecham pharmaceuticals team, which remained skeptical and recalcitrant. Whatever they were saying or not saying, Bob knew what they were thinking: "We just need to outlast them—the new chief executive, the consultants—they'll be gone eventually." With loyalty clearly weighted toward the old guard, everything moved far more slowly than he had hoped. It was hardly the environment in which to bring about the mandated change the board had charged him with.

A progress report on the research study was made in May 1987 at the EMC's meeting in Brockham Park, one of Beecham's U.K. research locations. The atmosphere was icy cold, the lines between old and new teams clearly drawn.

Basically, according to the report, Beecham had a very rich pipeline of potential new products, spread across nine therapeutical categories. The focus had become evenly balanced between chronic and acute care treatments. But Beecham had neither the millions of pounds to invest nor the marketing scale to realize the commercial potential of what was coming through its pipeline.

The EMC considered the different options proposed—strategic alliances, comarketing agreements, licensing out new products—and set up task forces to look at the different options. The task forces would work with the consultants and make their first report in December 1987.

Now that Bob finally had Pharmaceuticals management's participation, he wanted to keep the momentum going and deepen company ownership of the issues. The task forces helped him to do both, as each team leader reached further into the organization, selecting members from the next level of management to help with the specific task assignment.

Even as the discussions on strategy were proceeding, efforts had started on a number of different issues that would touch every part of the organization. With single-minded pursuit, the aim was to get the company to challenge its accepted way of operating.

ALIGNING SYSTEMS FOR PERFORMANCE

Most of the growth in Beecham's sales during the past fifteen years had been accomplished through acquiring new brands and then extending them, whereas profit increases had been achieved by both cutting costs and increasing sales. Consumed with near-term performance, margin-conscious brands management failed to acknowledge that some margins could not be reduced further and that some investment was necessary for growth. The company hit bottom in the mid-1980s because little had been done in support of the long term.

It was as if Beecham had been caught in a time warp. They had, for example, invested in very few, if any, of the management support systems such as information technology or human resources that could have helped to improve performance internally. Within six months of Hugh's arrival, the EMC had agreed to hire heads of information technology, internal audit, and strategic planning—plus a treasurer; each would be a new position to the company. They also considered Hugh's recommendation to list shares in the U.S. market to broaden the company's shareholder ownership.

Like Bob and Peter, Hugh was convinced that Beecham could not afford to stand still. He started to look at cash with an eye toward building a reserve that would allow Beecham to make a major strategic initiative when the time was right. Over and above the disposals already planned, Hugh identified additional cosmetic properties that could reap potentially high prices in the current market. By the end of fiscal 1987, Beecham's debt was less than £55 million and its leverage (debt/equity ratio) was less than 4.3 percent.[16]

With strategy discussions and the redesign of financial and human resource systems under way, attention turned to organizational culture—the *way* people at Beecham should work. As he had done with the strategy discussion, Bob tried to unite the disparate business and corporate managers by having them together work through the critical question: What kind of a company do we want to be? He initiated the discussion by circulating for comment the first draft of a one-page document called "Beecham Management Philosophy" in June 1987.

The discussion document set out key principles on how a manager at Beecham should manage. For example:

- ❖ Superior results can be achieved by being the best (excellence).
- ❖ Participation is believed to be the most effective way to excellence.
- ❖ What is best for the Beecham Group is top priority.

This philosophy marked the beginning of the attempt to create a single management culture at Beecham. (These principles became the kernels of what later grew into SmithKline Beecham's Leadership Practices.) It was an early try at instilling a winning attitude and getting the organization to strive for being the best. The simple statements focused on areas that were important to achieving this goal and were lacking in Beecham's existing culture. This included getting people to work together more often and as part of a team, to use more facts and data than intuition in decision making, and to put the company ahead of the individual business unit. It expressed a view that *all* employees, supported by managers, had a major part to play in achieving the company's goals. In other words, the organization could (and should) be the hero of the company's success.

But what he did not realize until later was that it was too soon to start working on soft issues like management philosophy, when so many of the hard issues such as strategic direction were still so unresolved.

The statement clearly placed the focus on the importance of people, a shift for the task-driven Beecham. Like that of many other companies, Beecham's management attention was often on everything else *but* people.

Human resources was an aside to the more important functions such as marketing and research and was run more as an administrative function than the strategically driven one it could be. In organizations where human resource systems support strategy, the way employees are developed, trained, and rewarded tells them what management values. If these systems are not consistent with what the business identifies as important, they can actually thwart the realization of strategic goals.

Underscoring his personal commitment to human resources, Bob had included management development as a key component of Beecham's overall strategy. Peter began to focus his energies on building a performance-based culture within Beecham. Beecham wanted to create a cadre of excellent managers for the long term; only the best people would deliver the best results.

In the United Kingdom in 1987 there were few management guidelines or human resource systems that actually linked employees to the business goals. Managing by objectives—setting measurable, assessable goals and being held accountable for their achievement—was in place in some companies, but only haphazardly at Beecham.

One of the earliest steps taken was to formalize a corporatewide objective-setting and performance appraisal process and create a standard bonus plan that would be tied more closely to company results. Managers would be judged on how well the unit did in meeting their financial objectives, as well as on their personal contribution. The automatic 10 percent annual bonus for staff paychecks would now vary, again based on how well the company did.

Instituting management by objectives (MBO) signaled the first time the organization was asked to change on a personal level, and the old and new styles of management clashed head-on. It took a great deal of energy and effort before the objective-setting process known as the Beecham Way was agreed on and implemented.

Shifting to the long-term view of how they could make sure they had the best people, Peter reviewed the available career training. He divided management development into two components: training to help managers do their present jobs better, and succession planning, a program wherein managers were developed for higher-level jobs. Both were directed to meet the strategic needs of the business.

Finally, he advocated that they communicate each of these initiatives to all employees. This included sharing all the information surrounding the new job-grading system and salary ranges, the calculation of bonuses, and the development programs—a fully transparent disclosure of how people were treated and why. Communicating was key to building trust and understanding of the underlying performance message.

If the old Beecham management considered these proposals on the edge, this suggestion was absolutely revolutionary. The attitude about employees at many British companies in 1988 was both paternalistic and secretive: employees were told as little as possible. Knowledge was power, and power belonged to management.

Clearly, the organization was gradually being pushed into a more open and involving management style, including the need for deeper, more direct—and more directed—communication with employees.

CREATING A NEW VISION

It was becoming clearer and clearer that changes in the pharmaceuticals industry were imminent. At its current ranking of twenty-third in the world, Beecham did not have the resources to compete in the changing industry, especially in the United States.

The more traditional approaches to growth such as new products or small acquisitions and strategic alliances would be helpful, but they were unlikely to achieve the major step forward that would be necessary to catapult Beecham from number twenty-three to one of the top ten. To become a global pharmaceuticals player, Beecham had to make a major move—such as a merger—or risk being relegated to a niche position.

For the traditional blue-chip Beecham, pursuing a merger would be a major step, and one that would be difficult for managers or shareholders to understand, especially in light of the firm's gradually improving performance. For the board to support the new management, it was essential to bring its members along with management's thinking as the strategy developed. It was well known that, historically, mergers had a poor success record. The ego-driven struggle for power among members of top management during the long negotiating period often resulted in mergers being aborted. By involving the board and management from the beginning, Bob reasoned that everyone would be able to see the business rationale and participate in the discussions as the recommendations unfolded. Then, ideally, they would all be able to support whatever made the most sense for Beecham Group.

One of the initial steps was to establish a reason for change of the magnitude that was required. The potential takeover of Beecham was clearly a present threat, and everyone knew it. Senior management understood the advantage of Beecham developing its own future instead of waiting for an outsider to do it. He could build on that concern. More important, though, was instilling the idea of not settling to merely survive or be in the ubiquitous middle, but of aspiring to win and become an industry leader. Such an aspiration would allow Beecham to sustain any success it achieved. Because of the significance of the Beecham team's accepting the idea of a merger, as well as their potential reluctance, the consultants were asked to do a rigorous analysis of the strategy. All the data pointed to a merger of equals, and their presentation supported this concept. The senior management's acceptance of the report would be a milestone in Beecham's journey. The first major meeting with the executive management committee took place in July 1987.

In their first complete report on corporate strategy the consultants opened their remarks by proposing three alternative goals for Beecham by 1990:

❖ To be a leading pharmaceutical company
❖ To be a leading consumer products company
❖ To be a leading company in pharmaceuticals and consumer products ("integrated healthcare")

They defined leadership as achieving the following conditions:

❖ Above-average growth rate
❖ A return on equity greater than the cost of equity
❖ Dominant global position

If Beecham decided to pursue pharmaceuticals only, the pipeline would be its sign of success; if it were to focus on consumer products, then the number of its leading brands would determine leadership.[17]

As the meeting continued, the EMC considered the different options available. Members agreed that the goal was to return to the company's roots: to focus on healthcare, which essentially meant over-the-counter and prescription medicines, and to build a capability in the world's largest market for both, the United States.

Their conclusion: Beecham could not achieve any of these leadership positions as it was presently configured. Furthermore, it ran the risk in its present state of not remaining a broad-based pharmaceutical company, but rather becoming a niche player. It simply did not have enough critical mass in marketing or geography, especially in the United States, to realize the potential of its growing pharmaceutical pipeline. The financial market was reflecting that condition, putting pressure on its share price, and making Beecham Group that much more vulnerable to a takeover.

This vulnerability added greater urgency to management's efforts in the near term to refocus the business and dispose of noncore businesses. Management knew that in the end its best defense was a strong and financially solid company.

As it looked to the longer term, the EMC considered the information presented that day against the background of the many individual discussions each member had had with the consultants over the previous six months. The consultants' unbiased view, challenging questions, and logical arguments—supported by industry, government, and economic data—could not be ignored. Gradually, one by one, EMC members had moved forward from their "it's just a blip" stance of the year before. Finally they agreed, with varying degrees of acceptance, that they should pursue a number of options, including a major acquisition or even a merger with a similar sized firm, all with the goal of becoming a global healthcare company.

The ramifications of what they were discussing finally sank into the minds of the men sitting around the table: this was revolutionary, not evolutionary, change. What had begun as a limited study of drugs in development had become a full-fledged discussion of corporate strategy.

The EMC asked the consultants to extend the study, analyzing the industry and all the options further, including a list of potential merger/acquisition candidates. The support for further study wasn't wholehearted; it was obvious that some members of the old guard were simply going along with the request. Still, even if the entire management team wasn't quite together, momentum to do something was finally starting to build, along with a sense of urgency that time was starting to run out.

On July 27—about two months after Bob's arrival in the United Kingdom—the same report on corporate strategy was presented to the full board of directors. After a discussion similar to that held by the EMC, the Board declared complete agreement with the EMC around the next steps.

The conclusion of this meeting coincided with the planned retirement of Lord Keith. The "revolution" he had started almost two years earlier in the boardroom had laid the foundation for what would ultimately be the complete transformation of Beecham from a diversified British consumer products/pharmaceuticals company into a global healthcare leader.

BUILDING CREDIBILITY

Even as efforts were being made internally to define strategy and shape a new culture, externally it was still necessary to reestablish Beecham's credibility with the city. It was a difficult task: the U.K. market was driven by a handful of security analysts from the major brokers. At this point few, if any, were recommending Beecham's shares; the jury on the new management was still out.

One way to offset the City's influence somewhat was to build the company's profile in the United States. Beecham had a large portfolio of well-known American products; why not see if it could broaden its shareholder base there? The EMC agreed to list Beecham's shares in the form of American Depositary Receipts (ADRs) on NASDAQ (National Association of Security Dealers), the second largest stock exchange in the United States, following the release of the results for Beecham's fiscal year ended March 30, 1987. Hugh interviewed an investor relations firm in New York to help support the company's plans.

One of the firm's consultants was Joanne Lawrence. Joanne had been head of communications and investor relations at Avco, where she had worked for fourteen years, the last four of them with Bob. Following the Textron acquisition, she joined IBM's corporate headquarters staff with the explicit goal of eventually working overseas. When later she realized that assignment would take years to materialize, she left for an internationally focused investor relations firm, with which she hoped to move to London.

When Beecham hired this firm in the spring of 1987, Joanne found herself working with Bob again, this time as a consultant. Her role was to raise Beecham's profile and position the company in the important

U.S. market, as well as help the small in-house corporate communications/ investor relations team with their efforts in London.

In preparation for the ADR listing, now planned for June 1987, meetings were scheduled with international equity fund managers, industry analysts at all the major U.S. investment houses, and editors at major business publications. The new management team at Beecham was introduced and positioned as the team that would restore Beecham to growth.

In November 1987 Joanne was in London for Beecham's interim results presentation. Although she was then considering an offer to become senior vice president, communications/investor relations for a major U.S. company, a discussion with Hugh and Bob turned to her interviewing for a position as the number-two communications person at Beecham.

From an upwardly mobile career perspective, the move made no sense. From position to salary, contrast with the U.S. job offer was dramatic. But Beecham offered the sought-after international setting plus an opportunity to work with Bob again. Better than most, she knew his propensity for change and that this was a unique opportunity to help bring that change about. It was still high risk. She was an American, another member of the new team, and joining at a time when few women occupied senior management roles in Britian. She had three strikes against her before she began.

From Bob's perspective, Joanne's ability to think strategically and use communication to help align various stakeholders with the company's overall goals was the key. Communications was a function he had always viewed as critical to creating strategic alignment, yet it was one he had found totally lacking in the company.

By the time Joanne arrived in the United Kingdom in January 1988, Beecham's head of communications had left. Joanne became responsible for first defining and then establishing a truly integrated, strategically oriented internal/external communications department, including investor and government relations. Like the other new members of the management team, she would find the first challenge was personal and lay inside Beecham.

Adding to her dilemma: she had totally underestimated the subtlety of working in a different national culture. Everything—from driving to work in the morning to drafting memos and managing staff—required an entirely new approach. Joanne went home exhausted each night, trying first to understand, then how to manage the differences. She began to wonder if she hadn't made a mistake.

MOVING FORWARD

About the same time Joanne joined Beecham, the Booz•Allen consultants reported back to the executive management committee.

Having hovered at twenty-third in the industry for a number of years, the Beecham pharmaceutical subgroup finally agreed on an ambitious goal: to become a leading player in the pharmaceutical industry within the next five years. That aspiration translated to growing profits 'at least equal to a peer group of (twenty U.S./European) pharmaceutical companies, or 15–20 percent growth per annum. To improve its position relative to the industry meant Beecham must achieve earnings per share growth rates in excess of 20 percent per year.[18] The EMC grew disheartened as it realized that organically there was no way Beecham could achieve that leadership.

Their report came down to proposing three strategic imperatives. To achieve its vision of becoming a leading healthcare company, Beecham must expand its therapeutic categories beyond antibiotics; it must build its global regional presence, particularly in the United States and Japan; and it must add a U.S. research presence.[19]

Beecham could license in some products, sign joint or comarketing agreements, enter into a joint venture, or make small-company acquisitions to achieve its 20 percent earnings growth goals. None of these options provided all the answers, and with nearly all of them it would be a long time before Beecham realized any benefit. In light of the current frenzied takeover environment, probably too long.

As the progress reports came in from the consultants, Bob and Hugh started to meet with different investment bankers, trying to piece together some alternative scenarios.

In the end, nearly all EMC members had reached the same conclusion: Beecham couldn't do it alone.

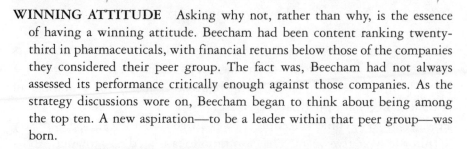

Phase I:
Strategy
1986–1989

WINNING ATTITUDE Asking why not, rather than why, is the essence of having a winning attitude. Beecham had been content ranking twenty-third in pharmaceuticals, with financial returns below those of the companies they considered their peer group. The fact was, Beecham had not always assessed its performance critically enough against those companies. As the strategy discussions wore on, Beecham began to think about being among the top ten. A new aspiration—to be a leader within that peer group—was born.

ORGANIZATION AS HERO Commitment to goals and involvement in their achievement must begin at the top and work its way down. This may mean some restraint by the chief executive: he or she must not impose a personal view on the senior management, but rather create the environment in which the management team can develop one together. Ideally, the top team in place will agree on the importance of making the organization the hero. If not, then it is up to the leader to get a sufficient number of players on board—including some from outside—before proceeding with any new initiative. Involving Beecham's top team hands-on in developing strategy eventually led to the revolutionary agreement to pursue the merger. Establishing the practice of involvement, it marked the beginning of engaging the entire organization in realizing the company's strategic goals.

CUMULATIVE LEARNING It was recognized early that convincing Beecham's skeptical, complacent management of the need for change would require both determined persistence and an outside perspective. A consultant, armed with industry data and an object viewpoint, was brought in to provide the indisputable evidence. By making all the hard issues clearly visible, management would be forced to address them at a rational and intellectual level rather than at an emotional and intuitive level.

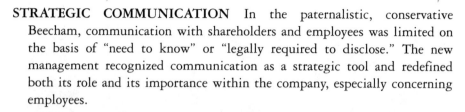

STRATEGIC COMMUNICATION In the paternalistic, conservative Beecham, communication with shareholders and employees was limited on the basis of "need to know" or "legally required to disclose." The new management recognized communication as a strategic tool and redefined both its role and its importance within the company, especially concerning employees.

ALIGNMENT OF BEHAVIOR AND STRATEGY One of the earliest goals was to instill a winning attitude and create a more performance-oriented management. Human resource systems constituted a tool that could support this goal. The first steps taken were to change the decades-old programs regarding compensation and tie reward more closely to individual and companywide performance.

Defining a Merger of Equals

BEECHAM'S CORPORATE HEAD-quarters building was located along the Great West Road in Brentford, just outside central London. Its principal structure consisted of a large rectangular block of stone and bricks, out of which rose a single tower, so called because it was about eight stories high compared with the one to three levels of the other buildings. The site was a maze of 1930s style buildings, each block designated by a letter of the alphabet (they were up to Q when Bob Bauman arrived) and linked through what seemed to be miles of bland brown rubber-tiled corridors. Its only distinguishing characteristics were the neon signs promoting its products—Macleans, Brylcreem, Lucozade— just visible from the busy A4, the main west road in and out of London. Upon entering the drab green-carpeted reception, new visitors had to study a directory of affiliated companies on the inside door and spot the familiar brand names to realize they were inside one of Britain's premier marketing firms.

The boardroom reflected the 1930s look: dark brown walls and camel leather chairs surrounded a huge, round, custom-built wooden table. It was here that the EMC sat pondering the consultants' recommendations that December afternoon.

To be a world-class player in healthcare, Beecham had to substantially increase its pharmaceuticals marketing and research capability, especially in the United States. It could try to do this alone, which would involve building and staffing a major U.S. research center (estimated cost: £100 million) plus more than doubling the existing U.S. sales force, from 600 to 1,500 representatives. Alternatively, Beecham could consider some other options:

1. *Form strategic alliances.* Beecham could find partners to help comarket specific products in the United States, adding significantly to its sales strength on an as-needed basis. It could contract with research laboratories to codevelop its new compounds, thereby speeding up the process.

2. *Buy several smaller companies.* By acquiring several smaller companies and folding them into Beecham's existing U.S. operations headquarters in Bristol, Tennessee, Beecham could try to build mass gradually. Considering the amount Beecham could afford to pay, these acquisitions would probably be too small to have much of an impact. In addition, as Beecham took the time required to digest each company, its competitors would be moving further ahead, and the gap between Beecham and its rivals would continue to widen.

3. *Make a large acquisition.* Acquiring another company of some substance could make a significant difference, but cost would be a major obstacle. Beecham's balance sheet just wasn't strong enough to finance anything that would be large enough to matter. Also to decide: if a friendly overture suddenly turned hostile, adding to the cost of acquisition, would Beecham continue to pursue it?

4. *Do a merger of equals with a U.S. company.* Financially and strategically, this was the best answer. It would require simply exchanging shares with no additional premium paid to shareholders, and at the same time it would increase Beecham's scale in the United States. Its achievement was also the most difficult, however, as designing equal financial structures could be extremely complex, and balancing the emotional management issues was enormously difficult. Furthermore, true mergers of equals were extremely rare. There had only been three in recent memory: Unilever, Royal Dutch Shell, and Ciba-Geigy.

   The long-term strategic success of equal mergers was even rarer, as most combinations ran into difficulties as soon as integration of the operations began. In some instances, two merged companies continued to operate separately, which meant the financial benefits of the combination promised to shareholders were harder to realize.

5. *Be acquired or spin off the two businesses.* The threat of a competitor making a takeover bid before Beecham management had a chance to pursue any of these options still loomed, so the consultants added another consideration: select the company Beecham would like to have acquire it, its own white knight. ICI emerged as the company that Beecham felt would be structurally and strategically most compatible. In light of previous rumors linking the two companies, the financial market obviously felt the same.[1]

In pursuing each of these options, the consultants had identified twenty-three U.S. and European pharmaceutical companies and organized them into three categories of possible combination:

❖ Major company acquisitions
❖ Extractive acquisitions (i.e., acquiring just part of a business)
❖ Merger of corporate equals (i.e., equivalent market value)

Each company had been assessed for strategic fit against Beecham's ambition to become an integrated healthcare company.

Pharmaceuticals:	Would it broaden their core anti-infective franchise, adding products in the antifungal and antiviral areas? Would it strengthen the cardiovascular and central nervous-system therapeutic areas?
Over-the-counter medicines (OTC):	Would it add to Beecham's scale in OTC medicines, putting Beecham into categories such as analgesics, where they were lacking a serious presence?
Global expansion:	Would it give Beecham the sales and marketing capacity to compete in both pharmaceuticals and OTC medicines on a global scale? Would it significantly strengthen Beecham's sales representation in the United States, and its presence in Germany and Japan? Would it give them a research base in the United States?

Each of the companies was then evaluated against a criteria of what could be done ("doability"):

❖ Could Beecham afford it? What was the impact on dilution? On leverage?

❖ Was it technically possible? What were the legal constraints? What about shareholders?

❖ What would the attitude be among the proposed candidate's shareholders? Among management?

The list of companies was narrowed to thirteen, then to six. Finally, each was considered against the broader picture of Beecham's entire product portfolio: what impact would the candidate company have on the consumer products and OTC medicines business, in addition to the pharmaceutical business?

At the end of that meeting, the EMC agreed to evaluate in detail the final merger and acquisition alternatives. Members wanted to look at strategic fit, particularly relative to the pharmaceutical business, and have a preliminary look at how the combined companies would appear financially. Finally, they wanted to know what would be required to complete a transaction.

On January 28, 1988, the EMC and board members gathered to hear the final presentation. The final candidates proposed as potential partners to address Beecham's most critical need were all U.S. companies. They included SmithKline Beckman and Sterling Drug. The consultants presented the six in descending order of attractiveness, which was defined as the optimal combination of strategic fit and doability. On the basis of geographical sales match and therapeutic categories, one of the most compatible in terms of strategic fit was SmithKline Beckman, but it was rated low for doability because of its market value. Its market capitalization at that time was just too large for a merger of equals to be possible. In another instance where timing was everything, Sterling was defined as a good strategic fit for consumer brands but was removed from the list when Kodak suddenly acquired it. (As if confirming the logic, SB would acquire Sterling Winthrop in 1994 from Kodak to bolster its OTC franchise.)

But it was still 1988, and the board was involved in one of those discussions that would shape the company's destiny. Conversations ranged far and wide as together the nonexecutive directors and executive directors brought their broad perspective to the issues at hand. Those outside the company wanted to know how the City would view these proposals, while those inside, seeing the company growing stronger, still challenged the necessity of doing something of this magnitude. At the heart of the debate: how real was the proposed shakeout in the pharmaceutical industry? They were, after all, putting the company on the line.

Finally, if they did agree to do something, how far were they willing to go? Would they enter into an agreement if Beecham retained less than 50 percent control? As the board considered the options, it became clear that the ideal approach would be a merger of equals—no premium paid, and friendly.

But the more they heard about the success rate of previous attempts, the more pessimistic they became. By the end of that session, they felt there was zero probability for a true merger of equals, and that perhaps a strategic alliance was a more practical alternative. But Bob disagreed: he felt the chances were more like fifty-fifty. For him, that meant he had to pursue it.

Bob and Hugh were charged by the EMC to find out more about what it would take to do a merger of equals—was it even possible, they wondered, between a British and American company? The structure would have to address both U.K. and U.S. financial regulations and tax laws. The discussion was put off the table for the time being as the practicality of the relatively unique solution of a cross-border merger of equals was pursued.

As the necessity for change at Beecham became more and more evident to the executive management committee and its advisers, the EMC itself began to undergo transformation. Whereas the propensity for change within the pharmaceuticals group had seemed virtually nonexistent, the early retirement of its chairman, Jim Pollard, opened the door to providing that operation with a leader more receptive to change.

To meet this requirement, they needed to look outside Beecham for Pollard's replacement. The executive search led to James Andress, then president and chief operating officer of Sterling Drug, a major prescription/OTC medicines giant in the United States. (As noted earlier, Sterling was one of the six potential partners identified by the consultants, but a few months after the December board presentation, Sterling was acquired by Kodak.)

Jim's industry background was solid healthcare. A former consultant himself, he had specialized in the pharmaceuticals industry most of his career. Before moving to Sterling Drug, Jim had headed Abbott Laboratories. Extremely bright and conceptual, he was a creative thinker and had very strong views about what was happening in the industry.

He would join, but only if Beecham was planning to become a real player in the industry and acquire greater scale. Reinforced by his experience at Sterling, Jim was adamant that the industry was due for consolidation. He didn't need anyone to tell him that Beecham would never survive on its own.

Bob explained where the company was in its thinking. Since the EMC had not actually agreed on any action, that's all he could do. On the strength of their shared conviction about the industry and personal commitment to change, Jim agreed to join Beecham in April 1988.

Jim's appointment was met with mixed reactions. Externally, while he was not that well known in Britain, his reputation and record in the United States quickly won over the U.K. security analysts. Internally it was another issue. He was being brought in above the seniormost person in pharmaceuticals, a long-term Beecham employee. In addition, the employees saw still another American coming in to head an important British business.

But Jim would prove to be one of those fortuitous appointments—a person whose period with the company would be short but whose impact would be enormous.

LAYING THE PERFORMANCE GROUNDWORK

As the EMC pondered the various alternatives, Beecham continued to focus on its present strategy—to grow as much as possible from within. The point was that no matter which alternative it chose, Beecham would need to have credibility to successfully carry it off. To win, it had to be seen as already winning.

So, even as Beecham reduced its presence in noncore businesses, management strengthened those it planned to keep. It increased R&D expenditure and focused more on nonantibiotic compounds. It continued the worldwide launch of Bactroban, the first new antibiotic ointment in twenty years, and Eminase, a drug to help heart attack patients, and awaited approval in the United States and Japan for Relifex, an antiarthritic compound, and Paroxetine, a promising antidepressant. In consumer products, Beecham's share of the U.K. cold and flu market grew to an unprecedented 60 percent, driving Beecham to first place. Cosmetics was expected to grow at 25 percent over the preceding year, and management agreed it was time to sell *all* of it.

An intensive study of headquarters' administrative costs was under way and a proposal for an Excellence program was being developed to help employees think more about how they were working. Could they do some tasks any differently, or maybe eliminate them completely?

The new management team was tackling issues on every front, all the time strengthening its existing business and seeking ways to build those critical areas where it knew it was lacking.

The massive efforts of the business units along with the unusually high number of outside appointments, a focus on reducing headquarters costs, and changes initiated by the new recruits in the human resource and financial systems now combined to take its toll on the employees. Morale steadily declined as the new executive chairman and his team continued to shake things up.

Employees saw lots of things happening but could not place them in any context. Still suspicious of the new team, their trust in senior management was tenuous. Yet they were key to changing the culture of Beecham. Bob knew it, but other than the occasional newsletter he had no way to reach 35,000 people directly. Joanne was asked to make employee communication her priority.

Bob made himself more visible, visiting with managers in their offices versus having them come to him, and placing communications on the EMC agenda regularly to underscore the importance to managers of creating an employee dialogue that would involve them more. He also set up the expectation that he planned to—and would—talk directly and more often to managers and employees, a first step in breaking the hierarchical barrier.

Joanne's new department proposed systems that would encourage more face-to-face discussions with employees in ways that were relevant and personal. Her staff initiated two-way systems, language translations for major publications and notices, an employee annual report, and most important, a more effective linkage and transmission system with Beecham's sites around the world to guarantee information was disseminated to local managers as widely and in as timely a manner as possible. (Until then, most of the focus had been in the United Kingdom). In a simple but symbolic gesture, press releases were distributed to ensure that employees knew the news before they read it in the newspapers.

All of this was still rather revolutionary in a British company in 1988. The environment being created—more egalitarian and participative, where every idea mattered and people were rewarded for their efforts—was a major departure from the authoritarian, paternalistic style that had been in place for some years. Step by step, the new systems that would support a performance-oriented culture started to take hold. Change might be inevitable, but it certainly wasn't going to be easy.

By April 1988 Beecham management finally reached agreement around the wording of the document to be called the "The Operating Philosophy for Beecham." The process had taken nine months, and had directly involved the discussion and thinking of close to 150 managers. It now incorporated the thinking of all those whose actions it sought to influence. The debate had proved more important than the content: it marked the first time Beecham management had actually talked about what kind of company it wanted to be. (The principle behind the discussion had been similar to that evoked for strategy: through management working out the issues together, each person involved could sign on to the end result, which was one more step toward making the organization the hero.) In its final draft form, the operating philosophy painted a picture of what Beecham aspired to be, which theoretically was a radical change from the old, hierarchical Beecham. Its goals were to supply customers with value-added products and services, to deliver financial performance superior to comparable U.S. and U.K. companies, and to create a work environment that encouraged excellence in everything employees did.

Resources would be allocated for the benefit of Beecham Group, rather than individual businesses. Through it all they would strive to get the balance right between operating as one company and operating individually as many businesses, investing for growth while contracting for efficiency, and managing short- and long-term objectives simultaneously.

"The Operating Philosophy for Beecham" concluded with these words:

> We must recognize that change is a continuous journey and not
> a destination . . . no decision is perpetual and there is no 'right'
> way of doing things that cannot be improved.

As a first step in involving the rest of the organization, it was agreed to present the new operating philosophy at the management meeting scheduled for June, and to determine the process for guaranteeing its widespread communication throughout Beecham soon afterward.

PURSUING A PARTNER

Consistent with their stated commitment to industry leadership, members of the EMC started to focus around what had been identified as the most doable near-term action—strategic alliances—and companies proposed as potential partners. They also went through the existing portfolio, trying again to identify businesses they should invest in, maintain, or dispose for cash to finance the proposed initiatives.

Still, Bob held out hope for the unique prospect of a merger of equals. The EMC studied companies like Unilever and Royal Dutch Shell, which had been among the few cross-border merger successes. They learned that a potential partner's strategic fit with the organization should be obvious and logical and, as critical, its management compatible. Individuals should be like-minded enough to work together.

Finally, during April, they learned it was financially and legally possible: a British company could do a merger of equals with an American company through a financial vehicle known as stapled stock. The parent U.K. company would issue two classes of stock: Class A for the U.K. shareholders and Class B, of which a certain number would be "stapled" to preferred shares in a U.S. subsidiary. The value of the Class A and the stapled shares would be equal. Both would trade on the London Stock Exchange and both would be listed as ADRs on the New York Stock Exchange. Dividends would be paid in pounds sterling from the U.K. parent to U.K. shareholders, and in dollars from the U.S. subsidiary to U.S. shareholders. U.S. shareholders would see no difference between the foreign security and a domestic share.

Bob wasted little time. He had already set up a number of top-management meetings to discuss growth through strategic alliance with the most doable of the six companies, and now he mentally shifted gears. As he approached each meeting, he studied the company carefully, confirming for himself the strategic fit. But his primary purpose in the meeting was to learn more about the company leader, trying to assess whether he shared Bob's view of the industry's direction and the kind of company it would take to compete effectively in the future.

Each discussion would begin around Beecham's desire to build its presence in the United States, perhaps in return for helping a U.S. company with its presence in key European markets where Beecham had a fairly significant business. But as the two spoke, Bob would steer the conversation to the industry and to what he believed were the inevitable changes ahead. He tested the integrated healthcare company concept, tying together prescription and OTC medicines, trying to spark a reaction from his host.

He listened closely to each response: did the fellow chief executive share his industry view, and the vision of the integrated healthcare company as the solution? Only then would he broach the idea of the merger of equals. This had been the soft approach discussed with the board—more in keeping with the industry's style of being noncontentious. But to that point not one conversation had gone that far. It seemed his industry colleagues did not share the same immediate concern.

ACTIVITIES ACCELERATE

Over the course of Spring 1988, talks continued with several companies, and developments were reported back to the EMC. While he remained outwardly optimistic that one of the talks would lead somewhere, he was personally very discouraged after each meeting. Each of the companies was doing fairly well and saw few threats on the horizon.

In May, Ken Kermes, someone Bob had known from his years at General Foods, was in London. He stopped by Beecham House on his way to Heathrow. Ken was executive vice president and chief financial officer for SmithKline Beckman (SKB), the U.S. pharmaceuticals company headquartered in Philadelphia. One of the six short-listed companies in November, SmithKline Beckman had ranked low in doability because its market capitalization was much higher than Beecham's at the time. For that reason, a meeting with Henry Wendt, SKB's chief executive, had not been set up. Bob now welcomed the chance to hear his former colleague's views about the industry.

After reminiscing about General Foods, Bob and Ken began discussing the industry they now both found themselves in. As they spoke, Ken noted similarities between his old friend and his present boss and suggested the two meet the next time Bob was planning to be in the United States.

SMITHKLINE BECKMAN

It was June before Bob met with Henry, and as usual he took the time to learn much as possible about the company, SmithKline Beckman.

Like Beecham, SmithKline Beckman had a long history,[2] having been founded in Philadelphia in 1830 as an apothecary by John K. Smith and John Gilbert. In the 1880s Mahlon Kline, trying to ensure product quality, led the company into research and manufacturing of its own products. In 1891 it absorbed French & Co., another wholesaler, creating Smith, Kline & French. The wholesaling interests were sold in 1929 to "concentrate on the discovery and manufacture of special drugs" as Smith Kline & French Laboratories (SK&F).

Between 1930 and 1965 the company introduced several revolutionary new therapies, including the Benzedrine inhaler for respiratory ailments, Dexedrine for depression, Thorazine for treatment of mental illness and Dyazide for hypertension.

But the medicine that catapulted SK&F into the big league was Tagamet—the world's first antiulcer treatment. Tagamet had been the result of some groundbreaking research by scientists at SmithKline's Welwyn Garden City research center in England. Its component, cimetidine, was a major breakthrough (its discoverer, Sir James Black, was knighted and received a Nobel Prize in 1988). Introduced in 1976 in the United Kingdom, Tagamet was hailed as a wonder drug that would revolutionize the treatment of ulcers, which had often required intensive treatment and sometimes expensive surgery. By 1985 it had become the world's first drug to reach a billion dollars in sales and had passed the tranquilizer Valium as the world's largest-selling drug.

Between Thorazine, Dyazide, and Tagamet, SK&F enjoyed a run during the 1970s as a Wall Street favorite, and saw its share price zoom.[3] The bubble burst when, in 1982, Glaxo launched Zantac. Through a comarketing agreement with Roche, Glaxo marketed Zantac aggressively and demanded a premium price. SK&F maintained its Tagamet sales for a while by expanding to new markets, and periodically raising prices. But then Zantac passed Tagamet. As fast as SK&F's share price had risen, it now plummeted.

In an effort to build for its future and stave off the imminent fall of its largest selling product, SK&F pursued a number of strategies. It embarked on an acquisition program in the early 1980s as part of a vision to build a broad-based integrated healthcare company. Believing that new technology would flow from diagnostics into medicine, the company added aggressively to some small clinical laboratories it had started acquiring in 1970, and expanded into diagnostic instruments and supplies through acquiring Allergan eyecare and Beckman Instruments, the latter for $1 billion, in 1980. That year it changed its name once again and became SmithKline Beckman Corporation (SKB).

An ambitious revamp of the research and development organization was undertaken, and R&D expenditures were increased to about 10 percent of sales, or $300 million. The number of therapeutic classes in which SK&F were working was broadened, and a brand new $200 million research center at Upper Merion, Pennsylvania was opened in 1983.

Considering, however, that it took ten to twelve years to develop a new therapy, some would argue that all of this was too much too late to save SKB from the predictable decline of sales when Tagamet went off patent in 1994. Adding to its problem, in efforts to fund Tagamet's development in the 1970s, the company had limited its other research efforts.

When Dyazide came off patent in the United States in 1980, threatening $400 million of SKB's annual sales, the U.S. Federal Drug Administration (FDA) had encouraged SmithKline Beckman to develop a successor, even postponing approval of a generic equivalent. In August 1987, despite these previous assurances, the FDA approved a generic version of Dyazide. While the approval was later found to have been based on fraudulent data, the damage to SKB was fast and devastating. Within two days of the announcement, it lost $1.3 billion in market capitalization, opening one morning at $6.1 billion and the next at $4.8 billion.[4] Within one year, sales of this important product had been cut by more than half.[5]

A few months later, another shock hit the company when misdirected attempts to limit eroding sales of Tagamet backfired. SKB had advertised the product's attributes directly to the consumers who used the medicine, generating greater demand even as it told wholesalers there would be a price rise. The result: wholesalers overstocked the product toward the end of 1987 to meet consumer demands as well keep their own costs down. Their stock build up dramatically cut into SKB's 1988 Tagamet sales: there was a 25 percent decline in the United States alone.[6]

As the financial markets disparaged SKB's fall from 1970s superstar to 1980s has-been, management was striving desperately to reshape the company to restore shareholder value. In an effort to refocus on its core business of pharmaceuticals, management planned to spinoff the recent acquisitions to the shareholders, reorganize the headquarters, and consolidate the various pharmaceutical operations; this meant closing the Philadelphia factory that had produced its products since the 1880s.

For the year ended December 31, 1987, SmithKline Beckman had annual sales of $4.3 billion, pretax profits of about $803 million, and employed 36,000 people in six principal businesses, the sales of which broke down as shown in table 3-1. A year later, reflecting these actions, pre-tax profits would decline significantly.[7]

Finally, in a decision parallel to the one reached by Beecham's management, Henry agreed in 1988 to refocus SKB on its core business—ethical pharmaceuticals—and to sell off the other three divisions.

By the time Bob met Ken Kermes in mid-1988, confidence in SmithKline Beckman had all but disappeared. It had been the subject of stock market speculation for months, and Henry was under enormous pressure to do something. He faced two options: for the shareholders, selling it at the highest possible price was the best alternative; for the employees, buying another company that would give it scale for the future was a logical choice. Ideally, he wanted to achieve the best for both groups.

With all this information as background, Bob now realized why Ken Kermes thought the timing was right for the two men to meet. The loss in market capitalization to approximately £3.5/$5 billion now placed SKB in the same tier as Beecham.

Table 3-1. SKB's Sales Breakdown, December 1987			
Ethical Pharmaceuticals	49%	Clinical Laboratories	10%
Instruments and Supplies	16%	Animal Health	7%
Eye & Skin Care	13%	Consumer Health Care	4%
Source: SmithKline Beckman, *Annual Report,* 1988, p. 26.			

A MERGER OF EQUALS

Bob was in the United States that early June week to continue his doable-company discussions. He agreed to meet Henry in New York at the distinctive Lowell Hotel on 63rd Street, just off Madison Avenue. They would have about an hour together before his return flight to London.

Henry had been with SmithKline virtually his entire career. After studying international diplomacy at Princeton University, he joined the company soon after graduation in 1955 as a sales representative. He opened Smith, Kline & French's first office in Japan in 1966 and launched Contac, the cold medicine, that same year. He returned to Philadelphia headquarters two years later and was named president and chief operating officer in 1976, the year of Tagamet's launch. In 1982 he became president and chief executive, and in 1987 was named chairman and chief executive, just a few months after Bob became executive chairman of Beecham.

Henry was pursuing SKB's plan, initiated in the early 1980s, to diversify into an integrated healthcare company; he was also taking steps to limit the impending effect of an off-patent Tagamet. So far, however, these efforts had generated more problems, including some with his own management team who did not share his view of the rapidly changing industry.

While they began the discussion by talking about Ken and about their personal experiences in Philadelphia, it took only minutes to get to the topic that was on both their minds: the dramatic changes they saw coming in the industry.

As they talked, they realized they shared the same view: the industry was facing some tough challenges as R&D costs continued to rise at the same time government interest in prescription medicines pricing was growing. Achieving critical mass in R&D and greater marketing capacity to get the returns from that increased R&D investment was crucial. As both men saw it, the highly fragmented industry had no choice: it would have to consolidate to realize the scale that would be necessary to compete more effectively. And they agreed that neither of their own companies could achieve that scale alone.

They talked about how they might work together, including discussion around a strategic alliance between the two animal health businesses (SKB was very familiar with this Beecham business, having actually tried to acquire it several years before). After some reflection, Henry noted, "But that wouldn't make a damn bit of difference in the long run to either one of us."

Seeing his opening, Bob grabbed it and shared his aspiration: "Forget an alliance, what about going all the way: a full-blown merger?"

Today, neither man can remember who actually said the phrase "merger of equals" first, but each remembers the other's favorable response to the concept. Bob remembers Henry asking, almost incredulously, "You'd would be willing to go that far?" and Bob responding, "Yes, and all at once, as opposed to working toward it, business by business, a piece at a time."

With time for this particular meeting running out, the two men agreed to meet again and take the discussions further. As they considered an agenda for their next meeting, they identified the issues they knew they would have to agree on before they could move forward. Clearly, they had to work out the numbers to ensure a merger of equals was feasible from the shareholders' perspective. But—possibly even more critical—they had to share the same vision of what the ideal entity would look like, and agree on all the decisions affecting the people who would lead the new company.

When Bob left the meeting with Henry, he felt hopeful. After all these months he had found someone who thought as he did about the industry—and just as important, someone who was open to exploring ways to address it. In his report to Beecham's EMC that month he shared his impressions of SKB but was careful not to raise any expectations. He also continued to meet with the other companies on his list, afraid to raise his own hopes too high.

BUILDING THE CASE FOR CHANGE

Later that same month, Beecham held its scheduled management meeting at London's Hyde Park Hotel.

Approximately fifty managers sat around the horseshoe stage as they heard firsthand the results for the year ending March 31, 1988:[8]

Earnings per share, up 16.3 percent to 31.68 pence (below average of competitors)

Return on equity, up to 17.4 percent, (but below the 20 percent target)

Return on operating assets, up 2.7 points to 37.1 percent, within the 35–40 percent goal

As the numbers were presented, Bob pointed out that these results, while good, were still below the targeted goals of earnings per share growth superior to comparable U.K. and U.S. companies and a return on equity of at least 20 percent. Resentment in the room started to grow.

When the goals for 1988–1989 were presented—20 percent growth in earnings per share for next year, consistent with the targets—the atmosphere became positively antagonistic. This was a management team not used to setting goals—let alone ones that were so obviously stretched.

"Not a hope in hell, we'll never achieve that," grumbled one executive. The emphasis on management performance grew even stronger as Peter, building off these stretch targets, illustrated how they would tie into the new performance appraisal and objective-setting process, eventually affecting management's compensation. Each step brought the U.K. company closer to becoming the performance-oriented culture the new management was trying to create.

Finally, the company's first five-year strategic plan was presented. The plan showed that without the minimum objective of 20 percent growth in earnings, the pace at which Beecham would fall behind its competitors would accelerate, eventually leaving the company far behind. The message was clear: the company had to do something now, while it was still in a strong position, to guarantee its ability to compete in the longer term.

It was the first management meeting Jim Andress attended in his new position as head of Pharmaceuticals and the last at which both Jim Pollard and John Robb would be present. With the departures of Pollard and Robb in September, some of the tension was relieved as managers felt they no longer had to split their loyalties. Gradually and softly, the management balance between the old and the new guard was starting to shift. The new guard was trying to instill a sense of urgency, trying to make the case for change seem inevitable. But for any change to be successful, they all had to support it. And they needed to do so soon, so they could get on with the task at hand, which was to change Beecham before someone else did.

DEFINING THE VISION

It was August 9 before Bob and Henry met again, this time over dinner. The discussion focused first around what the combined company would look like.

Having originally pursued and then abandoned the concept of an integrated healthcare company, Henry was in the process of returning SmithKline Beckman to its original pharmaceutical roots. He had under way the "ABC" strategy—the proposed spin-off of three businesses: Allergan Eyecare, Beckman Instruments, and Clinical Laboratories.

Beecham had also been in favor of pursuing an integrated healthcare concept but had defined it somewhat differently. Beecham saw healthcare in the future being driven by cost, and therefore the move would be increasingly to self-medication. Having an OTC business gave Beecham the potential of shifting its off-patent prescription medicines into the consumer market and provided them with an infrastructure—the distribution channel to get the products into the marketplace. Beecham was defining integrated by the life cycle of a compound: from its discovery in R&D, through marketing to doctors, then directly to the consumer.

The two company heads debated the question of a pure pharmaceutical versus an integrated healthcare company. Pharmaceuticals was a strong, stable industry, affected very rarely (if ever) by external events and thus had virtually no business cycles. But the companies within the industry did have cycles—often quite dramatic ones—driven by their propensity to pursue blockbusters. The lines on the sales charts would all be upward during patent protection, but the downturn would be precipitous once the patent was lost. An integrated healthcare company promised greater stability, more consistent earnings flow, and less risk since more of the factors were within company control.

Each defined what he meant by healthcare: it was diagnosis, prevention, treatment, and cure. In addition to the ethical pharmaceutical business, the definition encompassed SKB's clinical diagnostics business, while OTC medicines fit under the headings of prevention or treatment. They wanted a company that would have the best R&D and the best marketing among all the competitors. These were the areas that would form the heart of their merger.

Having now established a shared vision—to create an integrated healthcare company that would be better than the competition in both research *and* marketing—they shifted to a delicate question: Who would be the new company's chief executive? It was a conversation that proved to be far less difficult than most would have thought.

Obviously, both men wanted the job. But having convinced themselves of the strategic logic of the merger, they both were really committed to its success: the achievement of their shared vision had to be the overriding objective of every decision they made. To try to limit the obvious emotionalism in the discussion, they decided on some criteria. Foremost among these would have to be who had the ability to sell the merger to the analysts and shareholders.

At this point in their careers, they knew only too well the reality of external perception. Because of the difficulties that SmithKline Beckman had been experiencing, Henry's credibility with the financial community was not as strong at this time as that of Bob, whose own star had been gradually rising as Beecham continued to deliver against each of its stated financial objectives. Intellectually, they knew that for the benefit of the new company, Bob would have to be chief executive. Henry would be chairman. Both men would report directly to the board.

The conversation took far less time than anyone would have imagined. Unwittingly, in their effort to ensure fairness, the two men established the criteria that would drive every decision thereafter: decisions would be based on whatever made sense for the company they were trying to build and the vision they were trying to achieve.

With the most personally awkward and difficult of the questions resolved, it was time now to address the business and financial issues: what would be required to make it a merger of equals?

SmithKline Beckman had been proposed as a candidate for a merger of equals in October 1987.[9] One of the original companies on Beecham's list, it had been ranked as a less likely option than some others because at the time SKB's market capitalization was much too high to qualify it as a potential equal partner. As investors reacted to the dramatic loss in sales of its two principal products, Dyazide and Tagamet, SKBs market capitalization had dimished and was now the same as Beecham's.

As the two men talked, the fact that their pharmaceutical businesses complemented one another almost perfectly became very apparent (see table 3-2). At present, SmithKline Beckman had a strong R&D and marketing capacity in the United States but was weak when it went outside. Beecham was strong in the United Kingdom and Europe but had no significant American presence. The companies' therapeutic categories complemented, rather than competed with, each other. Both companies had aspirations to be leaders in the industry, rather than being niche players or also-rans. Their conclusion: a merger of equals was a real option.

But how could equal value be achieved? What assets would have to be retained/spun off, what parts would have to come together to achieve the vision of an integrated healthcare company, and how could the deal

Table 3-2. Beecham—SKB Comparisons		
	Company Statistics	
1988	*Beecham Group–U.K.*	*SmithKline Beckman–U.S.*
Sales:	£2.5 billion	$4.3 billion
	(57% Europe)	(62% U.S.)
Major Businesses:	Pharmaceuticals (23d)	Pharmaceuticals (6th)
	Consumer Brands	
Employees:	35,800	41,600
Capitalization:	£3.5/$5.6 billion	£3.5/$5.6 billion
Shareholders:	105,000	26,000
Listings:	London SE	NYSE
	NASDAQ (ADRs)	London
		Paris
		Tokyo

Source: Beecham and SmithKline Beckman, *Annual Reports,* 1988.

be structured so that the shareholders would find it attractive enough to support, despite its having no premium? Both companies would be in very vulnerable positions the minute the deal was announced, why shouldn't the shareholder wait for a higher bidder? There would be no room for error.

In the end, they agreed that Beecham would keep consumer brands, but sell cosmetics; SKB would keep clinical laboratories but continue with its plans to spin off Beckman and Allergan.

Using the merger-of-equals concept as their constant guideline, Bob and Henry agreed at this time to establish a board membership equally balanced not only between the two companies, but also between British and Americans. They agreed that another aspect of being equal was equal opportunity and so, in an unprecedented move, they agreed that only those top positions—that is, the senior corporate and business heads whose names were required by the regulatory authorities—be settled now. The others would be selected as part of the next phase, integrating the two companies.

Meanwhile, Henry continued to face discord among members of his own team over the strategic direction being pursued. Ahead lay some very tough discussions with a management group that clearly was not of one mind about going forward. In July the president of SKB's U.S. pharmaceuticals had resigned, and in August the head of research left as the embattled company tried to restore its credibility in the marketplace.

Following this second meeting, Bob felt comfortable enough to outline for Beecham's executive committee the terms he and Henry had discussed. The strategy presentation at the August 15 EMC meeting was bypassed, as some of the items had "been overtaken by events."[10]

It was only now—after the more sensitive agreements around a vision, equal value, and leadership had been agreed between the two chiefs—that external advisers were brought in. Each company briefed an investment bank and legal firm for the U.S. and U.K. markets.

Still, recognizing the enormous complexity of what they were trying to do, both chief executives continued to examine their other options. Leaving no stone unturned, Bob completed his meetings with the other candidate companies. As he did so and considered the possibility of the merger on the one hand, he kept a strong grip on what he was trying to achieve at Beecham with the other.

In early November 1988, the organizational steps and structures that Bob and Henry had agreed on were outlined. Subject to Beecham's EMC and board approval, and contingent on the SKB management and board doing the same, the two men would meet again that month to sign a confidentiality and standstill agreement and commence with the serious negotiations.

On November 7 the Beecham board was informed of the progress made with Henry to date. Having agreed on the path chosen months before, the board's main concern at this stage was whether SKB was the right company. Satisfied with the evaluation, strategic fit and compatibility of management style, the Beecham board gave the go ahead to engage advisers.

Until then, only the two company heads had been involved in discussing the kind of company they hoped to build. With those beliefs outlined only sketchily to the boards and senior management teams, they now needed to broaden and deepen that discussion if they wanted true commitment to what they were trying to achieve through this merger of equals. They appointed individuals from each company to develop a business plan for what the merged company would look like, especially in pharmaceuticals. In that process they were really trying to gain broader buy-in to the vision from a very important group, the group that would make it happen. Furthermore, by throwing together this group of strangers *now* they would also get some feeling for how well the senior management from both companies would work together later.

CREATING A NEW VISION

As autumn headed toward winter, the companies started to work out the actual numbers. In mid-November about twenty senior operating managers from the two firms began several weeks of seclusion in a Manhattan lawyer's basement office. Their primary tactical purpose was to make sure the proposed vision of the two chief executives actually was feasible. Their output was to be the first business plan of the new company.

The teams emerged with enthusiasm, clearly excited by the prospects. The major challenge, Tagamet's expiration, appeared manageable. Sales could be held for five years, they argued, and there were enough potential compounds in the Beecham pipeline to offset the loss of Tagamet sales once it came off patent in 1994.

Investment bankers were finally asked to confirm what the two chairmen had scribbled on the back of a napkin at their August dinner about financial values of the various businesses in their portfolios.

On the business-plan level, the initial output that emerged confirmed Beecham's view. In pharmaceuticals the companies' therapeutic categories were complementary, not competitive, and combined acute and chronic compounds (antibiotics, cardiovascular, gastrointestinal, central nervous systems, anti-inflammatory, and vaccines). They would add the marketing and research strength each had desired, as well as deepen their scientific and geographical reach, especially in the United States. In global sales, the combined company would rank number two in pharmaceuticals, number two in OTC medicines, number four in animal health; it would be the largest in laboratory diagnostics in the United States. In certain key markets such as Spain, the new company would be the country's largest in pharmaceuticals. With combined R&D expenditures of £300/$535 million, it would be ranked fifth in the world. The sales force and number of research scientists would double to 5,000 and 6,000 respectively, overnight.[11]

On a personal level, the people working on the teams exhibited a cooperativeness and a kindred spirit that boded well for the proposed new company. They shared the same strong desire to do well and to work together. By the end of the month-long process, the merger had its first group of disciples who would champion its cause in the tough months ahead.

Having first strategically developed their vision with each other and then confirmed it through their own managers' analysis, Bob and Henry now had a vision that was aspirational as well as logical and was owned by more than two people. The strength of their original logic, confirmed time and again, provided a compelling argument against any of the potential stumbling blocks. In the future, whenever there was a danger of the deal coming undone, they could refer back to that logic. This shared vision put everything in perspective and meant that most of the senior managers were willing to sacrifice personal ambitions for the greater good.

As more people became involved and traffic between New York and London increased, concern grew that a leak to the press might jeopardize the deal. Now, as people were drawn into the planning they signed a confidentiality agreement, swearing themselves to secrecy. At Beecham the project was named "Project Tokyo"—deliberately capitalizing on an earlier rumor that the company was going to list shares on the Tokyo Stock Exchange. Contracts were reviewed to ensure that managers had more to gain by adhering to the confidentiality code than by breaking it.

STOPPING AND STARTING

In mid-November 1988 Beecham announced its half-year results: earnings had risen 16 percent (versus 1 percent in 1985–1986), and Beecham was well on the way to delivering a similar increase for 1987–1988—consistent with, if not better than, the City's and Wall Street's projections. The analysts—some more begrudgingly than others—started to come around. The business was restructured, leading to significant cost savings, and major reshuffles had occurred in top management. Beecham was being perceived as a turnaround in the making. Bob was gaining credibility and now had a strong base on which to move Beecham forward.

Having confirmed the soundness of the integrated healthcare company vision, the practicality of a merger of equals and the compatibility of the people, the management teams moved into high gear during December. The two critical determinants of success—strategic and organizational compatibility—had been tested and proven. The numbers were crunched, and the equity structure that would make the value equal for both sets of shareholders had been agreed on.

Very early in the negotiations it was decided that the merger of equals would be in fact as well as in perception. The new organization would be a public limited company (plc), registered in the United Kingdom, trading on the London Stock Exchange. The U.K. standards on merger accounting coupled with certain tax advantages made it more advantageous for the fledgling company to be U.K. based.

With SKB's 150-year heritage in Philadelphia and long-standing profile as a major civic leader, the idea of the company being headquartered in Britain was one that Henry thought would be most difficult to sell to his shareholders. Political timing of the merger was not optimal, as the United States had grown increasingly concerned about the rise in foreign acquisitions of U.S. blue chip companies—Celanese (Hoechst) and Chesebrough-Pond's (Unilever), to name two. In an effort to again maintain the equality between the two companies, they agreed to trade off the London location—home of Beecham Group—for the name: SmithKline would come first. The new company would be known as SmithKline Beecham.

Negotiations continued. Outside, the rumor mill had started to grind, and stories circulated that SmithKline Beckman might be acquired. Was disgruntled management deliberately leaking information, trying to put the company into play? So far, Beecham had not been listed as a possible suitor. In the weeks leading up to Christmas, shares in SKB's stock climbed, adding 6 percent to its market value.[12] If the share price continued to run up, it would make the merger of equals impossible.

Bob and Henry did not want to be forced into making an announcement before they were ready. Too many issues remained unresolved. If they hadn't made the case for the merger airtight, if they were not able to communicate its unassailable logic, they would actually place both companies in extremely vulnerable positions. While they could run that risk at any time, it was just that much greater now. Left with little choice, they told the investment banks and management teams that the deal was dead. The raging speculation around SKB's shares ceased.

As far as the Beecham management was concerned, they were both furious and disappointed, having put much time and energy into the task during the past four months and becoming more and more committed to the vision. Some continued to work the issues—but behind the scenes. Their hopes were crushed, but none wanted to place the company in a vulnerable position.

The Beecham management never really thought the merger was off; the logic of it was still too apparent. They took the holiday period as time to consider what was at stake and hoped that SKB's management was doing the same. The cooling-off period actually bought the companies four more months of planning.

It was early January 1989 when Bob rang Henry to see if perhaps they could readdress the lingering questions. There were no plane trips; everything was done by telephone. No point in stirring the rumor mill or raising management hopes if the two men couldn't resolve the last remaining issue, which was the role of Philadelphia. While they had agreed that certain corporate staff functions would be based there, and that animal health and clinical laboratories would be managed from the United States, the lingering question had to do with where the worldwide pharmaceuticals' headquarters would be. One view held that locating the two major businesses alongside the corporate headquarters would ensure the consistent and ongoing dialogue required to realize the integrated healthcare concept. The other view proposed that, as the United States was the largest market for pharmaceuticals, it made sense to locate its headquarters there, with its management flying to London as required. After several weeks of back-and-forth telephone calls, the two men reached what each thought was the agreement. What they did not realize was that each had interpreted the decision differently. Their misunderstanding would later raise significant credibility issues within the business and teach both men a simple but valuable lesson: write everything down so there is no misinterpretation. But for now, the agreement reached via that last telephone call enabled the men to move on.

The investment bankers, lawyers, accountants, and external public relations advisers were called back in, as the complex finance, legal, and tax structure of the largest transatlantic merger done to date was put together and the early stages of a strategic communications plan to sell the deal were outlined. At each meeting, scores of advisers would take their places behind the company management of Beecham on one side of the table, replicated exactly on the other side for SmithKline Beckman.

Still, the insiders outnumbered the outsiders. In retrospect, having so many company people involved as early as possible meant that the merger always belonged to management, not the advisers. That this ownership by the organization was felt so early became a critical success factor in planning and implementing the integration of the two companies.

The companies, not the counselors, were running the show. And because members of the management tried to keep the bigger picture in mind, even as they found themselves facing the minutiae inherent in a deal of this size, they were able to work through it—even when the advisers thought they had exhausted every possibility. It really was "their" merger; the advisers simply brought the expertise required to execute it. Furthermore, by getting the issues involving the senior positions resolved up front, they were all freed from worrying about them throughout the difficult negotiations. Whatever decisions they made, they knew who would be responsible for executing them.

On Tuesday, March 28, the rumor trail that started in Philadelphia finally led one *Philadelphia Inquirer* journalist to telephone London. Someone had told her that Beecham had retained the Wasserstein Perella investment bank. Confirming this last piece, she reached her conclusion: SmithKline Beckman was definitely in discussions with Beecham.

On March 29, 1989, a headline in the *Philadelphia Inquirer* confirmed everyone's suspicions about a deliberate inside leak: "A Source Tells of SmithKline Merger Talks."[13]

Board meetings were hurriedly called for that weekend. Each chairman posed his question: "Do I have the board's approval to officially announce our intention to merge?"

The two companies had run out of time. It was now or never.

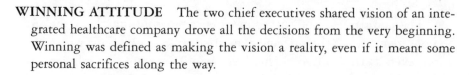

**Phase I:
Strategy
1986–1989**

WINNING ATTITUDE   The two chief executives shared vision of an integrated healthcare company drove all the decisions from the very beginning. Winning was defined as making the vision a reality, even if it meant some personal sacrifices along the way.

ORGANIZATION AS HERO   Despite the need for secrecy, a far greater risk would have been not involving as early as possible the managers who would make the merger work. Teams from both companies came together first to develop the business plan *before* bringing in any external advisers. This change in sequence made a fundamental difference in the implementation as a core group from both companies became both convinced and committed to the merger's success right from the start. This ability to work together early on was also the major benefit of having been an agreed-on merger rather than a hostile takeover.

CUMULATIVE LEARNING   While having a shared vision was important, it was equally important that it be substantiated through rigorous analysis and comparative data. The basement planning team showed that having a disciplined process to evaluate the proposal was extremely effective in helping them reach a logical decision. As the team tried to pull together the data in a meaningful way, it illustrated early on the dilemma the merged company would face due to fundamentally different financial and information systems.

STRATEGIC COMMUNICATION   Communication is given priority at a management level as the topic takes its place as a regular EMC agenda item for Beecham, and the chief executive personally demonstrates his expectations of it as a management responsibility by visiting employees regularly and directly. Striving to create a more participative environment through building greater awareness of the company's goals, new systems to address employees in their own language and in a timely way are initiated to encourage and support local management's efforts. Communication is also brought into the merger approval process at the beginning.

ALIGNMENT OF BEHAVIOR AND STRATEGY   To create a high performance culture, new reward, performance appraisal, and MBO programs were introduced into Beecham, linking reward directly to company performance.

Selling a New and Better Company

S UNDAY, APRIL 2, WAS A typical gray day in London, with some drizzling rain. As on most Sundays, London was quiet, and traffic in front of Beecham House was light. But cars had been arriving since 8:00 A.M. and by midday, activity inside the eight-story brick building had built to a crescendo as copy was redrafted, stock exchange disclosure regulations were checked one more time, and distribution plans for the announcement were finalized yet again.

In Philadelphia the twenty-four-floor glass and stone headquarters of SmithKline Beckman stood silent as dawn approached. Yet inside, keyboards had been tapping since 5:00 A.M. as numerous legal and management "editors" wrote and rewrote the same few sentences. Faxes blurred back and forth to ensure absolute consistency with their London counterparts.

During the preceding twenty-four hours, the wording in the final three-paragraph press release had been reviewed and agreed by all eight sets of advisers (legal, banking, U.S. and U.K. brokers, and PR consultancies for each firm) plus twenty members of management. Compelled by the stock exchanges in New York and London to address the swirling market rumors and newspaper innuendoes, the two companies had been forced to announce the merger discussions before the final terms had been agreed upon. Without any of the deal's details, and abiding by the markets' stringent disclosure regulations, the wording of the press release was almost innocuous, raising far more questions than could possibly be answered.

With approval finally given, at 2:00 P.M. Joanne telephoned her counterpart at SmithKline Beckman, and with that, the release was read to the Reuters and Dow Jones newswires, ending eight months of speculation about a possible liaison. SmithKline Beckman Inc. and Beecham Group plc announced that "discussions were taking place regarding a possible merger of major parts of our respective businesses. . . ."[1]

It was done. The news was officially out.

Telephones rang well into the night, as analysts from each major market called in turn. The last contact was made at 2:30 A.M. in the United Kingdom, as one analyst telephoned from Los Angeles, anxious to know who would be leading the combined entity.

Announcing the deal before the terms had actually been completed was almost as if each company had announced to the financial markets that it was up for sale. Both sets of management knew they had increased their vulnerability to an unfriendly takeover almost overnight. Bob went to bed that night haunted by one question: What would the headlines read? He knew they would make or break the deal.

The next morning, the newspapers were delivered to Beecham House by 7:00. There was hardly time to clip the stories as everyone hovered around desks, scanning the headlines, virtually oblivious to the hallway chatter of employees who had been completely surprised by the announcement. The response of financial markets and media in both countries was absolutely critical: it would shape initial opinions about the entire merger. Were the analysts and the press for the deal, or against it?

With an audible sigh of relief, the Beecham team agreed that the first hurdle had been overcome. In general, the analyst comments reported in the press were favorable. While it had been difficult for them to make a quantifiable assessment without financial details, they could make a strategic assessment by looking at the two businesses. And on that criterion, they made their initial judgment, ranging from "it's not the best possibility, but it's a good fit for both companies" to "the fit is remarkable."[2] Overall, concluded the press, the deal made sense.

The analysts appreciated the logic of the merger—the very thing Bob and Henry had spent so much time making sure was right from day one. Just as the strength of the business logic had guided the companies through myriad negotiations, this single message now guided the security analysts as they drafted their first reports and awaited more details.

But the financial markets, calm since the takeover spree of the early 1980s, jumped on the news by proclaiming the obvious: announcing the merger—especially before its terms had been finalized—put both companies in very vulnerable positions. In a flurry of speculation about potential bidders, the share prices for both companies soared. The pharmaceutical sector indices also rose sharply, as analysts saw the SKB/Beecham merger as the first move in the long-predicted restructuring of the drug industry.

With the announcement made, teams on both sides of the Atlantic moved into overdrive. Monday afternoon they mapped out an ambitious timetable, agreeing that the detailed terms of the deal for shareholders would be resolved and announced by April 12—less than ten working days away. Everyone went right back into negotiations and started hammering out the remaining issues.

The aggressive target was based on their fear of losing the favorable analyst and press opinion achieved so far and having a bidder step in, leaving no alternative. The ambitious deadline also created a tremendous sense of urgency and self-induced pressure to achieve their aspirations. It forced everyone to clear their thinking. They found they were able to resolve issues in an hour that normally could have taken them a month. The self-imposed stretch goal was the first of many that would characterize the process of building the new company.

The teams met every day the next ten, often leaving U.K. investment banker Kleinwort Benson's offices on Fenchurch Street just as the sun was rising. Gradually the final merger terms were defined. The clearly stated intention of the two chairmen—to create a true merger of equals—guided every discussion: financial considerations for shareholders, business disposals, the composition of the board. There was enormous sensitivity to detail as Bob and Henry realized that everyone, inside and outside the firms, was looking for the slightest clue that would tip the merger into a takeover. They became very conscious of symbolism and its role in communicating key messages.

Finally, at 3:00 in the morning of April 10, 1989, with just hours to go before the board meeting at which they would have to present the final terms, the two men stood in the bank's simple conference room on Fenchurch Street. They shook hands, and the champagne cork popped.

Bob felt elated. After all these months, the agreement to create SmithKline Beecham had finally been reached. His euphoria was short-lived, however, as he soon recognized that the real challenges still lay ahead. They had to sell the deal they had struck; and if successful, they had to realize the promise of the tentative business plan.

The next day, April 11, each chairman met with his respective board to present the final terms of the agreement and request approval. Bob had until midnight to advise Henry, who would be meeting with his board at the same time on the other side of the Atlantic. Starting promptly at 4:00 P.M. the Beecham Board began its momentous discussion.

The investment bankers gave their view of what the outside market would say, addressing the major concern: what was the risk of putting Beecham into play? After they left, each EMC member was asked for his view. The votes were along expected lines: longer-term Beecham people were reluctant, whereas the newer team members were very positive, captured in Jim Andress's all-endorsing "No guts, no glory!"

The nonexecutive directors then grilled the EMC: Could they generate the cost savings required? Was the potential of the combined pipeline real enough to generate the growth they were promising? And (their major concern) could the new company hold the sales of Tagamet at current levels—£50/$80 million per month—for five years until the new products in the Beecham pipeline would begin contributing significantly to sales? Satisfied with the responses, the board moved ahead and voted unanimously in favor. The discussion had lasted close to five hours. The EMC members were exhausted, but exhilarated.

Meanwhile, Henry was going through the same process with his board. The issues he faced primarily focused on value for shareholders. Given they would receive no premium on the transaction, was the merger of equals the best option? SKB board members focused on assessing the potential growth of the new company: was Beecham's pipeline really strong enough to generate results in the near term that would be better than SKB could achieve on its own, or with another partner?

At 9:00 P.M. in the United Kingdom and 4:00 P.M. in the United States, the two men spoke. All signals were go. There would be no turning back.

On April 12, right on target, the firms announced the agreed terms of the proposed merger. The merger transaction would be completed through a complex share exchange, with no additional equity raised. The stapled stock equity structures assured that each shareholder was receiving equal value. The achievement of equal value of each firm had proved very complex and required several divestments. In exchange for its existing shares, SmithKline agreed to distribute shares in its Allergan eyecare products unit and Beckman Instruments to SmithKline shareholders, along with the stapled equity unit in the new company. Beecham agreed to divest its cosmetics and fragrance businesses and to present each Beecham shareholder with the "A" share in the new company and £1.75 in loan stock. Until the cosmetics sale was completed, there would be a substantial debt outstanding from the funding of the loan stock. In both instances, while the businesses to be divested had been earmarked previously as part of each company's plans to focus more on their core businesses, cosmetics would prove to be the more difficult to dispose of, taking far longer than expected. The final company would look like table 4-1. Its businesses would be organized into four business sectors as shown in table 4-2.

The next day—April 13—Beecham and SKB jointly announced a strategic alliance to copromote five major drugs in the United States, including Beecham's leading antibiotic Augmentin and SKB's leading ulcer drug Tagamet, "in order to integrate our marketing efforts from

Table 4-1. SmithKline Beecham at a Glance, April 1, 1989	
Sales	£3.7/$6.6 billion
Profits before taxes	£544/$974 million
R&D expenditure	£337/$603 million
Market capitalization	£7/$12 million
No. of employees	62,800

Source: Excerpt from the pro forma statements, Merger Documents, p. 42.

Table 4-2. The Business Sectors of SmithKline Beecham	% Sales	% Profits
Pharmaceuticals	52	63
Consumers Brands	29	24
Animal Health	8	7
Clinical Laboratories	11	6

Source: Based on segment data, SmithKline Beecham, Annual Report, 1989, p. 66.

the outset." The comarketing agreement—while beneficial to both companies—was actually a deterrent to an unsolicited third party, since its terms would remain enforceable no matter who owned the companies. As an added benefit it underscored management's belief in the strategic logic of the combination, reinforcing the message about added sales strength and complementary products. (It also meant that they could begin working together much sooner to realize one of the merger's major benefits: the increased sales potential.)

In the three months between announcing the terms of the deal and winning shareholder approval, the management of the two companies faced three streams of activity—each one major in itself, but absolutely overwhelming when placed side by side, which was how they had to be managed. Managers found themselves split in three directions:

1. Gaining regulatory and shareholder approval, the timetable for which was outside their control

2. Running the business, the pace of which had to be maintained at a constant level

3. Planning how the two companies would come together, the schedule for which was mainly within their control

The third priority added pressure that some felt, in light of all the effort the transatlantic deal was requiring, could have been avoided if they deferred the planning discussion until after the shareholder vote. Yet Bob was adamant. From what he had learned about other mergers, becoming one company—structurally *and* emotionally—as quickly as possible was a critical factor in a new entity's ultimate success. Once he knew the merger was going to happen, he was committed to not just achieving the promised savings, but to creating a brand new company. He believed he must resolve the business and people issues before he could focus on creating the culture that would give the new entity its true competitive advantage. The integration had to be done quickly by the organization, not a small group of management, if they were to start building a company that would realize the full promise of the merger.

STREAM 1: COMPLETING THE DEAL

Announcement of the merger terms began a legally imposed quiet period for both companies. Securities laws in the United States and the United

Kingdom permitted no further communication about the merger, internally or externally, until the shareholders had received the detailed merger documentation on which they would base their vote.

Hugh Collum, finance director, and Fergus Balfour, legal counsel, took this time to write out a detailed timetable that would guide the merger approval process. Their goal was to simplify what was an incredibly difficult process in any merger, but its complexity was virtually doubled because of the deal's transatlantic nature and equal merger terms. The timetable had to start with the regulatory requirements for each country and the completion of shareholder documents according to the different U.K. and U.S. accounting standards and tax laws. Then they had to work through which advisers were dealing with which issues and what information was required in order for each to complete and sign off on their portion. Compensation consultants had to be brought in to help define compensation programs for senior management consistent with the new company's intended global compensation plans, and to design executive option plans for approval by the shareholders. Public relations advisers were not only planning how to best position the merger with analysts, press, shareholders, and employees, but also defining a defensive strategy in case a third party stepped in.

With all this activity, the master timetable Hugh and Fergus were devising was extremely tight. U.K. shareholders would vote at an extraordinary shareholders' meeting on June 20, and U.S. shareholders at a similar meeting on July 26. Given all the requirements, July 26 was the earliest date they could win approval, assuming everything went smoothly and they met every other deadline on schedule.

It was too short a time to get all the work done, but too long to manage the growing uncertainty—and fear—that was arising at every level. Compounding the concern was the difference in shareholder approval dates, which meant a protracted period in play for the United Kingdom.

As management struggled internally to manage the advisers, it had to focus externally on opinion-formers such as the media, who would be key to shaping shareholders' views. Because this was the first major merger in the pharmaceutical industry as well as the largest transatlantic all-equity deal ever done, the two companies received an unprecedented level of attention from both analysts and the press. But because of the imposed quiet period, most of the questions were unanswerable, creating frustration on both sides. It also meant that no more could be said to those inside the company than had been said to those outside.

Hordes of people, including the teams of accountants, then lawyers, then investment bankers for each company, worked feverishly to complete the submissions in time. The very nature of the due diligence meant there could be no shortcuts, and tempers grew short as the same company person often had to answer the same inquiry from each of the six different advisers. Adding to the frustration: in some cases, the legal requirements of the two countries actually conflicted. For example, obeying U.K. regulations meant details of the deal would be in the 200-page U.K. document sent to the U.K. shareholders nearly a month before the U.S. shareholders received their 400-page version and the quiet period imposed by the U.S. Securities and Exchange Commission (SEC) had ended.

While the SEC required that no American investors receive data in advance of SmithKline's documents reaching its shareholders, realistically, as soon as something was released as required by the United Kingdom, it was on newswires all over the world within minutes.

The other challenge resulting from the deal's transatlantic nature was trying to sell the proposed new company to individual and institutional shareholders in the two financial markets, each of which had unique perspectives. To address some concerns, the financial structure was devised so that the securities traded locally, and dividends would be paid in local currencies. The U.K. company agreed to report quarterly, as was custom in the United States, rather than on its normal half-yearly basis.

The communication plan segmented investors by holdings and by country, identified potential objections and issues, and created a single platform of messages for both companies that would not just address those concerns, but aggressively market the benefits of the combined new entity in a way that was consistent, yet locally relevant. The business logic of the merger was captured in phrases such as "a new and better company," "together, greater results than either one could alone," "leading positions in each of our industries," and "two plus two equals five." Specific examples from the business were used to reinforce each message.

(It was not only important that the U.K. and U.S. shareholders understand the company's true global presence; there was concern that in some places, growing nationalism and concern over unemployment could mean government rejection of the merger. The merger had to get through the Hart-Scott-Rodino Act in the United States, the Office of Fair Trading in the United Kingdom, and certain European work councils.

Conscious of the xenophobic concerns of both markets, the new company was positioned as U.S. for the American audience, and U.K. for the British by exploiting the amount of sales, research, and famous brand names the new company would have in each country.)

While the business logic was recognized as sound, the number one issue for most security analysts and major shareholders was management. Without a strong management, the promised benefits would remain just that: promises.

Once the U.K. shareholder documents were posted in mid-May, a concerted effort began to get the entire management team better known in the two markets. Nearly every day, management team members found themselves heading for a different airport, as they met with large institutional shareholders in London, Edinburgh, Boston, New York, Chicago, and Philadelphia. Press interviews were set up in which each member of the management team would elaborate on a particular strategic message, such as the combined company's increased sales and research strength.

But the merger's strategic sense and management's credibility weren't always enough; the management teams encountered hostile audiences on both sides of the Atlantic. In the United States, arbitrageurs who had anticipated a SmithKline Beckman takeover were very angry that their large stock positions would now bring no takeover premium. On the Beecham side, most shareholders believed that Beecham had made a lot of progress and wondered why its senior management wanted to take the risk of such a merger. Even as the Beecham management focused on selling the merger, it also had to make sure that the old way didn't look bad, in case the merger didn't happen.

One of the toughest moments came in Scotland, as a major shareholder challenged, "But why merge? Beecham is doing well, you've turned the corner. Shareholders won't get a premium out of this merger, and besides, mergers never work. Our rule is that once a company enters into a merger agreement, we drop the shares."

That was it: mergers never work.

Finally, on May 10, the first comprehensive analysts' report on the proposed merged company was issued in the United Kingdom. With the banner "Deal of the Decade!" the Shearson Lehman report became a watershed, setting the tone for the reports and media stories that followed.

But six weeks remained before the U.K. shareholders' vote at the end of June, and ten weeks before the U.S. shareholders' vote at the end of July. The communication team kept a pipeline of story ideas focused around the business logic, trying to maintain the press and analysts' positive tone.

STREAM 2: BUSINESS AS USUAL

While management had to concern itself with completing the deal, it was equally worried about maintaining business as usual.

Concern grew that employees, increasingly distracted by the merger activities, would neglect the day-to-day running of the business. If allowed to go unchecked, any decline in the business could place management credibility in serious jeopardy. It proved to be an enormously difficult task, with people feeling pulled in myriad directions at once. Managers who were helping gather the data for the new company were expected to maintain the day-to-day morale, order, and productivity of their employees. Employees were expected to be excited about the enormous opportunity presented by the merger even as they read press stories citing analyst estimates of potential job cuts. In some places employees remained far removed from the work associated with the deal, whereas in other areas the work was exclusively merger related. And in many cases the people who had always had the answers, their own supervisors, knew no more than they did.

Beecham employees couldn't understand why the merger was necessary: it just didn't make any sense to cause all this turmoil if they were doing so well. Some felt they were selling out to the Americans.

Communication was the way to keep employees focused. The emphasis was on maintaining a steady flow of information about what was going on and why, what would happen next, and what was expected of them. The objective was to ease their concerns about the merger as much as possible first by placing it within a strategic context, such as why the merger was unnecessary (the changing government environment and growing competition, using specific data), and then anticipating their questions by sharing information about the new partner and the approval process, including the timetable for completion. Care was taken that information given internally was the same as that given externally, minimizing conflicting messages. By creating an information network and using it regularly and systematically, the communication team tried to supersede and manage the ubiquitous grapevine.

The message "business as usual" was delivered as often as possible by as many members of management as feasible. News of business successes were communicated widely, and efforts were made to ensure that employees saw no change in their day-to-day environment. A special publication, *Merger News,* was issued within twenty-four hours of any news release to ensure that employees learned of developments internally at the same time outsiders heard about them.

Despite all their efforts, they never seemed to answer all the employees' questions. With their time and energy focused externally, members of the senior team could do little at first to calm the enormous angst and emotional turmoil employees were experiencing.

Gradually things settled down, and the focus on their day-to-day work actually provided employees with some relief from uncertainty. Their business was real; their achievements against targets were tangible victories. They could still feel they were somehow winning.

The business-as-usual message was somehow getting through, and reports from each of the Beecham business units during this time indicated some significant successes, including new product launches and extensions, and entering new markets such as the former Soviet Union. Reports for the first three months of the fiscal year 1988–1989 showed that profits were running ahead of plan.

Ultimately, while Bob was saying "business as usual" what he really wanted was business *better* than usual. Having a strong foundation going into the merger was the only way the new company was going to deliver results better than either one could alone.

STREAM 3: PREPARING FOR INTEGRATION

Even as management focused enormous time, energy, and effort on winning shareholder approval, reassuring employees, and maintaining business momentum, it was already taking steps to make sure the new company hit the ground running once approval was received in late July.

Although they couldn't actually *do* anything with the business until the shareholders voted, they could think and plan the integration so they got off to a strong start as soon as SmithKline Beecham (SB) was official.

In the few months prior to their announcement, Beecham's top team had taken time to learn more about mergers. Why had so few—despite good strategic logic—failed to achieve their financial objectives? What distinguished those that succeeded from those considered to have failed?

The key differences seemed to be organizational. Beyond the near-term financial and strategic considerations, long-term success was directly related to the amount of emotional turmoil and uncertainty that existed, the length of time it had been allowed to go on, and whether it had been used constructively to build the integrated company. It seemed the longer the period, the lower the productivity, and the less likely that the new company could achieve its promised potential.

In many instances, after initially slashing operations to realize obvious savings, members of the top team would grow increasingly worried about the business. Accepting the organization's concern about overwork or fear about integrating too quickly, they would delay tough decisions. Everyone would stay with what they were doing, even so far as allowing the businesses to run separately for a while. Failing to capture the promised cost savings and business opportunities offered by the combined entity, management lost the potential of the original vision.

Three actions appeared to be fundamental for SB's integration to succeed:

1. Establish a plan, and move as quickly as practical.

2. Involve as many people as practical.

3. Provide clear guidelines and standard procedures so that decisions are all data driven.

The Case for a Swiftly Executed Plan

Mergers create a built-in crisis that provides management with a unique opportunity: employees are waiting and expecting change to happen. Rather than allowing things to slow down, management must maintain the momentum and capitalize on the opportunity to make change happen.

The urgency behind the drive to become one structurally was to realize cost savings as early as possible and get on with building the company for the long term. Bob knew the financial market—the ultimate judge of the merger's success—would never give him the time to build the company if he didn't deliver the promised savings fast. He was also aware that hasty decisions could jeopardize the ability to achieve longer-term goals. Management needed a big picture for the future against which it could make near-term decisions. So, even as the teams were completing due diligence, meeting the regulatory requirements, and visiting with key shareholders, the first integration planning meeting was set for April 17—only five days after the merger details were announced and a month before documents to the U.K. shareholders were posted. Setting the meeting date ensured that the merger approval process would not sidetrack the integration planning process.

The Case for Involving People

The simplest and fastest way to have achieved the promised savings and benefits would have been for senior management to simply (and some could say arbitrarily) merge the two businesses. This top-down approach is favored by many security analysts as the quickest way to realize synergies, and while employees may find it painful, it is the most expeditious way to eliminating job uncertainty.

However, best-practice research clearly indicated that dictating merger plans from around a table at corporate headquarters did not always mean successful implementation or long-term effectiveness in the business unit. The reason many mergers fail is that they start and stay at the top. When a merger is viewed as top management's, rather than the whole company's, the momentum to win is never instilled beyond that top layer. Furthermore, where mergers are driven top down, integration decisions may appear to be quick but usually take a long time to implement, especially in companies where operations are spread across the world. Twenty people cannot achieve what 2,000 people can.

If SB was to achieve its financial objectives as promised, it would need to address integration on a global scale and involve the organization right from the start in designing the new company. The challenge was to move quickly *and* ensure involvement and ownership by more than just a few. This would involve highly structured teamwork.

The Case for Guidelines and Procedures

Believing the team approach to be the most efficient and effective way of accomplishing the mammoth integration, management knew the only way to deliver both was to establish a disciplined process and clear and stringent guidelines by which the teams would operate. This would ensure alignment and consistency, yet allow for employee empowerment.

Many companies address integration country by country and unit by unit, with managers from each firm instructed simply to integrate.

The quality of decisions and their implementation may vary across the company. One manager is likely to emerge the stronger, which leads some employees to feel they are not merging but being taken over. They become demotivated as they see one company "winning" over the other.

SmithKline and Beecham had entirely different business heritages. Where one had been scientifically driven, almost genteel, as part of the gentlemanly pharmaceutical industry, the other was commercially driven, hard nosed and aggressive, used to battling it out in the tight-margin, diversified consumer-products arena. While these differences made the businesses complementary, they offered the potential for enormous conflict. That there was also an American and British way of doing things just added to the complexity. One of the features they had in common—a long history—also meant that both were bureaucratic and somewhat paternalistic, prone to decisions based more on intuition and emotion than on analysis and data. Management had to design a process that would bring these two disparate groups together effectively and efficiently.

PLANNING THE PLAN

On April 17, as scheduled, the new executive management committee (EMC) gathered in a drab hotel conference room at New York's JFK Airport—a location that bespoke the enormous time pressures on the transatlantic group.

The ten members of the EMC included Henry and Bob as chairman and chief executive, respectively, Hugh Collum as head of finance, Ken Kermes as leader of planning, Peter at the helm of human resources, and Fergus Balfour as corporate secretary. Also included were the operating heads of the two major groups, John Chappell for Pharmaceuticals and Jim Andress for Consumer Brands, along with the regional heads of pharmaceuticals for the United States and Europe. Representation was evenly divided between the two companies, with Beecham managers assuming the majority of the corporate positions and SKB managers the majority of the business units.

On their agenda that day: to plan how they would integrate the two companies starting the day following shareholder approval.

A subset of the EMC was formed which was to be known as the merger management committee (MMC). The MMC was composed of seven members, again almost equally divided between Beecham and

SmithKline Beckman, and chaired by Bob. His role was deliberate. Despite his strong belief that members of the organization had to do it themselves, he was not quite confident that the new company would realize the savings and sales goals set if he was not personally and deeply involved in the entire integration process.

The MMC comprised the key managers who would lead the integration of the two companies and shape the future SB's destiny. Their role would be "to provide guidance, philosophy, strategy, receive recommendations and make decisions, but not to do it all."[3]

As MMC members looked at the issues posed by global integration, they realized that nothing had prepared any of them for the enormity of the task that lay ahead. The new company just didn't have the experience or the resources to provide all the assistance the teams would require. If they were serious about building something new and better, they would need some outside advice. They agreed the consultant had to be global and capable of handling the enormous complexity of bringing together operations in four businesses throughout forty-five different countries. In addition to analytical and problem solving skills, the resource could provide the latest industry data and best-practice advice. Most important, the consultant would act as a neutral voice, bringing a perspective that was different from either of the two companies.

The competence of any firm selected against this criteria was taken for granted. What the new management felt extremely strong about was the caliber, attitude, and facilitation skills of the individual consultants. It wanted outsiders who would act like insiders, people who would work alongside SB managers rather than direct them—or worse, actually *do* the work. For the plans to succeed, the organization, not the consultants, had to own them. The consultants had to accept a subordinate role to the task forces.

In the end, McKinsey was selected based on its willingness to put together a team of the best from anywhere in the world, and to roll up its sleeves *with* SB rather than *for* SB. (The last point was heavily emphasized. So that the consultants did not stay on at SB, the contract stipulated that all integration plans were due, and the consultants' role completed, within six months of the merger: December 31, 1989.)

While the role of the MMC as an integration body was very important, creating it at exactly this point in the merger process and announcing it to the organization a month later accomplished two additional things. First, it reassured employees by letting them know that other people were worrying about the merger; they could focus on their jobs. Second, it was symbolic. While nothing could be done until the merger was approved, creation of the MMC told both organizations that management was already planning and was intent on becoming one company as soon as possible.

The MMC agreed to meet a minimum of every two weeks, on alternate sides of the Atlantic, determined that the integration process would proceed simultaneously with the merger approval process.

INVOLVING THE ORGANIZATION

The June planning meeting, which was held in McKinsey's offices in London, lasted three days. The agenda reflected the enormous complexity of what management was dealing with. Some issues were immediate, such as addressing the SEC's comments on the documents that would be mailed to the American shareholders days later. Others were more medium term, including how to expedite the copromotion of Tagamet and Augmentin in the United States, the United Kingdom, and Europe. Finally, they moved on to planning the merger integration process and the decisions that would shape the new company for the longer term.

Having shared the key lessons about integration, members of the MMC were in agreement about the need to involve a large number of people. The success of the twenty strangers who had been thrown together to create the company's first business plan reinforced the MMC's belief in the organization's ability to design the new company. From a practical standpoint, involving more people meant addressing more areas and generating more aggressive results than a small management team could do in the same period of time. More important, it was likely to yield better-quality answers and greater commitment, as had emerged from the first team. The quality of that team's plan was evidenced again by its use as a template for much of the merger documentation process. Thus the task-force approach that created the first business plan became the model for planning the integration.

Compared to the initial plan, however, the size of this task was daunting. How would they bring the remaining 57,000 people, working in four separate businesses at more than 150 locations in forty-five countries together to create one company, at the same time reducing positions by 5,000 and achieving savings of £500/$807 million over a targeted three-year period?

It look straightforward enough, but as the MMC proceeded, it realized that all the interdependencies among these areas, including those that were cross-sector and cross-geography, had not been worked through. Planning teams were created for areas critical to realizing the necessary cost savings and business opportunities, but clear principles were needed to guide their work.

Behind the guidelines was a desire to integrate in a disciplined, orderly way while instilling in the organization the need to set new, higher standards, thereby laying the foundation that would ultimately deliver new and better results. The guidelines were approached in a clear spirit: create discipline without bureaucracy, instill entrepreneurship but not an "every man for himself" mentality, and set targets that were ambitious but clearly achievable. In a way the guidelines would be the new company's expectations for itself. The vision would set out *what* the new SB was trying to achieve, and the guidelines were the *how.*

First the MMC needed to create the context in which all the integration decisions would be made. Bob had used the concept of meaningful work to build commitment within Beecham's EMC, and now he invoked the same principle with the new committee. Members began by trying to rearticulate the vision for the new company: in the end, what was their goal? What were they trying to achieve through the merger?

They revisited the key messages they were communicating about the merger and reconfirmed their belief in the strategic fit. But now they debated the points that could determine how they shaped their future: What did they really mean by "a new and better company" and "striving to be the best"? What did it mean to be transnational? Even as they strove to create something new, they were also determined to build on what had been the best of each company. They considered Beecham's management philosophy and SmithKline's personnel policy statements and identified some common principles that would guide their future.

After a day of discussion, Henry offered to integrate the MMC's comments into a single, inspirational statement that would become the framework for defining the kind of company they wanted to be. He penned the first draft of what became "The *Promise* of SmithKline Beecham": the statement that would capture the business logic of the merger and set out the company's higher purpose and longer-term aspiration:[4]

The purpose of our merger is to build a new and better healthcare company. "New" in the sense of being well-prepared for the future . . . as a global competitor; "better" in that, from the strengths and traditions of both companies, we seek to build SmithKline Beecham as a company which sets the standards for the industry.

Even more fundamentally, the Promise set forth the philosophy towards employees that became the bedrock for the culture SB would later shape under the banner of *Simply Better:*

. . . teams of skilled and dedicated employees . . . performance-oriented managers . . . pursuit of innovative products based on scientific excellence and commercial promise . . . bringing new products to market in an efficient and continuous manner . . . to achieve our potential rests on the spirit and dedication of employees and the ability of managers to lead, organize and motivate. . . .

The Promise set out the new company's definition of winning and its commitment to becoming the best, not only in terms of financial performance, but also in terms of the kind of company SB hoped to be. The word itself was an inspired choice. More than a vision, the word "promise" implied a commitment.

The way the Promise was developed—as a team—was as important as what it said. In those three months before the shareholders voted, the new management group worked hard, debating each idea, slaving over each word, conscious that the result would set the direction and tone for the brand new company. The more they worked together, the more consensus they reached around a common purpose. The more ingrained the words became, the more committed they grew to their achievement. "To become a new and better company" became more than a vision of two men; it became the single-minded goal of the entire MMC.

The Promise provided SB with its purpose: where it was going and why. Still missing was the how: what were the specific guidelines that would help build a company that could deliver against this Promise? The task forces would need more specific guidelines for designing how the two companies would actually integrate. What would be the criteria for keeping locations or closing them? How would they identify and agree on those who would be asked to lead the new company? How would SB treat those who must leave? As they worked the questions through, committee members realized they were developing SB's operating and management philosophy.

In discussing structure, for example, they examined issues fundamental to how they would manage the business. The vision was to be an integrated healthcare company, but the company was divided into four business sectors. The resulting MMC document addressed three areas: structure, resources, and organizational style.

The guidelines created enormous debate, since the history in both companies was one of separately run businesses, each with its administrative, geographic, and distribution network. Now each business sector was divided into major geographic regions. Each region would have its own series of line and staff functions. Within each country of a geographic region this organizational structure would be replicated. The guidelines were aimed at reducing the organization's layers. In one sector, for example, there would be fourteen layers in one country between the CEO and the salesperson. This was far removed from the guideline of six layers required to deliver the promised performance.

Implications of the guidelines were far reaching. Every role would have to be justified in terms of its *specialized value.* Task forces were to consider each job based on its contribution to ultimate performance. Activities that were required but not unique should be outsourced, while others should be shared to avoid redundant facilities and personnel.

The logic looked powerful on paper, but the MMC totally underestimated the political dimension behind the concept. Eliminating regional structures and sharing services would prove very unpopular with some of the EMC and regional business heads. (SB would back off the concept of shared services in 1990, only for its managers to raise its potential again following acquisition of Sterling Winthrop in 1994.)

The final guidelines on organizational structure and resources attempted to get at the heart of corporate waste:[5]

> The country operating unit will be the basic building block of the organization and primary profit center within the corporation.
>
> This structure requires delegation of responsibility and authority to the lowest level possible in the organization.
>
> We will strive to attain the "best cost" (i.e., the marriage between cost and quality) industry positions in all our businesses.

Resources should focus on adding value, and should not be used to sign off decisions, or check on line activities.

These criteria are intended to help us achieve greater productivity than our competitors, which means not only savings in the area of direct costs, but also minimizing the indirect costs of excessive organizational layers and corporate bureaucracy as evidenced by too many meetings, reviews and paperwork.

We intend to create a climate of action, flexibility, innovation and productivity as priority features of the new SmithKline Beecham. Scale and size must work for us, not against us.

The merger was not just about reducing costs, it was also about realizing opportunities. As the discussion moved to how it would maximize its enhanced capabilities, the MMC started to talk about organizational style, and how an ideal employee would behave within the new SmithKline Beecham. While less specific than the guidelines for structure, these guidelines laid the cornerstone for what would become SB's new culture:

Our focus must be—today and in the future—on delivering superior value to our customers and consumers, and we will strive to continuously improve that value.

To meet our objectives, we will continually strive to improve our performance, challenging today's approaches and search for better ways to achieve our goals.

To be a truly successful, world class, global corporation we must seek ways to harness the value and global use of certain strategic and specialized core skills and capabilities while maintaining local independence and responsiveness.

Finally, the very last principle summed up how the "new and better" vision would be realized:

There are few, if any, organization precedents for the new Smith-Kline Beecham. No such uniquely transnational company exists today. We can—and will—learn from the experiences of others but, ultimately, we will build our own model for the future.

Their goal was to complete the integration plans within six months, with the actual integration of major parts of the business to be finalized within one year of shareholder approval.

Once again aggressive milestones were being set deliberately to create a sense of urgency and maintain the momentum for change. The goal was not only to realize the savings necessary to retain their credibility with the financial markets, but also to put the merger behind them quickly and focus on building the new and better healthcare company.

They were setting up what would be an ongoing conflict between speed to satisfy financial markets and time required to guarantee organizational ownership. It was a conflict that would plague them throughout the entire process. (In the end they would favor ownership, believing it key to building the company for the long term.)

LEADING THE CHANGE

Ever conscious of the messages their every move sent back to the organization, MMC members faced the critical decision of determining who would lead the planning teams.

During the drafting of the merger agreement, Bob and Henry decided that no appointments beyond the top ten executive committee members would be made until after the design of the organization had been completed and senior management had a chance to see individuals from both companies in action.

While they recognized the immediate need to reduce uncertainty and establish clarity by appointing the leadership as quickly as possible, their overall objective was to have the right structure and to then select the right person to fit that structure. This was reflective of their absolute commitment to creating a new and better company, which would require a well-thought out design and to having a high-quality management team to lead it.

They were concerned that if individuals were named to positions before the new company had actually been designed, this would seriously preempt the organization's role in creating the new company. If jobs were awarded before individuals had accomplished anything within the context of the new SB, their appointment could be seen as arbitrary, or even more problematic, they could be a mistake.

They did not choose new management at this time, thereby ensuring that:

❖ as many managers as practicable would fully participate in designing the new company. Furthermore, the managers would be encouraged to think more openly and "outside the box," as long as it was for the benefit of the new company, rather than for a particular person or job.

❖ the current business momentum would be maintained during the months of planning; the existing managers would remain in control even at the beginning of the massive integration planning effort.

❖ individuals would be judged on their displayed talents and performance within the teams, rather than preconceived views of former supervisors.

This last point was one of the most important aspects of the integration process. Members of the MMC had to be certain they were not prejudging people and that everyone knew they had the same chance for the senior positions. Decisions had to be based on who was the best, not on which company they came from. This had to be about creating equal chances and selecting the best person. How they chose people would reflect the underlying value system of the new company, as well as help build a key competitive advantage: the best management in the industry.

They agreed the MMC would focus on ensuring the integrity of the integration planning process and the fairness of the management selection procedure. People would be named to their new positions as quickly as those carefully executed processes allowed.

Their concern now was that team leader assignments could be viewed as management appointments. They finally agreed that each team leader would be selected by the MMC member responsible for the area/function, but only after the MMC member was reminded that the selected individual—as well as the organization—might interpret the team leader assignment as a final appointment. This early in the integration process, such a perception could destroy the spirit of fairness and equality critical to achieving the best the merger could offer. For the chosen individuals, it could affect the way they led the team; and it could potentially demotivate and disenfranchise individuals not chosen.

The MMC member was careful to advise the leader of the position's tenuous status, even as they were considering the criteria by which the final appointments would be made.

Those named to head the teams inevitably were viewed as extremely competent and who had headed the function/area in one of the two companies. His or her counterpart was also on the team. Those participating as team members had been chosen primarily for their expertise in the particular area, rather than on their ability to manage or work as part of a team. There was not time (nor thought given) to train people in team skills. Yet, in the end, these would be the skills that would determine the success of the integration planning process.

While the rationale behind the planning and selection processes was sound, the reality was more stressful, as none of those participating knew whether they would have jobs once the teams' work was completed.

By the end, those who had been most competent at leading the teams and achieving the integration targets became obvious. When it finally came time to announce the new management positions, there would be little dispute as to who the new appointees should be.

And while time would show they may have made a few mistakes, the organization was far more tolerant because they knew that the process had been fair.

As the MMC neared the end of the three-day session, members realized that all the tactics they had discussed would force the structural creation of one company. But they had to start pulling people together emotionally to get them to buy into the *concept* of one before they would actually *be* one company. How could they build a one-company mentality among 57,000 people?

ONE IN SPIRIT

The required documents had just been posted to the U.K. shareholders, and the communications people were preparing for the first major merger presentation to the U.K. analysts. At the same time, the MMC had set up a task force chaired by Henry Wendt to address corporate identity. In making corporate identity a priority, the MMC again illustrated the importance it placed on symbolism. While the task forces would involve some employees, a new logo was one way to tangibly reach every employee, *each* of whom would be required to truly make the merger a success. It would allow them to see, not just hear, that something had happened.

Like every task force to follow, the corporate identity task force used the principles now embedded in the Promise to guide the new graphic identity's development. The merger of equals was reflected in the name and the unique bonds that tied the two letters together, while the Promise to be a new and better company guided the choice of initials, S and B (SKB had been the stock exchange symbol for the former SmithKline Beckman), and colors. For colors the team chose teal green and gray because both companies—in fact nearly every pharmaceutical company— had used various shades of blue for as long as anybody could remember. Symbolically, they had to be certain the new identity was a clean break with the past.

Conscious of the goal to integrate as soon as possible, a few weeks later Joanne proposed that the new graphic identity be used to help create the desired single mindset by building around it a campaign that informed employees about management's intentions.

When she said, "From day one we are one," Bob knew she had captured what he was trying to achieve.

The phrase "Now We Are One" was intended to carry a message of momentum and integration. Meant to both inform and inspire, the message that everyone was now part of the new SmithKline Beecham would be illustrated symbolically through the unveiling of the company's new name and graphic identity around the world at the start of its first full day as a new company.

Consistent with maintaining a single voice, Now We Are One would be the same message for all of the new company's constituents. Internally, it would be used to get employees thinking about the future. Externally, advertisements in the financial and trade press would send a message that the new company would operate as quickly as possible as one company, SmithKline Beecham. Now We Are One would be the theme for all communications efforts that first year, constantly reinforcing the integration goals.

On July 10 the MMC approved the new design and the Now We Are One campaign plans. The communications team shifted into high gear, working around the clock; there were fewer than fifteen days to Now We Are One.

"NOW WE ARE ONE"

On Thursday morning, June 20, at the Barbican Center in the City of London, Beecham shareholders voted overwhelmingly in favor of the merger, and the High Court of England and Wales quickly sanctioned the vote. In the end, the absolute strategic logic of the merger and the credibility of the senior management team had sold the new company to the U.K. shareholders.

One month later, on Wednesday, July 26, at about 11:30 A.M. SmithKline Beckman shareholders were in the Philadelphia Hotel awaiting the final count of the proxy votes. In the United Kingdom it was 4:30 P.M. and Fergus Balfour, Beecham's legal counsel, was in the City, waiting to hear the outcome. Joanne was at her desk at Beecham House, ready to issue the announcement the minute Fergus gave the word. Finally, at nearly 5:00 P.M., news of the shareholders' approval and announcement that the shares would begin trading that day were released simultaneously in London and New York. After months of uncertainty, hard work, and anticipation, the moment had finally come. The first milestone had been reached exactly on target. SmithKline Beecham was a legal reality.

In that instant, management's full attention shifted dramatically to focus exclusively on the employees. At 3:30 the next morning, the large teal green and white sign reading *SmithKline Beecham* was raised in place at the top of Beecham's headquarters, while across the parking lot an enormous poster proclaiming "Now We Are One" replaced the poster promoting Beecham's Lucozade drink.

Over three thousand miles away, at 10:30 P.M., the facilities crew in Philadelphia affixed the bronze letters of the new company name to SmithKline's headquarters at Franklin Plaza. While the corporate identity task force hadn't managed to get a sign on every single building around the world (their original goal), as symbols no two buildings could have been more appropriate than the former companies' headquarters.

On the morning of July 27, employees walking into their offices all over the world were greeted by posters in their native language (a first) that proclaimed "Now We Are One." On each desk was a small gift personally introducing the new corporate symbol, and a letter to each employee from Bob and Henry, expressing their appreciation and sharing their vision:

Dear Colleague,

. . . We have a unique opportunity, to create a new kind of global company, one dedicated to excellence . . . a constant drive for excellence is our dominant corporate value, and the foundation for realizing our Promise.

Around the world every single Beecham and SmithKline site had been encouraged to celebrate that day, with corporate providing not just posters and mementos, but also nominal funds for a party—in itself a gesture that said things were different.

After months of outside focus and and efforts to minimize disruption below top management, Now We Are One specifically focused on the employees. It said not only that SB intended to be one company as quickly as feasible, but also that management recognized the individual employee stress as well as the exhaustion of all those who worked so hard to meet the first major milestone. The celebration told every employee that achieving this first milestone was part of winning.

For many people, Now We Are One captured the moment, the day when SmithKline Beecham actually began. As one employee later related, "The celebrations of that day were a very important symbol to me. It meant that we were not just going to put the two companies together, but were going to make one new company."[6] By focusing on the employees, Now We Are One made the merger personal; it also helped to position people for the changes to come.

But the merged firm's honeymoon lasted only a few hours. Even as its employees celebrated the birth of SmithKline Beecham, Bristol-Myers announced its intention to merge with Squibb. Overnight, SmithKline Beecham dropped to fifth in the revenue rankings of pharmaceutical companies. The new company's moment of glory vanished as newspapers and analysts focused on the next pharmaceutical industry titan.

The days that followed would bring constant comparisons between the two mergers. As an unprecedented merger integration process involving the planning efforts of nearly 2,000 employees began, everyone at SB realized that selling the merger had been relatively easy compared to the task that lay before them.

Now they had to make the merger work.

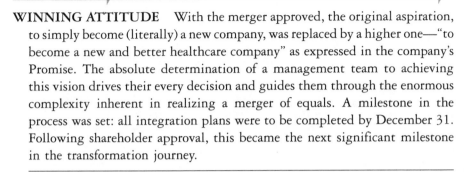

Phase I:
Strategy
1986–1989

WINNING ATTITUDE   With the merger approved, the original aspiration, to simply become (literally) a new company, was replaced by a higher one—"to become a new and better healthcare company" as expressed in the company's Promise. The absolute determination of a management team to achieving this vision drives their every decision and guides them through the enormous complexity inherent in realizing a merger of equals. A milestone in the process was set: all integration plans were to be completed by December 31. Following shareholder approval, this became the next significant milestone in the transformation journey.

ORGANIZATION AS HERO   In agreeing to involve as many people as possible in planning and implementing the integration of the Beecham and SKB operations, management took the first step in making employees the heroes of the new SmithKline Beecham. By defining the criteria and identifying the goal, the MMC created a disciplined process aligned with its aspiration, but those on the teams were responsible and accountable for determining the outcome.

CUMULATIVE LEARNING   The positive experience of using a task force comprised of members from both companies during the merger period to create the new business plan became the model for planning the integration in the new company.

STRATEGIC COMMUNICATION   Expressing the rationale of the merger to the media and analysts influenced how shareholders and employees viewed the merger and helped to shape their thinking and attitude on why the merger should be supported. Constant attempts to ensure "one voice" both internally and externally, yet still tailor the messages to meet the segmented needs of the two major financial and national markets was pivotal to gaining shareholder and employee acceptance. Even more powerful was the role of symbolism, expressed in senior management behavior, the use of the graphic identity unveiling, and the deliberate crafting of the "Now We Are One" statement, to focus and prepare people for the integration to come. Simple messages, built around the desired outcome and constantly repeated, helped bring about its achievement.

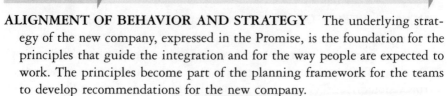

Phase I:
Strategy
1986–1989

ALIGNMENT OF BEHAVIOR AND STRATEGY The underlying strategy of the new company, expressed in the Promise, is the foundation for the principles that guide the integration and for the way people are expected to work. The principles become part of the planning framework for the teams to develop recommendations for the new company.

CHAPTER FIVE

Now We Are One

B Y LATE J ULY THE SENIOR team was being bombarded: no sooner would it make a decision than a number of others would be needed in its wake. Some that seemed simple actually had wide implications. Introducing new business cards, for example, meant deciding the names of sale forces, which meant determining country sales structures. As much as possible, Now We Are One guided them as they sought to create an environment that would have everyone looking to build the new company rather than trying to protect the old.

But as members of the EMC struggled over the integration issues, slowly and almost without realizing it, they were mirroring what they hoped would be the output of the task-force approach: they were coming together more and more as "one" management. As they worked each task through to a decision, it mattered less which company they had come from and more what their actions would contribute to the new company. Increasingly they were being viewed by those who watched and worked with them as a team of equals. The message was not lost on a highly sensitized organization, and would set an example for all the teams that would follow: what was best for SB came first. Nothing would be allowed to detract from its creation.

DESIGNING THE INTEGRATION PROCESS

The formation of planning teams had been based on those areas where the synergies and business opportunities were the most obvious; therefore they evolved primarily around Pharmaceuticals. There were eight, and they fell into four categories:

- ❖ Those that were self-contained, such as sector management
- ❖ Those that were a global resource, such as manufacturing and R&D
- ❖ Those that supported the business, such as information systems and finance
- ❖ Those areas where there was a potential to share resources

For each planning team, the MMC had sketched an initial charter, which included the team's purpose, objectives, and targets. The planning teams were asked to complete work plans illustrating how they would develop recommendations to dramatically reduce costs, sustain business momentum, and radically change the way SB did business in the future to achieve a true competitive advantage. In the course of agreeing on their charters, the planning teams would propose specific project task forces to help them plan the actions and timetable for implementing the planning team recommendations. (For example, the planning team for information systems would recommend the creation of four project task forces such as office systems, telecommunications, finance, and information technology.) A sample project team charter appears in figure 5-1.

Once the one-page charter was agreed, the planning team was given a template for developing its work plan. Work plans identified the necessary steps for each team to follow in developing its recommendations and had been designed against the framework of the guiding principles. The steps required that each team do an unaccustomed amount of data gathering from both inside and outside the company. How were other companies organized to do the same work? What resources were required? By following the analytical, logical approach, the teams would (ideally) generate the objective, high-quality recommendations the MMC was seeking.

The work plans would be checked rigorously to see that the teams had thoroughly thought through their integration task, thereby ensuring that they would complete their work using its disciplined process. The work plans were to be approved by September, to be followed by all the recommendations by December 31.

Team Charter	Purpose
	• Set the overall design for where responsibilities will lie in the organization
	• Guide and oversee the integration of all Finance staff
	• Assure that effective policies and procedures are developed for Finance
	• Develop structure and staffing for all corporate center activities

Finance Design

Project team structure
Core members: J Barnes
                     H Collum
                     R M James
                     K Kermes
                     W Packer

Target
- Define required activities to support SB and design the organization to deliver these more effectively
- Apply a stretch target of 40% head-count reduction

Key dates (preliminary)
- July 25, July 27 and August 10: Project Team meetings
- July 17 and July 29: Presentation to MMC on preliminary design
- July 28: MCC presentation - corporate center organization; proposal on information to units on Finance design

Decisions already made

Objectives/mission
- Assure aggressive objectives for rationalization are met throughout all levels of Finance staff
- Develop a finance organization able to support SB objectives effectively and efficiently
- Initiate and oversee all project teams needed to resolve financial policies/procedures or to manage the integration of specific corporate staff

Key issues/tasks
- What should be the responsibilities of corporate center Finance staff?
- Which activities can be delivered across businesses within a given market?
- Which activities are unique to the needs of business, area, or unit level?
- What structure and staffing levels will cost effectively meet the design?
- Through what processes/time frames should the Finance organization at all levels be integrated?

Merge Integration Team (MIT)
designated contact: F Downing

Figure 5-1   Sample Project Team Charter—Corporate Center

Source: Excerpted from SB Merger Management Committee documents, August 14, 1989.

Note: Team tasks will be conducted in conformance with MMC guiding principles for planning/project teams.

The need for discipline and control versus a lot of action during this time was heavily emphasized. The MMC wanted the teams to balance their desire for quick hits with the longer-term view—the one that would allow them to find "the better way." Not every member of the MMC agreed with the tight discipline and control of the work plans. Some found the centralized review process highly objectionable, especially where tradition had been to set targets for a unit but leave it to unit members to determine how they would generate the results.

But the work plan approach was deliberately intended to specifically define the how. Having the defined, standardized process driven by the teams completing the work plans was extremely important for several reasons. First, team members were from two original companies with different ways of working. They needed some common methodology to be certain that they were getting at all the fundamental issues. Second, since most people were not trained in problem solving or process improvement techniques at this time, the work plans guided them to do in-depth analysis by providing a step-by-step methodology. Third, and just as important, they needed to get the emotion out of the decisions. By requiring team members to focus on gathering data about their specific areas, then having them look at that information against other companies in the industry, the process would force them to be more analytical in developing their recommendations. It meant looking to the future rather than the past. It kept personalities out of the process and focused them on achieving their goal of going for the best. Finally, the consistent approach allowed them to consolidate the recommendations to create the bigger picture.

Unwittingly, the company was creating its own reliable process for integration, which the work plans then helped standardize among all the teams. As a reliable process, the work plans would be controlled from the top, but the output—the recommendations for integration—would be generated by those responsible for its implementation. The process was designed as described in figure 5-2.

The work plans identified logical steps such as do research first and gather data around the basics (e.g., existing job descriptions, numbers of people, budget, etc., of the function/business as it presently existed in both companies). Team members were then required to contact their counterparts at similar companies and learn how they were organized.

By forcing the team members to do fundamental analysis and begin with a clean sheet of paper, the MMC was saying that "what was" from

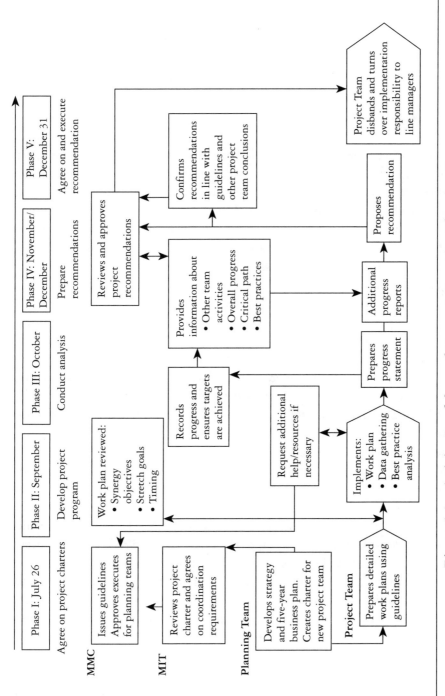

Figure 5-2 Activity Breakdown of Merger Integration Planning Process

either company was not a consideration; what they wanted was the *best* there could be. The way to learn the best was to look both inside and outside the company.

Given this information as background, they were to shape their recommendations according to the Promise and the guiding principles and any detail that could be drawn from the business plans. For example, in sales and marketing, the guideline was that decision-taking activities should be located closely to the customer. Where key data was known, such as when a new product would reach the market, the team was given the data generated from the original business plan to help guide their target projections and the steps that would be required to realize the new product's potential. For staff functions, the teams were to use an activity-based analysis approach: every task was to be evaluated based on whether it was adding special value or could be eliminated or outsourced. Only after this rigorous analysis was the task force to recommend what the function or area could ideally look like in terms of people and responsibilities, and identify what savings their redesign would contribute to the corporate target.

This target had changed substantially over the months of negotiating final merger terms and planning the integration process. In the first business plan the savings predicted at that time had been at least £350/$550 million. As the MMC started to review these numbers, trying to set ballpark targets for each of the planning teams, McKinsey challenged them. Based on McKinsey's experience in similar circumstances, the numbers were too low; there was much more that could be done. Was this about creating more value, or more of the same value? the McKinsey partner asked. Was the new SB really serious about being a winner?

By the end of that session, the MMC had decided that they would be seeking *the best* margin structure in the industry. Here it was late July, and the planning teams were being told to go back and redo their numbers, setting much more aggressive targets. This was especially painful for SB Pharmaceuticals, which had despaired of attaining even the initial targets. (SmithKline Beckman had gone through two major reorganizations before the merger, trying to trim an organizational structure that had grown geometrically with the wealth generated by Tagamet; it just couldn't see where else it could cut.)

The planning teams kicked off as near day one as possible: the final charters were approved July 29. They worked feverishly through the remainder of the summer at refining their charters and defining their work plans, with documents being couriered around the globe as people tried to squeeze in desperately needed summer breaks. The teams would meet the first critical target date of the integration phase: September 1, when the project task forces would actually begin to develop their detailed recommendations for implementation.

AIR TRAFFIC CONTROL

To help manage the implementation, the MMC agreed that planning and project teams would be coordinated and monitored by the Merger Integration Team (MIT).

The MIT was the critical link between the MMC, and the planning and project teams. It acted as an air traffic controller. If the MMC was about creating the reliable process, and the planning teams and project task forces were about creating ownership of the recommendations, then the MIT was all about managing the complexity and logistics of the massive exercise. Its role was first to be certain that all the tasks necessary for integration were identified; then it would collect and codify all the tasks, creating a master checklist. The MIT was responsible for ensuring there were no overlaps—or where there were, to make certain they were coordinated. It would set priorities and determine the order in which work would be reviewed by the MMC. Once the review was completed and the MMC approved the recommendations, the implementation steps outlined by team members would be monitored by the MIT. All the information would be put onto a computerized master plan to help manage the complexity of integrating all the operations on a global scale.

Composed primarily of the strategic planning department members, the MIT's primary responsibility was evaluating progress against the work plans, which ultimately would allow the MMC to measure progress against the savings target that was ultimately a compilation of all the planning teams' projections. For example, if a planning team had targeted closing a location by a certain date, the MIT would check whether it had met the milestone, which would also indicate whether the expected savings would be realized on time. If the team needed to coordinate more closely with another team, the MIT would suggest or confirm that they had. Basically, the MIT would determine whether the teams were doing what they said they would do.

The MMC had originally expected about 100 project task forces to be operating alongside the planning teams at any one time. But the pace at which the project task forces were created astonished even the MMC. Where people had been skeptical at first about the approach, they soon realized that by not being involved they were missing an opportunity to help shape the new company's destiny and, with it, their own.

That autumn there were at least 250 task forces involving more than 2,000 people all around the world—a number far greater than the MMC had prepared to support. (To this day, no one is really sure of the number, for while the major planning teams and project task forces were known to the MMC and MIT, each one spawned others, involving that many more people. As a result, some have put the estimate of those involved as closer to 3,000!) The global scale and companywide scope of the effort, magnified by the telescoped time frame and inadequate information systems, would later swamp the small MIT. It would also provide a major lesson about the critical role of information systems in helping to manage future reengineering efforts.

REVIEWING THE WORK PLANS

Once the work plans were reviewed by the MMC and approved, the teams were given the go-ahead to develop their recommendations based on their agreed roadmap.

It was at this point that that one of many problems emerged as the four members of the MIT couldn't handle the sheer volume of information they were receiving. Where the theory of having the MIT assure quality was sound, in practice it was controlled chaos. The quality of the plans varied enormously. For example, where the work plan said a team would use customer and market data extensively to develop its recommendations, the outcome would most likely be logical and the MIT review process simple and straightforward. But where the work plan had not identified the data the team would seek, the potential implications were far less clear and the conclusions far more suspect. The atmosphere when the MIT reviewed these nonspecific work plans was charged and emotional, and both groups were exasperated by meeting's end.

Sometimes the variance in the work plans resulted from the team's level of commitment, but more often it was because of inadequate training and support. When the MIT failed to provide the needed guidance, the teams tried to do it themselves. In some cases, they ran out of time. The work plan bypassed MIT and went to the MMC, where it was inevitably sent back to the team for violating one of the core guiding principles (e.g., not the best way, only a refinement of an existing way).

Being absolutely fanatical about the quality of the work plans was the only way Bob knew to force the organization to look ahead, to really stretch its thinking about how SB was going to be different from either of its component firms. He felt strongly that if he got the process right through the work plan, the integration would be successful. Eventually he personally reviewed over 100 work plans.

Where few had used McKinsey as an available resource at the beginning, the consultants now found themselves working alongside SB managers in every area of the company as the teams, realizing they had not got it right, sought McKinsey's advice. The consultants provided the critical objective view that helped stretch a team to think outside its normal parameters. But the consultants were deliberately few in number. With no training, and with access to McKinsey difficult, the teams' level of dismay grew with each resubmission. It seemed no matter how hard they were working, it just wasn't good enough.

These were tough times. Not only were team members fighting for their own jobs, they were fighting for their own people. If one person "won," it might mean that hundreds would have to move or even leave. All the work was being done in an atmosphere where people still barely knew one another—and despite high levels of goodwill, at this point trust between strangers was far from complete.

In an effort to help build that trust, the MMC insisted that no "minority opinions" be included in the final recommendations. The teams would have to reconcile their differences before their recommendations ever reached the MMC. This was particularly difficult in situations where available data did not lead to obvious conclusions. It meant the team members had to trust that no one was manipulating information and that all judgments were made in the spirit of Now We Are One.

As the teams' pain and consternation grew, so did the resentment. But at this point the EMC was not prepared to deal with it, and much of the resentment was allowed to build, always bubbling just beneath the surface. The inadequate training and support for the teams plus the MIT's lack of a master plan and failure to provide enough external resources provided painful but valuable lessons. The EMC would later remember how much lost time and frustration resulted from their inadequate planning when they invoked the team approach to process improvement.

REVIEWING THE RECOMMENDATIONS

Dates were staggered for reviewing team recommendations, enabling the MMC to assess each and still allowing time for resubmission and approval before the year's-end deadline.

The MMC and MIT came to dominate—and some managers would later say, drown—this period in SB's history. The whole process was viewed as cumbersome and overly bureaucratic. The amount of paper generated by an organization that had been far more intuitive than analytical was staggering. The review process was even worse. It was compared most often to the Spanish Inquisition, conjuring up an image of relentless, grueling inquiry.

The first review meetings were held in early October, about three months after the merger: Consumer Brands, Canada, and U.K. Pharmaceuticals presented their recommendations for integrating the operations in those countries. Horror stories abounded from this period as one by one the early teams reported back their experiences. Of particular interest, of course, was Bob, their new chief executive. "Tough," they would say, "relentless, detail-oriented, stubborn." "Be sure you can back everything up," they advised their colleagues.[1]

This was clearly the period in which Bob was at his most controlling. His personal behavior was a dilemma even to him. As he reviewed the first set of budget figures, he could see that the 15 percent growth target in earnings per share would not be achieved. Here it was—SB's first goal—and they weren't going to make it. Bob just could not, would not, accept that. SB's credibility as a new company and his credibility as its chief executive were both at stake. Without tight controls, he felt SB would never get the numbers it needed to satisfy the financial markets. Yet he was equally convinced that the organization, not the MMC, had to generate the recommendations. It was a very tough period for him. He knew the organization felt he was being overcontrolling, and some were very resentful. While he was not going to tell them *what* to do, he was determined to tell them *how,* and that meant the process outlined in the work plans—all of which had been thought through carefully—would be followed strictly. While he had taken personally the goal he had articulated on behalf of the new company—that it was to be "new and better" and "deliver results better than either one could do alone"—he wasn't certain the rest of the EMC felt as strongly as he did. Rather than risk SB failing because his commitment was not equally shared, he felt the company would realize the promise to shareholders only if he was deeply involved, questioning everything from assumptions to analysis to recommendations. The only way to achieve the goals they had set would be to stretch everyone further and demand more than either company had ever done in the past.

The problem, of course, was that they were essentially breaking new ground with every step they took. While the EMC had agreed to using task forces and had provided fairly specific guidelines, the time available did not allow for training in either process analysis or team work. The guidelines were helpful but conceptually broad. Interpretations varied by manager, making alignment of the results difficult. There was inconsistency even in MMC's planning of the teams: all were geographically and functionally oriented, yet some of the guidelines suggested that cross-sector, cross-functional teams would have been more effective. There was simply not enough time to consider all the complexities within each area optimally. For example, in addressing manufacturing and trying to seek some cross-sector opportunities, the SB pharmaceuticals team included representatives from the areas of animal health and consumer brands. But the sectors' requirements differed widely, and in the end only some of pharmaceuticals and animal health operations could be combined.

Finally, there was no baseline to use for comparison. At this point the two companies were operating under their previous budgets plus the financial targets generated in the November business plan. (This made each manager responsible for meeting three goals.) The only means for quantifying the integration plans and measuring progress were the projected sales and savings. Because one of the simplest measures of the latter was reduction in people, headcount became an obsession.

As one manager remembers it, the review process before the MMC was like an interrogation scene from an old movie: seven men in their shirtsleeves sat around the oversized board table. Open in front of each was a 100–200 page document containing the planning team's recommendations. An overhead projector was turned on, making the team leader look even more ashen than he or she felt. As the presenter spoke, the team leader tried to gauge the MMC's reaction.

In reviewing the recommendations, the MMC looked for four key points:

❖ That implementation would lead to the creation of a new and better company, not just a combination of the two old ones
❖ That the guidelines had been met
❖ That coordination between teams was fully reflected
❖ That the promised financial targets would be met or exceeded

The MMC tested the team's reasoning, trying to assess whether it had really approached the task with a clean sheet of paper or had simply adapted what had gone before.

MMC members questioned the use of data, checking to see if it drove the recommendations, and challenged the financial goals if they did not meet or exceed those set at the time of the merger. For example, if a team failing to achieve the projected savings suggested adding salespeople, they challenged the market data surrounding the product. If a team suggested moving production from one site to another, they questionned the cost assumptions. Violations of the guiding principles were not automatically assumed to be aimed at protecting people or preserving the past, which is why the MMC spent so much time trying to understand the rationale behind those plans it did not accept. If the MMC wanted to encourage an open, risk-free environment, then it would consciously have to do everything it could to build that environment. The MMC deliberately paid close attention to those areas not typically seen as important in pharmaceuticals, such as manufacturing or purchasing, sending a strong message to the organization about the importance of *everything* in the new company.

The symbolic role of the EMC was very clear as it approached the integration of corporate staff, one of the last groups to be integrated. (Until now, the staff groups had been supporting everyone else.) Just prior to the merger SmithKline Beckman had been decentralizing corporate staff, whereas the trend at Beecham had been the exact opposite. The different philosophies about the role of corporate staff in the two merging companies, together with the question of U.K. or U.S. location for certain competencies, meant that this area posed issues as difficult as those encountered in the business integration. The standards that had been set were just as stringent. Senior managers struggled with how they would oversee staffs that crossed the Atlantic. It took several months and enormous diplomacy and patience as one by one the role of each staff member was reviewed, adjusted, and redefined. The focus for the analysis was activities—was the task adding value? If it was not, it would be eliminated, outsourced, or located wherever the majority of the expertise lay, creating centers of excellence on both sides of the Atlantic that would be managed from the U.K. headquarters.

While the recommendations were meant to ensure effective integration in the near term, they were in reality setting out the new company's objectives and business strategies and actually agreeing on the company's first business plan. This meant the discussions were long and tedious and the questioning relentless. Unused to having their thinking and reasoning challenged to such a degree of detail, most of the managers found the reviews overcontrolling and the MMC overbearing.

"The guys on the MMC drove us crazy; they were absolutely relentless," said one manager, describing his team's frustration at being told to rework and resubmit.[2] As frustration levels rose, tempers flared, and team leaders and the MMC began to direct their dissatisfaction toward Bob. No matter how hard they had worked, it seemed they just couldn't meet his expectations.

Most reviews were expected to take three hours and were scheduled back-to-back, three per day. As the autumn wore on, and more plans were submitted, the MMC found itself running out of time. Outside the boardroom, team members sat in chairs along the wall waiting their turn. On one particularly testy occasion, one of the country planning teams that had flown in for its review returned home without being heard. When Bob apologized to them, he found team members more frustrated than angry. Intellectually they accepted the delay, but emotionally they had reached their limit. They knew they would have to wait that much longer before they could get on with actual implementation.

In the end, everyone learned from the experience. The MMC learned that because the organization had not helped to define the guidelines, they felt less commitment to achieving them. The organization learned that "new and better company" was more than a slogan; it was the strategic reality they were expected to strive for.

TWO STEPS FORWARD, ONE BACK

Managers busy working on the merger-related issues yet trying to maintain business as usual soon found an inherent conflict in what they were trying to do.

To keep the business momentum going, they had to maintain the existing systems and business plans of the former companies and continue to operate separately: any changes could put the business at risk. To keep employees focused on the business, all but those on the teams were discouraged from meeting until the integration planning was completed.

At the same time, in the spirit of Now We Are One, managers were trying to bring the businesses together as quickly as possible. It meant some people—usually the same people whose job it was to deliver the business performance—*had* to start working together. As members of the task forces, their role was to challenge virtually everything that had gone into creating the old business plans—even as they were charged to continue implementing them. It was as if key managers had three employers at this point, SmithKline Beckman, Beecham, and SmithKline Beecham—each demanding their absolute best. Balancing efforts became a personal dilemma: how much time and energy should go into delivering the actions outlined in the former plans, and how much should go into developing the new plans? All were beginning to feel like players in a tug of war between the past and the future.

During the same six months, these same beleaguered individuals were responsible for preparing the first budgets for the new company—another major undertaking requiring assumptions about combined businesses that were not yet combined. Adding to the difficulty, each company had multiple accounting and information systems, all of which had continued running in parallel (rather than integrated into one system) so that business could continue as usual.

The only plus was that employees of sales and research and development—cornerstones of the merger and critical to SB's present and future performance—had been assured from the outset that their jobs were safe. Because they felt no threat, those working in these areas not only continued current performance levels, but were able to start focusing on the promised potential of their combined efforts. Employees in other areas could not help but envy their security.

To help SB managers realize that they actually had to do all these things, and do each one equally well, the EMC advised them that all bonuses and incentives for 1989 would remain tied to the objectives set against the old plans, while those set for 1990 would focus on achieving development of the new structure and new objectives. The senior team's acknowledgment of their struggle helped boost their spirits, and the managers responded to both challenges with renewed energy.

Meanwhile, the nonexecutive directors were also playing a valuable role as models of Now We Are One. The five nonexecutive directors who had come from each of the former companies had taken the Promise to heart, and championed working together right from the start. As the EMC listened to these ten nonexecutive directors debate issues, they could see clearly by the questions, discussions, and decisions that the nonexecutive directors were committed to doing the best for SB. There was no sign of protecting the old companies or their practices.

The nonexecutive directors also respected and were supportive of the enormous effort being taken to achieve the merger's goals and recognized the challenges and demands the work was placing on senior management and the organization. They looked for opportunities to recognize and reward heroic behavior, and took actions such as encouraging management to award special bonuses and double options in 1989.

THE FIRST MANAGEMENT CONFERENCE

While the EMC was encouraging "get it right, not fast," the organization was pushing to do both. Their feeling was "let's get this over with so we can get on with the business." Driven by both the process and the uncertainty, the managers experienced enormous stress as they "did their regular jobs during the week and the merger work on weekends."[3] And most did not know whether they would have jobs at the end of it. By autumn, the enthusiasm and high energy level of those leading the teams had begun to dissipate. Adrenaline waned, replaced by an aching sense of exhaustion.

It had been agreed in June that sometime in autumn the senior management should be brought together to meet and hear firsthand the vision of the new company. At that time, their goal was to ensure that more than just their small-group were aligned in spirit and committed as well as actively involved in Now We Are One. What they didn't know then was that the timing could not have been better; by then the strain had become almost unbearable.

In late October the top eighty managers from around the world gathered in London. They heard SB's strategy for leadership that was building on the strengths of both businesses: the heritage of scientific research that lay at the heart of the pharmaceuticals business, and the low cost, market-oriented, customer-driven mentality of the consumer brands business.

One by one the presenters ran through their overheads, each forcing energy into his voice to hide the fatigue. Then a country manager whose team already had been through the MMC process came to the podium. He shared with the audience a graph that charted his team's emotional roller-coaster ride from the task's start (euphoria) to the review (abject despair) to final approval (rising optimism). The weary audience grasped the single beacon of hope, making the graph a symbol from that period that would be remembered long afterward.

People were pleased to finally meet those whose names they had only heard, yet there remained an uneasiness about becoming too friendly. After all, not all the jobs had been designated officially. The individuals in that room still had big question marks around their own futures.

On the second day, the audience was broken into discussion groups, each with an EMC member present. When asked how things were going, participants hesitated, trying to assess just how frank a discussion it was meant to be. Gradually they opened up, giving the EMC more than an earful. The managers questioned the need for what they considered an onerous amount of analysis; they challenged the constantly stretching targets and balked at the demands of the tight deadlines.

Until that meeting, EMC members had not realized the strain they were putting the organization under. On one hand managers were being pushed to keep the business going, on the other hand they were required to complete their recommendations for integrating the two companies by year's end. These plans basically determined their fate. The stress was enormous both from the sheer work load and from the personal uncertainty: would they be part of the company six months from now?

ALIGNING FOR CHANGE

From the very beginning of the merger process the EMC realized that the morale of the employees and the chemistry between the people of the two companies would be the most important determinant of the merger's success.

While the plans for integrating structures were under way, the EMC continued to seek ways to make the new company tangible as quickly as possible on a personal level. Signifying the importance of people, much of management's early effort focused on defining global human resource systems that reinforced the spirit of Now We Are One. At the top of the list: employee benefits and compensation. By changing what was rewarded, the EMC could begin to encourage the behavior they knew would be required to achieve their longer-term strategic goals.

Now We Are One became increasingly important as time passed, for while management wanted employees to "feel" as one, it was still discouraging them from meeting their counterparts until the disciplined integration planning process was completed. Having some evidence of being one company—like SB paychecks and a common compensation system—helped calm the tendency to move too quickly and gave the task forces time to help plan how they would structurally become one.

Some of the human resource systems had already been designed as part of the process to gain shareholder approval. Most of these dealt with senior management, since information about compensation, share options, and pensions had to be included in the shareholder documents. Despite being driven by the tight deadlines, drafters of those plans had tried to invoke criteria they would later be able to apply consistently as they defined programs for the entire organization. As each proposal was put forward, the first question was what effect it would have on the organization at large. Could its principles apply to everyone? Every decision was examined against its wider implication: what it would mean for the longer term.

In creating these programs managers looked again to the guidelines and the Promise, in which the stated goal was to "have the best talent." Their objectives:

❖ To create plans that would keep those managers they wanted to keep
❖ To ensure that those who would be leaving were treated fairly
❖ To build a system that would help in the selection of future leaders

The first objective was met by allowing for rollover of key option plans and assurances that existing bonus plans (in both companies) would be honored through 1990 against goals each manager had set originally as part of each company's MBO process. The second objective was met by guaranteeing that severance programs were philosophically consistent on a worldwide basis.

For the third, it meant identifying what becoming a new and better company meant for management. How would those leading the new company be appointed? It was then that the MMC agreed to appoint only the best, even if that meant going outside the company or promoting talent from within over others more highly graded. This in itself was radical thinking: both companies had followed fairly traditional policies of promoting from within and on the basis of hierarchy. Although changing both practices was potentially demotivating, it was absolutely essential if SB was serious about achieving its goal of having the industry's best management. They decided to make a concerted, focused effort to develop greater talent internally that would transcend either company's past attempts.

Augmenting the initial work that had been done for the shareholder documents during July and August were a global compensation plan, an SB benefits philosophy, and a worldwide job evaluation system, all with the explicit goal of making Now We Are One a reality for the employee as quickly as possible.

But at the Grosvenor House conference that October the participants' questions showed clearly that the top management had some educating to do; this included educating itself. When the new compensation plan was explained, for example, the British were amazed at the size of the bonuses, while the Americans challenged the normal U.K. practice of providing employees with cars. Such responses brought home very clearly and very early that the EMC must keep the organization with it every step of the way. It had been running too far ahead of even its most senior managers for them to understand the thinking behind the decisions. Yet, these managers were expected not only to commit to the decisions, but to help implement them.

MEETING SB'S FIRST MILESTONE: THE FIRST "WIN"

There was no open space in any MMC diary in October, November, or December, including weekends. As the year drew to a close the meetings were held almost daily. They would begin at 7:30 A.M. and continue throughout the day. Coffee/tea breaks collided with lunch. Rooms were filled with the scent of half-eaten sandwiches and fruit on trays. Sometimes one MMC review would end, and the same team, with the addition of a finance person, would come back to present its budget.

Everyone was drowning in paper. Finally, the MMC agreed that Christmas weekend was it: that would be the end.

Of the 250 teams created, those remaining on December 31 were R&D and several of the European operations of SB Pharmaceuticals. These had proven to be areas where the MMC had totally underestimated the complexity, interdependency, and fundamental disagreement in managerial approaches to the market or the function.

The strain on those involved had been enormous. Although the EMC had said "no divorces, no heart attacks," everyone was working to absolute full capacity and many knew they would not have jobs for long. Yet SB lost very few people to competitors during this period. To this day, most think it is because those who participated believed their opinions truly mattered and appreciated being consulted as experts in their particular jobs. As one project team member remembered, "Redesigning your own function is something you don't get the opportunity to do very often. In the end, despite the incredible sacrifices, the process was tremendously satisfying, particularly if the alternative was the top-down rationalization you see in most other mergers. I don't think any of us would have done it any other way."[4]

In the end the word via grapevine was that most felt the process fair and believed the best person would win the job. Each sector's management looked at how well a team was managed and the quality of the decisions it generated. But it was impossible to eliminate politics entirely, and in most cases, despite management's assurance that no jobs had been predestined, most team leaders were selected by the four sector heads for the top positions. But by then most team members would agree they deserved them. The appointment process appeared to have engendered far less bitterness than it might have.

Overall, the organization was exhausted but satisfied. In the six months since the merger's approval, more than 250 teams had submitted recommendations for review. Their efforts had identified sixty operations for closure, generated more than 150 bulletin board announcements, and led to a promised savings of approximately £500/$800 million. Despite the frustrations, rework, and resubmissions, nearly all recommendations had been approved for implementation beginning in 1990. The organization had achieved the new company's first critical milestone and the plans showed it would reach the targeted 15 percent growth in earnings. In the process the EMC learned what enormous capacity the organization had. The organizational structure, business plans, and human resource systems—systems that could have taken years to complete—were all realigned within six months.

Management had delivered on its promise: most of all the senior positions had been announced by year's end, and the massive flow of bulletin board notices began to dwindle by late December. As employees left for the reprieve of their Christmas break, they knew at last what jobs they would be holding on their return in January 1990. Not all team members were pleased with the outcome, of course; but having been part of the process, most at least understood.

Amidst the relief of a milestone completed was a measure of sadness, as some who had been instrumental in helping to bring the two companies together knew they would not be staying. One of these was Jim Andress, whose own role had been diminished in the effort to keep the new EMC a balance of SKB and Beecham managers. Believing the merger's ultimate success to be more important than keeping a job that clearly was not essential, he volunteered to leave the company he had helped create.

Uncertainty behind them, everyone looked toward January as a new start.

MANAGING EXPECTATIONS

During the months of the complex integration planning process, senior managers were dealing with uncertainties, but they at least understood the process. For employees not directly involved, stress and uncertainty were magnified because those who normally had the answers—their own managers—were either unavailable to explain or lacking answers themselves.

In a continuing effort to manage employee uncertainty and maintain business momentum, the communication department tried to supply a consistent flow of information. A telephone hot line was installed in the United States and United Kingdom, and Beecham's *Merger News* was converted into a monthly publication for worldwide distribution. As the year drew to a close, the only other worldwide system—the bulletin board—was laden daily with announcements of new appointments, resignations, reorganizations, and office and site closings. At this point SB was marketing two things to employees: (1) the purpose of the new company and what it was striving to achieve, and (2) the progress being made in bringing the two companies together. The bulletin boards may have been overloaded, but the sheer number of announcements conveyed clear progress reaching the December 31 milestone.

However, as employees began to feel more certain, external concern was growing. The period following the merger was a complete reversal from the period before, when external constituents were optimistic, but employees were worried. By the first quarter the financial markets had grown increasingly concerned.

One of the reasons for the market's growing uneasiness was the Bristol-Myers/Squibb merger. Within a few weeks of the merger announcement, its management had disclosed their restructuring plan and merger provision. Where analysts had once been sympathetic with SB's desire to say nothing until it was ready, they grew less patient as Bristol-Myers Squibb disclosed more and more numbers. They kept challenging SB to reveal what the savings would be and the number of redundancies planned. But the task forces were still working, and Bob refused to preempt them by providing quantifiable responses to the outside world before receiving their recommendations. He was determined that the teams, not the accountants, would find the answers, and that took time. During the six months of planning, SB provided no guidelines by which analysts could judge its progress in the near term. To their constant questions, all management said, in effect, was "Have faith." In the absence of SB's providing any parameters, the analysts set targets, driven largely by Bristol-Myers Squibb's numbers, which soon included headcount reductions, disposals, and expected cost savings. But—and this was the fundamental difference between the two mergers that would be realized over time—Bristol-Myers Squibb was being managed more as an acquisition than a merger of equals, with a more top-down than lateral approach to its final design. The difference in approach was making all the difference in the perceptions now being shaped of the two new companies.

It became an important lesson about managing expectations. Whereas internally the company provided milestones by which the employees could judge their progress, externally it failed to do so. In retrospect SB should have given outsiders something to meet their short-term needs and help them assess SB's progress, so they could see that in reaching each milestone the company was winning. In the absence of any specific information, analysts chose their own way to measure SB's progress, and they decided the measure would be how quickly SB brought down the debt level. This meant that the anaylsts focused on the sale of the cosmetics business as the single largest disposal. When that sale was delayed and its market value decreased, analysts viewed SB as failing.

One by one the analysts' reports turned from neutral to negative, particularly in the United States. One stated in late September 1989, "Earnings will surge for the next two years due to cost savings and cross-selling, but decelerate thereafter . . . the stock lacks the takeover/ restructuring appeal of others in the group."[5] Another headline read "Restructuring going slower than expected; stock rated neutral."[6] SB's share price tumbled.

Questions coming from the financial community, major shareholders, and the press reflected their exasperation and exacerbated employee unrest. Management had to field tough questions: Don't you have to admit the merger is a failure when you measure it in terms of share performance? Why is the implementation plan taking so long, particularly when compared to Bristol-Myers Squibb? How is effective management of the operations being maintained if your best people are all on task forces?

Joanne tried to manage a balance between what was said externally to maintain support of the financial community and what was needed internally to sustain employee motivation. Any discrepancy could easily destroy management credibility—and with it trust in the new management team. In the effort to speak with one consistent voice, she had to weigh every answer given to an analyst or the press (and consider its potential for starting a domino effect) against the background of the bigger picture they were trying achieve.

Finally, in late November at the height of budget plans and MMC reviews, a two day briefing session was held in London for the top twenty-five U.K./U.S. analysts in an effort to diffuse their concerns. To a group whose faces clearly read "show me," the new SB management shared the new company's integrated healthcare strategy, explained the differences in the U.K. and U.S. accounting standards, and walked the analysts through the integration planning process, hoping they would gain an appreciation for the magnitude of what SB was trying to do. The SB managers were nervous: for some this was their first exposure to the two markets and they felt their reputation was as much on the line as SB's share price. While the seminar helped—some analysts were convinced SB was truly trying to build something new—there remained a feeling of impatience and a why-don't-they-just-get-on-with-it attitude.

To defend the analysts' perspective, they were seeking justification for their earlier "buy" recommendations. The last thing they wanted was to be wrong: if the company wasn't going to deliver, they needed to know *now*. But management was just as impatient with the analysts, frustrated by their lack of sympathy for what SB was trying to achieve. Where the analysts were focusing on the immediate gains to be made from the merger and the quick hits that would add to earnings that year, management was trying to build a structure and a workforce that would be right for many years. How many analysts, they asked themselves, had tried to do what they were doing? Couldn't the analysts see how hard it was?

Despite all the effort, the share price began to slide, even as all the project task forces submitted their final work plans and met their first major milestone as a new company: MMC approval by December 31.

Meanwhile, of course, the organization was in the throes of pulling together its first set of annual figures and preparing its first annual report as a new company—two processes that are strenuous in the best of times. For SB it became an absolute nightmare as those responsible tried to appeal to two different financial markets, two sets of shareholders, and two different management styles.

Although the intensity of the period took an emotional and physical toll on some parts of the organization, it provided those who were working side by side with some valuable insights about one another. As they began to plan implementing the recommendations, it became clear to the EMC that not all its members were challenging the status quo in pursuit of becoming a "new and better healthcare company." Some remained far more comfortable operating according to the ways of the past.

At this point Bob began to realize that the best of the former two companies and their management wasn't "best" enough for the new SmithKline Beecham: SB still wouldn't be the best managed in the industry. Rifts in opinions over the long-term direction started to arise among the senior team. The merger had hit a crisis stage.

WINNING ATTITUDE   The process by which the targets had been defined and agreed became a critical part in achieving them. In meeting the company's first milestone—December 31—with implementation plans that would "deliver results better than either one could alone" and reflected the higher aspiration to be a "new and better healthcare company," the new company had experienced its first win. Each task force was encouraged to go out and celebrate, and the letter to employees that Christmas reinforced the spirit of their achievement.

ORGANIZATION AS HERO   By having a well-defined, rigorous process, challenging the assumptions rather than the conclusions, the MMC allowed the task forces to shape the new company. Not appointing people immediately allowed for open-mindedness about organizational design and for natural leaders to rise to the top. It also reinforced the spirit of equal chances. The more each task force struggled to meet the demands of the MMC, the more confident it became of its recommendations and the more united in its commitment to implement them. Gaining MMC approval and receiving its congratulations was seen as the ultimate victory, attributable to the heroic efforts of all those on the team. This period was all about pushing forward and focusing the organization's collective energy to complete the task at hand.

CUMULATIVE LEARNING   Management and the task forces learned the power of working together and acquired some skills in teamwork, as well as benchmarking as they struggled with their "best practice" instruction. Insisting on a rigid process meant decisions were based more on logic than on emotion, helping guarantee the quality of the desired outcome and fairness of the decisions. With hindsight, more might have been achieved if some training in teamwork and problem solving had been made part of the integration planning process; the extra time might have been compensated by less rework.

STRATEGIC COMMUNICATION   Consistently invoked were the vision of the company as "new and better" and the integration message of "Now We Are One," two themes that actually drove the actions of the teams internally and positioned the company externally as management disciplined itself to maintain "one voice" with all its audiences. Internally employees had milestones by which to gauge winning, but where previously Beecham had always provided quantifiable objectives against which investors could assess the company's progress, the external messages this time weren't made measurable enough. The new company learned that articulating milestones could have helped manage expectations for those both internal and external to the company.

ALIGNMENT OF BEHAVIOR AND STRATEGY   Becoming a "new and better" global company required human resource systems different from those in place in either company. Defining these systems as quickly as possible would make "Now We Are One" a reality. Less than three months after the merger was approved, the new global compensation plan was introduced to the new management group, and within six months all employees in the company's major markets were on a combined payroll, receiving SB paychecks that reinforced the one-company mentality.

CHAPTER SIX

Starting at the Top

A S PEOPLE CAME BACK FROM
the holiday break that first week
in January 1990, it was as if a refreshing wind had blown through the
corridors of SB House and Franklin Plaza.

With the majority of recommendations approved and the most senior
jobs decided, the way forward was clearer than it had been since the
merger announcement. Those remaining recognized that months of hard
work lay ahead of them but felt relieved as the anxiety of nearly nine
months' uncertainty slowly abated. The people who had developed the
plans had been given the authority and the responsibility to implement
them. Now they tackled the tough work of actually integrating the two
businesses country by country, function by function.

With the outcome of the integration recommendations known, it
was time for Bob and Henry to share the vision with the employees
directly. An exhaustive series of what came to be called employee road
shows were planned, to begin in late January. Except for the celebrations,
there had been little direct contact between them and the employees
until this point.

They started with each visiting different locations beginning with
the furthest point, Tokyo. Over the course of the next three months the
two men would separately visit nearly one hundred sites in over twenty-
five countries, taking to the employees directly many of the same messages
they had shared with the eighty managers back in October at Grosvenor
House. In the end, what they learned was that no amount of paper

could replace the direct interface between them and the line employees. Employees needed to hear them explain the key message—Now We Are One—to believe it, and to see firsthand how serious Bob and Henry were about SB becoming a new and better healthcare company.

Given their demands, the visits took enormous time when time was scarce, but they reaped enormous benefits. The visits said that employees were important: this was SB's vision, and they were critical to making it a reality. In terms of motivating and reassuring a global employee population, the symbolism of those road shows has never been lost. (As one former Beecham employee remembers, it had been the first time in his thirty-plus years with the company that he had ever met the executive chairman.)

Communicating face-to-face gave Bob and Henry a chance not only to share information, but also to inspire employees through their own personal commitment. It also helped to build a climate of trust as they reassured where possible but were forthright where necessary, no matter how tough the questions were, especially around acknowledging there would be job redundancies. The employee road show had an added benefit: it enabled Bob to meet and talk with all the local management teams directly. In the end, these were the managers who would have to be the champions of SB. Meeting as many of them as possible was important in winning their support.

BECOMING ONE STRUCTURALLY

Corporatewide implementation of most recommendations was scheduled to be completed within eighteen months, between January 1990 and June 1991, with the remainder to be completed by February 1993. The detailed analysis and enormous effort that had gone into creating first the work plans, then the recommendations of the highest standards possible was reflected in the relative ease with which implementation of most of the more comprehensive plans actually occurred. Having assured themselves that the recommendations would yield the results required, the MMC retreated visibly from the forefront during this phase, while the MIT assumed increasing importance. The MIT's role would be to monitor the teams' activities and report to the EMC on their progress in meeting the targets they had set. Having created the plans, reworked them, and then defended them, the managers were committed to their achievement. This really was the organization as hero.

If Now We Are One as a concept had guided each of the integration decisions, the phrase now took on much more meaning as employees were finally encouraged to meet and learn directly from one another. Planeloads of people began flying back and forth, especially between the United Kingdom and the United States. And as more people came together in the positive spirit of trying to build one company, the trust that had been so elusive during the merger and integration planning phases began to grow.

This trust continued to grow over the coming months, even as those who had not been given roles in the new company started to leave SB. They considered their severance packages fair, which was as important for the message it sent to those remaining as it was for those departing. (Confirming the sense of fairness that pervaded the company: not one merger-related lawsuit for wrongful dismissal or discrimination was filed against SB during this time.) There was a quiet sadness throughout the organization as individuals, some with more than twenty years with one or the other company, departed.

Not everything was perfect: there were still some apparently flagrant violations of equal chance and the principles that had guided the recommendations' development. It was only when the recommendations appeared to seriously undermine the spirit of Now We Are One that a member of the MMC would step in and confront the team leader head-on, challenging the proposal and conducting its own analysis.

In Australia, for example, the need to choose between Melbourne and Sydney for the country's new headquarters cost SB many of the key people it wanted to keep when Melbourne was selected as the site that offered more potential development opportunities. In another country, when the manager proposed a management team composed entirely of old colleagues, Peter flew in on a day's notice to speak directly with managers from both prior companies to understand how the positions had been decided. After hours of one-on-one meetings, he learned the violation had been more an error of judgment that an attempt to protect people. The country manager had based his decisions on the business's near-term prospects, which would be driven by sales of existing products known best by his present team, rather than considering who had the best competence and expertise to drive the business for the long term. Peter had the country manager reconsider his recommendations, and worked closely with him to redefine the new team with more of a look to the future.

From the very beginning of the merger, the management of both companies had agreed that a critical factor in its success was maintaining management morale. Having exercised so much control in the planning stage, the EMC believed any interference now that was not perceived as significant would undermine the organization's belief in the importance of its role and therefore its commitment to creating SB. How their actions were perceived by others was something of which all EMC members were acutely aware; everything was still fragile. Just one action out of sync with what they were saying could shatter the prevailing positive spirit most managers were feeling towards the merger. With trust still somewhat tenuous, they knew that the way they behaved had consequences far beyond the immediate decision or action at hand. They knew that mutual respect had to operate at every level of what they were doing.

MONITORING PROGRESS

For the monthly EMC meetings the MIT prepared progress reports that were quantitative and finance driven, focused on the targets for sales and savings, especially those generated by reducing numbers of people.

At this point Bob's reputation for being Mr. Performance had expanded to include an obsession (as the organization saw it) with headcount. But at this stage sales and people were the only two measures by which management could judge whether they were achieving the promised synergies, and he felt personally responsible for ensuring that the new company achieved them.

The biggest concern was that the creeping headcount characteristic of both firms would continue in the new company, that three years down the road SB would have eliminated 5,000 positions but added 10,000. Bob believed very strongly that the only way to realize the promised savings and achieve the commitments made to the shareholders was to prevent the organization from falling into that trap. While the organization didn't have a problem with the concept at the macro level, its perception during the integration period was that the EMC was managing by headcount.

Other difficulties were encountered during the months of implementation. One area that had been totally underestimated in terms of importance throughout both the merging and planning stages was integration of the information systems function. It now took on enormous magnitude. The MMC had agreed to let the systems run side by side to help maintain business as usual and guarantee business accountability, but the lack of an integrated information system at this point meant that as the businesses came together there was no way to keep track of the newly combined operations or measure (accurately) how well they were doing against the restructuring provisions. Their failure to appreciate the magnitude of the task and plan adequately for a system fundamental to making SB one company was constraining the pace of implementation. Bringing the two information systems together should have been given higher priority in the integration planning process.

In other cases the teams that had been most successful in defending their recommendations in the review process were now the most successful implementers. They welcomed the chance to think differently about their work to become an industry leader. The converse was almost true for the other teams: those who had struggled with developing and getting their plans approved during the autumn, continued to struggle during the implementation phase. Both sets of teams had been competent but for this fundamental difference: where one welcomed change, the other kept looking at the issues in the same old way. It was a problem mirrored at the very top of the new company.

EMC members were anxious to move ahead, and patience was wearing thin. It seemed that every meeting still focused on rehashing integration rather than moving the one company forward. The reason for the endless debate became more and more obvious: some EMC members were having a difficult time looking at things from a new perspective.

INTEGRATION ISN'T ENOUGH

It was February 1990 when the executive management committee met on a Wednesday in Philadelphia. Members faced three days of back-to-back meetings.

The major issue on the EMC agenda was the 1991 annual budget. After several hours of discussion no agreement was reached, and one didn't seem likely to emerge soon. Despite all the months of pushing relentlessly, the proposed budget featured a substantial gap between what had been promised to the shareholders and what had been proposed in the integration recommendations, and what the businesses were now saying they could deliver. That profit gap—£60/$112 million—was huge, and responsibility for most of it—£40/$75 million—fell squarely on the shoulders of the SB Pharmaceuticals team.

As the members debated the feasibility of the target, Bob insisted on its attainment. For SB to achieve the desired shareholder value, the new company had to build credibility, and the only way to do that was to keep delivering on its promises. He could not—indeed, would not—waver.

While some of the shortfall could be attributed to the slowness of the corporate disposal program, as they talked it became clear that much of it resulted from slippage in SB Pharmaceuticals' expectations for both sales and projected savings against the merger and integration targets. Pharmaceuticals attributed the shortfall to the time and effort involved in planning the integration, which meant delays in implementing some of sales training and comarketing efforts as well as in closing some locations. While the current year's sales reflected the immediate success of comarketing the major products, targets set for the following year had not built on that success and were uninspiring. Two plus two was still equaling four, not five. But the merger had been sold to shareholders on the basis that SB would reach higher levels of performance than either company had reached before and generate better results than either could have done alone.

Bob was furious, and those in the room knew it. Unwilling to accept the forecast, he challenged the SB Pharmaceuticals team again, questioning the assumptions and thinking behind the projections. What alternatives were there, he asked, to close the gap between what the merger plan said and the current forecast, yet not jeopardize the long-term business plan? Some EMC members tuned out, frustrated and angry at the amount of time consumed by the debate (which actually had been going on for some months), especially since they had tried so hard in their own areas to achieve the merger targets. Rather than continue an argument that apparently was going nowhere that day, they agreed that Pharmaceuticals should have another budget review meeting in a few weeks, giving the sector's management time to reconsider how it could deliver what it had originally said was possible.

But in the end the budget wasn't the real issue. While the managers worked together for the greater good of the whole company to get the merger done, individual differences had been suppressed. Now they were getting into the heart of how they would manage the business.

Achieving the targets meant challenging the conventional ways of operating in the industry—for example, looking at cost structures in nontraditional ways. As had often happened in recent EMC meetings, Bob was going head-to-head with members of the Pharmaceuticals team, who completely disagreed with his fundamental belief and—they would say—stubborn persistence on the importance of SB becoming the industry's lowest-cost producer.

What a few still had not grasped was his absolute commitment to deliver on a promise. Unless it could be argued convincingly that a goal's achievement could seriously hurt the company's future, he felt it his duty to deliver the goal that management had set on SB's behalf. It was as if his personal word were at stake. Later they would find him more flexible in certain areas, but when it came to SB's meeting an agreed, stated goal, Bob was resolute.

The debate had started nearly a year earlier with the first draft of the Promise which included the wording "SB aims to become the low cost competitor in the pharmaceutical and healthcare industry." Somehow the reality behind the concept and what it would mean for actually managing the business had not been appreciated at the time. Putting it into practice could affect the entire structure of the company.

A PIVOTAL DINNER

As Bob prepared to go downstairs for dinner that February evening, he was very troubled. After just seven months, he felt the merger was starting to lose its momentum. It frustrated him that the business that lay at the core of the merger and accounted for more than half the company's profits and employees—Pharmaceuticals—was the source of constant disagreement. As he walked along the way to the restaurant, he was joined by Peter.

As was usual during EMC weeks in Philadelphia, the entire hotel dining room was filled with SmithKline Beecham management. When they crossed the threshold, they noted that everyone had regressed to their premerger cliques. There was something very insular about the way people had gravitated to their own corners, sector sitting with sector, Beecham colleagues together, SmithKline people elsewhere. There was little animation or excitement; the atmosphere was subdued. It was as though the wind had gone out of everyone's sails.

That evening Bob and Peter shared a dinner discussion that five years later both would agree was a watershed. While they believed they had achieved the best they could through the merger itself, they knew they needed to do much more in terms of getting the best for the long term. The bad news was that integrating the two companies just wasn't enough.

Peter agreed with Bob that teams, not individuals, would be key to the merger's success, and that real teamwork started at the top. As both men saw it, teams are just individuals who have been pulled together by a single purpose that overrides everything else. In the beginning, everyone was working toward the same purpose: the creation of SB and its approval by the shareholders. But at this point EMC members were starting to develop their own agendas, which could ultimately mean none of them would be realized.

In Peter's view the stalemate in the EMC was not about the budget or the businesses or the incompatible and combative personalities. It was more fundamental. It was about people—about their willingness not just to accept change, but to welcome and seek it aggressively in pursuit of a common purpose that was bigger than themselves.

If the first phase of the merger had been all about the present, about creating one company from two, the second phase had to be about the future—about building the foundation that would take SB into the next century. It was a very discouraging time as it became apparent that the team at the top, as it was presently constituted, could not make the change that would take the company where it needed to go. Furthermore, it was becoming increasingly evident to senior managers outside the EMC that things really would have to be done differently for SB to achieve a truly competitive advantage. As the two men lingered over their coffee, they reviewed the attitudes, skills, and competencies they thought would be needed to carry the company forward.

The Case for Management Change

Clearly, if SB truly wanted to become an industry leader, they were *all* going to have to change. The way each company had always done it—even with major improvements—was just not going to be good enough as the industry increasingly came under attack by politicians, government, and consumers. Managers needed to focus on every element: to do much more to reduce costs, realize the potential from integrating the businesses, and focus their R&D efforts, particularly in pharmaceuticals.

They had the best people from SmithKline and the best people from Beecham, and they'd done a fine job on the merger. But during their dinner Bob and Peter realized that SB did not yet have a world-class management, and without it SB was not going to be a world-class company.

Sitting in the empty dining room, they agreed that SB needed a team more committed to what *could* be, one that would pursue the vision with a sense of urgency *before* the impending industry changes became a sweeping reality. While some EMC members would be able to support and lead the necessary effort to change, others truly believed that "the way we've always done it is right, we just need to do it better." Peter's recommendation: Bob would need to get the right team before he could get the team right.

Moving On

The lengthy conversation about the top team led to a discussion about the organization itself. As they revisited the day's events, the men discovered they had reached the same conclusion: the momentum generated by the merger was fizzling out, and the organization was rapidly running out of steam. Both felt the organization was falling back into old habits: employees, considering the merger "done," were drifting back to their premerger behavior. SB was losing the winning spirit that had driven the merger and was settling for less than what it could be—less than it needed to be to become a world-class player. Given the EMC complacency reflected in the meeting that day, the top team as it stood could not revitalize the organization's winning spirit.

If they allowed the organization to drift back now into the old SmithKline or Beecham frame of mind, the moment was lost; with it would go SB's opportunity to *ever* be an industry leader. Management had to seize this chance and deliberately shape the organizational behavior SB needed to get them where they wanted to go. A new culture for SB to succeed *had* to be developed.

While establishing a new culture had been planned as the next SB phase, their dinner conversation that night convinced Bob and Peter that it had to begin immediately. It was a logical time and a logical way to restart momentum in the new company.

The time was right to take the next steps in the journey toward their new and better company. SB's strategy and integrated structure would be meaningless unless they had the right team to lead it and the appropriate organizational behavior to support it.

Two important decisions had been made at dinner. One was to focus on getting the right team, the other was to accelerate and intensify the efforts that had been quietly under way to further develop the new company culture.

REBUILDING THE MANAGEMENT TEAM

When Bob met with Henry to discuss reshaping of the senior team, Henry's advice was to wait. He was concerned about moving too quickly, before things had a chance to work themselves out naturally. The company was deep into the anguish of totally reorganizing; to make changes in the seniormost team now could be very unsettling.

Bob viewed it differently. Understanding full well the risk, he still believed keeping the same members when they knew it wasn't the right team would slow down the development of the new company culture. He preferred to address the issue there and then—however disturbing it was—and get it behind them as quickly as possible.

The discussion led to a different, and, in some respects, an even more important question: did they have anyone in place now who could succeed Bob as chief executive? Consistent with his original contract with Beecham, Bob had agreed with the new board to step down in 1994, five years after the merger. Who would be groomed as his successor?

The critical succession issue finally went to the nonexecutive directors, and Bob and Henry presented their position. As head of SB Pharmaceuticals, the company's largest business, John Chappell was in a key role. John had been in charge of SmithKline Beckman's pharmaceuticals business before the merger, and his presence helped ensure equal representation in the EMC between the Beecham and SmithKline Beckman management. Without John, the organization—still sensitive to changes that might tip the balance—might feel the merger-of-equals concept had somehow been violated. But in the end, while Henry believed that John was appropriate for his current position, he recognized that the philosophical differences between Bob and John were too great for John to be Bob's successor. A few weeks later John agreed he would step down.

His agreement had implications beyond the one position: it gave Bob and the board a chance to review the sector's entire management structure, an opportunity that was quickly seized as they sought to build a world-class management team.

Meanwhile, the existing team had to continue to manage the new company.

External Criticism

Members of the senior team were about to face sixty of the City's top industry analysts at a London hotel. It was March 14, 1990, the merger was just about eight months old, and SB was reporting its first results as a new company.

The numbers showed a 16 percent increase in sales from continuing operations of £4.3/$6.9 billion. Profits before taxes were £724 million/$1.2 billion and, considered on a pro forma basis (i.e., as if SmithKline Beecham had been one company since 1988), were up 15 percent. The numbers were right on target with the merger goals.[1]

In addition, SB announced the £500/$807 million restructuring charge. The restructuring provision covered estimated costs of plant closings and redundancies and would give some indication as to the amount of restructuring that was planned. The number reflected the culmination of the 250 planning and project teams' work and was within the ballpark amount that the premerger planning team had estimated. While the actual provision had not been disclosed to analysts these many months as the teams completed their work, SB's management had tried at least to position its magnitude. Therefore, they felt it would be fairly well accepted and were decidedly unprepared to hear negative reactions from both national constituencies for two totally different reasons: Wall Street, well acquainted with all the high financing deals of the 1980s and still comparing SB to Bristol-Myers

Squibb (its pre-tax charge had been about U.S. $850 million), felt it should have been larger. The U.K. financial market was surprised by its enormity. Clearly SB was in a no-win situation.

Adding to the difficulty were the analysts' nagging questions about the high levels of debt, continued delay of the sale of the cosmetics business, and sales of Tagamet versus rival Zantac.

While SB had generated positive results, the performance did not get reflected in the share price. Between July 1989 and March 1990, it had fluctuated between a high of 630 pence and a low of 508 pence. By March 14, the company had lost 26 percent off its shareholder value since the merger, and the amount of U.S. holdings was starting to decline. It seemed as if SB management had done everything humanly possible toward what it believed to be right, and it still wasn't enough, at least not in the market's view.

Internal Anxiety

One week after they faced the critical market analysts it was announced to the organization that the head of Pharmaceuticals would be leaving.

The news sent tremors through the company. For all these months the organization had accepted the ambiguity, the uncertainty, and the disruption as something temporary, something to be endured until things could get back to normal, which in people's minds was the time before the merger. Where management was talking about five years out, the organization was still trying to get through the first year. Because everyone thought there would be at least two years' peace before any further upheavals, for most employees the announcement came as a incredible shock.

EMC members themselves could hardly believe the timing. Although they had recognized that differences between Bob and John were building, none thought that significant changes in the top team would occur only nine months after the merger.

In symbolic terms the departure of John Chappell was actually bigger than the event itself. It made real the message that SB would no longer be as it was; clearly they were all moving on, creating a new company with new attitudes. That meant people had to change. For the organization, it was as if a light bulb had come on. People finally realized there was no going back.

Anxiety levels rose again among employees, as those in the SB Pharmaceuticals sector started to speculate on who would be the new head of Pharmaceuticals.

Seeking Outside Advice

If there was no going back, then where was SB headed? EMC members knew the kind of culture they didn't want; they despised the old "if it ain't broke, don't fix it" and "not invented here" philosophy. They knew that the business needed to be more responsive, productive, and innovative, but they weren't sure how all that translated into employee behavior.

Around the time of their February dinner Bob and Peter agreed they were going to need someone from outside SB not only to help build the EMC into a team, but also to help them define the organizational culture they were trying to shape. They drew on their experience to put together a list of experts in organizational change. But it was difficult: they were seeking an expert in organizational behavior who could also win the trust of an EMC made up of strikingly different business and national cultures.

Consistent with their past practice, they identified several consultants for consideration. In March 1990 they met with Warner Burke, professor of organizational development at New York's Columbia University. Warner's style made him a natural facilitator for the EMC. He also brought a proven methodology on how to effect transformational change, the Burke-Litwin Model (see figure 6-1). Based on Warner's expertise and experience in both team building and cultural transformation, after meeting with the EMC, Warner was hired.

The Burke-Litwin Model consisted of twelve boxes. At the top was External Environment, changes to which usually drove a shift in business strategy and the need to transform in the first place. Along the left-hand side were the factors most commonly tapped to address the changes, the so-called hard stuff: mission, strategy, structure, and tasks. Along the right-hand side were the factors most senior management felt less comfortable with and usually delegated to others or ignored: culture, systems (policies and procedures), individual needs, and values. To truly transform a company, every one of these elements would have to be addressed. But—most important—they would have to be addressed in such a way that each reinforced the others: the arrows connecting the boxes were

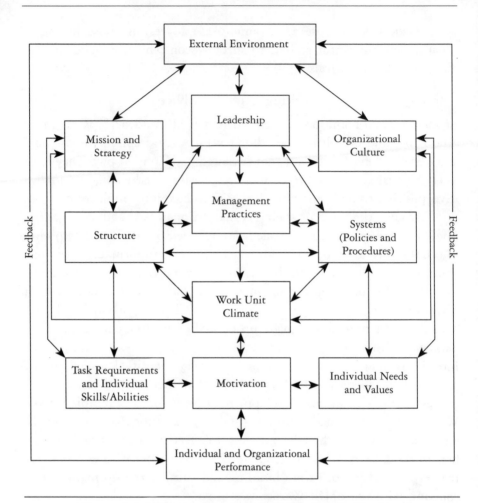

Figure 6-1 ***The Burke-Litwin Model of Individual and***
Organizational Performance

Source: W. Warner Burke and George H. Litwin, "A Causal Model of Organizational
Performance," extracted from *Developing Human Resources* (San Diego: University
Associates, 1989): p. 280.

Reprinted with permission from W. Warner Burke.

almost more important than the boxes themselves. The model's underlying
premise and fundamental message was that business strategy and organizational culture must be inextricably linked to promote individual and
organizational performance.

Directly below the box labeled "External Environment" was one
labeled "Leadership." Before SB could do anything further, it had to have

those in the top management team together, all moving in the same direction.

At the next meeting it was proposed to the EMC that it consciously pursue team building, using Warner as an outside facilitator and implementing some actual team-building exercises. A series of one-on-one interviews followed to assess EMC members' opinions on how well they thought the merger was going, whether they were working as a team, and what they would change if they could change anything. The goal was to find out how far apart members really were and why.

The EMC reaction to the team-building effort ranged from interest or concern to a so-what attitude. After all the months of merging and integrating, EMC members were at last trying to focus on the business. Organizational culture just wasn't a sufficiently high priority for them. But Bob was insistent. This was to be a new and better company, and it would never achieve that goal if people kept behaving as they always had. That session marked the beginning of a concerted effort to gain personal insight that would build the EMC first into a team, and then into a team that could lead behavioral change.

Recruiting Top Talent

With the John Chappell decision behind the company, the focus was now on getting the right team. The February conclusion was reinforced: the best of both companies' management teams wasn't enough for the future. It wasn't going to get SB where it needed to go to become a world-class company.

There just wasn't enough management depth for the long term. In Pharmaceuticals, three of the four senior members were within a few years of retirement. One of them was Fred Kyle, the U.S. head, actually filling the sector's two most critical roles since he had stepped temporarily into Chappell's shoes.

Fred's successor as head of the U.S. business had been a concern for some time, since the U.S. market had always been considered crucial to SB's overall success. (In fact, gaining a larger presence in that market had been one of the driving reasons Beecham had pursued a merger with an American company.) With changes in the U.S. healthcare market increasingly imminent, executive recruiters had long been advised to keep their eyes open for a potential replacement for Fred.

Furthermore, as was common in a major restructuring, other members of management would assess their personal comfort level with the new organization, and some would decide to leave. The head of Japan, for example, resigned within a few weeks of John Chappell, and the person in charge of Europe would leave SB in several months' time to return to the United States. Other sectors faced similar situations.

Until they got the right team in place, trying to build a new corporate culture would be very difficult if not impossible. But Bob didn't want to slow up any part of the process of creating this new company, fearful that it would never happen if any momentum was lost. They simply had to work harder, smarter, and faster.

A list of criteria and possible external candidates for the potential head for SB Pharmaceuticals was developed. It was difficult. SB needed someone who would see and manage the changing demands on the industry, be a positive force in shaping the culture that would help SB achieve a competitive advantage, and, perhaps most important in the longer term, be viewed as a potential successor to Bob.

Any of the four candidates eventually identified would be up to the business task, but Bob personally was looking for someone who would be passionate about changing the organizational culture. His other two requirements: an absolute commitment to winning and a personal belief in the principles and vision already outlined for the company. Bob was adamant about all three, and unwilling to compromise on any one of them.

At about that same time, a long-time associate suggested that Bob meet Jan Leschly, who had been president of Squibb at the time of its merger with Bristol-Myers. Danish and a pharmacist by training, Jan had joined Novo As, Denmark's largest pharmaceutical company, in 1972 as assistant to the vice president of marketing. He was hired by Squibb in 1979 as vice president, commercial development and two years later was named president of Squibb's U.S. business. Jan became president and chief operating officer of Squibb Corporation in 1988, just months before its merger with Bristol-Myers. A former professional tennis player (ranked tenth in the world in 1968), Jan was highly energetic, competitive, and enthusiastic, as well as highly regarded in the industry. Jan had been extremely successful in building Squibb's business and in developing and launching new products such as the blockbuster cardiovascular treatment Capoten, which became a

$1 billion-plus product. He also had a reputation for attracting talented managers to his company.

Jan left Bristol-Myers Squibb soon after the merger but continued to be involved in the pharmaceutical industry. He had one unfulfilled personal ambition: to become a chief executive of a major healthcare company. That ambition had been thwarted with Squibb's merger.

However, as far as the world was concerned, SB was not looking for a chief executive; it hadn't even officially launched the search for the head of Pharmaceuticals. But here was Jan, so Bob agreed to meet with him on an April day.

As the two men talked, Bob became more and more comfortable with Jan's values. Jan shared what he had tried to do at Squibb to create a corporate culture that would reward productivity, personal performance, and risk taking. Jan also shared his view of the future of the industry and the need for SB to be an integrated healthcare company.

It was two months before the next meeting could be arranged, this time between Peter and Jan. Peter, too, was struck by Jan's high energy and enthusiasm as well as his ambition. Given his proven track record, Jan's desire to continuously improve his own leadership skills was also both impressive and attractive in a potential chief executive. It meant he would be open minded, which was critical to guaranteeing a seamless top management transition.

That said, Peter still checked numerous references from superiors, peers, and subordinates. (Seventeen in the end!). The merger, after all, was not even one year old, and here they were not only bringing in an outsider to head the largest business, but actually considering him as a potential CEO. The appointment was not one to be done in haste: the company's entire future depended on it.

In all of the discussions, Jan was never assured of the chief executive role, only that he would be one of the lead candidates. Too much was at stake to make promises now that might not be kept. For despite having all the right credentials and a wealth of highly respected experience in the industry, Jan would still have to earn the role within the context of SmithKline Beecham. This was the culture they were trying to create, and it would apply at *every* level.

The prepared agenda for the May board meeting was postponed as Jan's appointment was presented to the nonexecutive directors. What followed was a long and arduous discussion about the quality of senior management, Bob and Henry's own plans for retirement, what would constitute a world-class global management team, and how they could guarantee the continuity of such management.

The standard that the board was now setting for determining the executive management team included some of the same criteria that had been used in determining the board. For example, at the time of the merger the number of board members had been equally divided between the British and the Americans, each bringing a discipline and expertise to the board that complemented that of the management team. In a deliberate effort to reflect the company's desire to be truly global, as these original board members retired, they were to be replaced with more directors from Continental Europe and the Far East. And as SB moved further in its efforts to transform, it became important that the board bring a competence in line with the new requirements. In addition to scientific and technological expertise, they began to seek board members experienced in culture change. The appointments eventually included a chief executive from France, the female head of privatization in East Germany, the Japanese head of research at the University of Michigan Medical Center, and two chief executives of American companies renowned for their quality efforts. (From the original twenty members—ten from each side—the Board was eventually reduced in 1990 to seventeen, of which ten were nonexecutives. Five nationalities were eventually represented.)

Following the three-hour discussion around SB's overall long-term management plans, the board members gave their approval to hire Jan.

On June 7, it was announced first to the SB pharmaceuticals team, then to all of SB and the newswires that Jan Leschly would become SmithKline Beecham's Pharmaceuticals chairman, responsible for more than half of SB's sales and close to two-thirds of its profits.

Later in the summer of 1990 what would prove to be another spectacular hire reached its rather bizarre conclusion. It was August, and there was Peter disembarking from the company plane and walking across the small, empty Grenoble airport (the French air-traffic controllers were on strike) to meet Jean-Pierre (JP) Garnier, president of Schering-Plough's U.S. pharmaceuticals business. The retiring Fred Kyle had suggested JP as a potential candidate to head SB's U.S. pharmaceuticals, and JP had been enthusiastically endorsed by Jan, who knew him from previous contacts.

JP held a Ph.D. in pharmacology, an M.S. in pharmaceutical science, and had been a Fulbright scholar at Stanford University from which he received his M.B.A. in 1974. During his fifteen years at Schering-Plough, he held a number of management positions, including general manager of several overseas subsidiaries, before moving to the U.S. division in 1983. There he progressed from senior director of marketing for both ethical and OTC products to U.S. pharmaceuticals president in 1989. While at Schering, he had an unprecedented record for superior performance and was considered one of the industry's most capable leaders.

Born and raised in France, JP was spending his summer holiday there, high in the mountains. Having met Henry, Bob, and Jan, he agreed to come down to the airport for one last meeting, this time with Peter, out of both curiosity and genuine interest. He still wasn't certain about leaving Schering for the new SB.

As they sat on the tarmac talking and eating lunch in the small executive plane, Peter found an individual with a keen intellect and sharp business acumen who also showed all the signs of being a highly proficient change agent. For the head of a country business considered crucial to the company's long-term prospects, Jan had already confirmed that JP displayed an in-depth understanding of changing U.S. healthcare trends and their implications, yet also came across as instinctively global. Most impressive: JP appeared to challenge everything. He took nothing for granted, assumed nothing was absolutely right; nor did he consider anything sacred. He was dedicated to winning, and that meant everything could always be improved or changed for the better. While finally convinced of SB's potential, in the end it was JP's respect for SB's leadership that finally convinced him to join the new company, where he would report directly to Jan.

In discussing JP's appointment with the Board, Bob advised the nonexecutive directors that he believed having both Jan and JP would assure SB of high management quality well into the next century.

One month later, in September, SB announced that Jean-Pierre Garnier would join as president of North America Pharmaceuticals, SB's largest and most profitable pharmaceuticals market.

Internal Appointments

The appointments of Jan and JP reflected the new company's commitment to build the best possible management team, even if it meant going outside the company to fill positions. The message underlying the appointments both internally and externally was that SB was determined to build the best management team in the industry. The markets and analysts were extremely pleased, but internally there was some management disappointment that SB had gone outside to fill such key positions with the merger barely a year old. On the other hand, both Jan and JP came with a reputation among the former SmithKline pharmaceuticals team for being highly competitive and hard driving. The appointments sent a strong message about what being the best would mean in the new SB. There was an added benefit—these new people would bring in fresh thinking and expedite the creation of a new company since neither was tied to what *was* but both were driven by what *could be.* Jan's first message to employees reinforced this spirit: "We have a fabulous opportunity . . . Our goal is to be the best . . . We need to think big and to develop the strategies now so that we can really get to the top."[2]

Once Jan was in place, he undertook further the task of totally rebuilding SB's pharmaceuticals team. Between June and December 1990 the entire pharmaceuticals management committee (PMC) had been (or would be) changed. Half the appointments were people from outside, half were from within SB. Whereas it had once been thought it would take two years to make management changes in Pharmaceuticals, Jan and JP condensed those two years into six months.

Of the internal appointments, the naming of two young managers with great long-term potential to senior positions further symbolized how old cultures were crumbling. These candidates jumped several grades overnight—unheard-of moves in the two previous company cultures—as senior management acted on its belief in the need to place the absolute best in the top jobs.

These management changes sent an important and consistent message to the organization: people would no longer be promoted on the basis of behavior that had been acceptable in the past. This new company would require different competencies and skills, and the senior team would seek them out wherever they had to, whether inside or outside. The new appointments became another symbolic watershed, reinforcing to the organization that the times really were changing.

With his team in place, Jan Leschly led the SB pharmaceuticals sector through another round of integration during early 1991. Much of what could not be done before was accomplished as the newcomers brought fresh insights and new energies to an organization that had grown weary with restructuring. While his team ran SB pharmaceuticals operations, Jan focused his energies on where he felt the company could gain its greatest leverage: R&D, which had from the very beginning been the most difficult part of the two companies to integrate. With an outsider directing the effort, the disparate groups came together much faster. Jan also helped ease the transition between the retiring head of R&D, Dr. Keith Mansford, and his successor, Dr. George Poste.

George had joined SmithKline & French Laboratories in 1980 and held a number of research positions until 1988, when he was named president of R&D. Upon the merger, he was named president of SB's research & development technologies, with 85 percent of the 5,000 R&D staffers reporting to him. British by birth but now a U.S. citizen, he held doctoral degrees in veterinary medicine and virology and had held positions as a principal cancer research scientist and a professor of cell and molecular biology in the United States. He was also an elected fellow of the Royal College of Veterinary Surgeons and the Royal College of Pathologists, both in London. He would work very closely with Jan to rationalize the discovery programs and decide which sites to consolidate and in which therapeutic areas to focus. George succeeded Keith in November 1991.

Keith had been with Beecham's research staff for close to forty years and had been named chairman of Beecham Pharmaceuticals' R&D in 1984. He left knowing that his work had been instrumental in the merger's approval and would be important to its future success. The product pipeline he nurtured had helped convince the financial markets of the merger's logic, and the three new compounds ready for launch would carry the company through the decline of Tagamet.

Because Pharmaceuticals had been the focus of the merger, this was the management team that SB had to get right first and fast. But there were still management issues surrounding the other sectors. In Consumer Brands and Animal Health, for example, both chairmen were nearing retirement. With Pharmaceuticals now in control under Jan's leadership, Bob and Peter turned their attention to the other sectors. A search for successors, both inside and outside the company, was quietly started.

Of the thirty-seven members of senior management introduced in the 1989 annual report, less than one-third would be in the same positions by the end of 1991. Still, the feeling within the organization was not of a management revolution. Somehow the changes seemed to have evolved naturally.

1990 BUSINESS PROGRESS

Despite the information systems difficulties, the management conflicts, and the relentless push on the budget, SB made enormous business progress in 1990. While the integration work continued, employees within SB Pharmaceuticals continued to move ahead, and significant business milestones were reported during this time. Some success from comarketing Tagamet and Augmentin started coming through in the first half of 1990, as Tagamet held its share in the critical U.S. market. And, in an enterprising turnabout, SB signed a supply agreement with a generic distributor to participate in the sale of Dyazide as a generic. In SB Consumer Brands, certain products gained all-time market share, and new products were launched, one of which was an energy variation of Lucozade. By summer, Lucozade Sport was selling a million cans a week.

Clinical Laboratories acquired additional laboratories in the United States and introduced customized computers that would link doctors and hospitals straight to them, enabling test results to reach clients faster. (This technology would later be viewed as a core competence for SB.)

At a corporate level, the disposal program progressed as some of the noncore consumer food products such as Marmite and Bovril were divested. Finally, in July, the major part of cosmetics was sold for £350/$675 million—half of what had been expected. But these sums, together with funds generated by issuing some auction-rate preference shares and—most important—over £900 million/$1.7 billion cash created by the businesses, meant debt by year's end had declined almost two-thirds. The annual interest payment was halved, moving from £110/$212 million in 1990 to £59/$110 million the following year.[3]

Slowly but surely SB management was progressing toward the vision. First it had addressed the so-called hard stuff—headcount, plant closings, business performance—all of which had to be done to maintain credibility outside and eliminate uncertainty inside. Rebuilding the team was the first of many major soft-side changes that would be required to achieve

SB's vision. Compared with the quantitative side, the soft side would be more difficult to address.

Once again, the steps toward change would have to start with the top team.

WINNING ATTITUDE   The winning spirit is consistently promoted by focusing on achievement of the next set of milestones, namely implementing the integration recommendations by the agreed-on dates and achieving the financial targets to which teams had committed. Also illustrated is how critical it is that the leaders of a company share a common vision of winning and an understanding of what that vision implies. The way SB had defined winning—i.e., to become a "new and better" healthcare company—forced management to think differently about how it ran the business. It became necessary to go outside the company for leaders who believed in SB's vision and relished the personal challenge to change.

ORGANIZATION AS HERO   To create an organization where people are the hero of its success requires leaders who are concerned equally with what is achieved and how it is done.

A major organizational change affects everyone, including the leaders, with uncertainty. Leaders are decided initially on the basis of competence as well as personal circumstances such as impending retirements. In a friendly merger most of the issues are discussed openly in premerger phases and management changes can be anticipated. As time goes on, questions arise on the way things are done, and some elect to leave as they recognize that their management style is not compatible with that of the new company. These are straightforward, and departures are sad but amicable. More difficult are cases wherein people whose behavior is not consistent with the new company direction want to stay. While every effort should be made to help talented managers adapt and stay, if those in key positions cannot change, they must be replaced before management loses momentum.

CUMULATIVE LEARNING   The success of the integration planning process became manifest as the teams started implementing their recommendations. In the six-month process, members had learned much about how to work together in teams, including how to resolve major impasses, the importance of their interdependencies, and the need to work more across processes, businesses, and functions. They began to recognize the value of discipline and using data generated through analysis and benchmarking to problem solve. These stepping stones would become part of the company's core values and later be built into its training.

STRATEGIC COMMUNICATION The employee roadshow brought the message of a new and better healthcare company personally to managers and employees and allowed time for explaining more definitively what that meant by including the specifics of the integration Recommendations. It established a two-way discussion with the company's most senior management. Hearing the vision first-hand from the chairman or the chief executive enabled employees to respond directly to senior management and was an important step toward aligning the organization with the company's Promise. Some would have liked this to happen earlier, but many questions could be answered only after the teams had completed their work. However, more effort could have been made to ensure that managers had the answers and to help them establish a systematic dialogue with their employees, thereby easing some of the massive uncertainty.

ALIGNMENT OF BEHAVIOR AND STRATEGY The Promise and integration guidelines along with the five-year goals provided a consistent framework for all the teams and therefore alignment of their business and integration plans. The milestone (Now We Are One), goals (synergy targets), and enabling systems (team charters, work plans, McKinsey facilitators) were centrally directed from corporate, while developing the integration plans and assuming responsibility for implementing them took place in the business and belonged to the organization. Controlling the process centrally ensured overall alignment with the vision, while requiring the content be developed and implemented locally gained the organization's commitment. It was guided empowerment.

CHAPTER SEVEN

The Launch of *Simply Better*

T HE DRIVE TO CHEWTON GLEN on England's south coast took only two hours that Wednesday afternoon. Traffic was surprisingly light.

It was July 17, and the merger was approaching its first anniversary. Bob pondered the past twelve months as he drove along the highway to the EMC retreat. How had they done?

He mentally outlined some of the positives: SB had met or exceeded most of the goals it had set for the integration—the number of sites, the amount to be saved, the timing for implementation. The first-half results were in line with analysts' expectations; some of the analysts were starting to turn more positive on the fledgling company.

But while SmithKline Beecham had become one company in structure, it was not yet one in spirit. Not only had Beecham and SmithKline come from different national and corporate cultures, but distinct differences existed among the four business sectors. If SB were ever to achieve its ambition of being an integrated healthcare company, all the barriers to better performance—including those between the businesses—would have to be destroyed. SB needed one culture absolutely consistent with its strategy and shared by every employee so they could work more effectively *across,* not just down, the company. And the commitment of top management was necessary to shape it, develop it, and champion it.

As the car pulled into the long driveway, the sky was turning the dusty yellow of dusk. Other EMC members had been arriving throughout the day. They would meet for dinner, scheduled at 8:00 P.M.

It was time to focus on building SB for the future. As top-level managers, they had done what they could do with what had been: the operations had been put together, the savings squeezed out, the noncore businesses sold. Now they must build on the merger's momentum to move SB forward. But the question kept echoing in their minds: "We know what we want to become. But what skills do we need to get us there?" And should they try to answer that question now, *before* they had the right team—one that would lead SB into the next decade—on board?

This last point had been a source of constant discussion. If they waited until they had all the right members on the team, they risked losing the opportunity for change created by the merger.

As Bob and Peter had considered this trade-off between the team and momentum, they also had recognized that the entire EMC was not committed to the new direction. They decided all they really needed was a core group that had the following characteristics:

❖ They were key influencers both in terms of the organization's respect and in their understanding of the need for behavioral change.
❖ They were committed to staying with the company (three-to-five years minimum).
❖ They were in positions of leverage—that is, they could affect large numbers of people.

Speed was important. "Change while you can" was one of the lessons they had learned through the integration process. They decided to move ahead while they still had some momentum. (Later they would advise others to err on the side of moving too fast versus too slow: just be sure to have a plan.)

The Chewton Glen retreat had been planned as a time to work together as a team to develop the behaviors that would help SB realize its strategy. To work as a team meant building trust. Many of the participants were still relative strangers, and the time spent together so far had been fraught with overactivity.

The team needed to be built quickly from relationships that were still somewhat fragile. Before the EMC could have an open debate around defining organizational behavior, it would be important for members to be able to speak openly about their own. With this thought in mind and to minimize any risk of failure, the session was structured in two parts. The first part would focus on team building, using some mechanism to help bridge the strangers gap and create the desired atmosphere of openness. The second part would focus on one key issue that would carry SB into the future, something bigger than each individual's interest that they could work through together.

The goal: by the end of the session, the EMC would see itself as an *SB* team and have agreed to a set of values that would become the foundation for SmithKline Beecham's one corporate culture.

Because each person brought with him not just the culture of his national origin and previous company, but also the culture of his sector and function, the task was far greater than simply merging the two company cultures. But defining SB's culture would *have* to start with them: they would have to shape it, model it, and be seen to be driving and living it before the rest of the organization would get on board.

The EMC agreed that they would not move forward into the culture discussion unless they concluded that the first day had been successful and some steps had been taken toward understanding how they functioned as a team. There was no point trying to move SB forward if they couldn't move it *together.*

The session opened the next morning with a question: How are we doing as a team? It was a day dedicated to getting the issues out in the open in way that signaled "we are all in this *together.*" To do this they would use the results of Warner Burke's interviews and the nonthreatening Myers-Briggs personality assessment test.

The test data helped identify individual behaviors and how these influenced the team. Members learned that personally they were far more intuitive than they cared to admit and great at generating ideas but poor at following them through. It was as if once they had spoken an idea, they considered it done and then moved on to the next challenge. The implications for the organization were far-reaching: no sooner would employees be given one task than another would come hurtling toward them. Warner's explanation of the test findings created a forum that was nonthreatening and nonevaluative as EMC members tried to gain insight into the collective impact of their individual behavior. That was when they realized the real value of the simple team-building tool. The test data was incidental to its true purpose: providing a legitimate opportunity to talk through their differences.

The EMC gained two important insights from the results. (1) Given the chance, they would try to tackle everything at once. (2) There would have to be a more definitive decision-making process to ensure that each proposal was completely thought through. To work more effectively as a team, they would have to work harder at setting priorities and be more focused and consciously disciplined about their demands on employees. As a simple first step, members agreed that future EMC meeting agendas would be limited to ten items (compared with the present average of eighteen), permitting greater focus and more discussion time.

As the discussion continued, EMC members grew more relaxed. Tension seemed to dissipate as strangers took their first steps toward becoming friends. By the end of that day Bob knew he had the core team he needed to move forward, and EMC members had a clearer idea of how they could all work together. When they met for dinner that evening, everyone agreed the day had been a success.

In preparation for the second day's session, advance work had been done in three areas:

❖ Finding a tested model for change that could help guide SB's culture-building efforts
❖ Outlining some suggested values from the principles that had guided their work so far, such as those contained in the Promise and the merger integration guidelines
❖ Gathering statements that captured what these values looked like in action based on best practice of other companies

The idea was to deliberately guide the session constructively in hopes of achieving their goal by day's end. (This reflected another lesson learned through the integration process: guided empowerment was more effective than unstructured, freewheeling brainstorming.) The next day, the EMC moved to its next challenge: building a culture for the new SB.

DEFINING THE FIVE VALUES

The morning opened with an introduction of the Burke-Litwin model (figure 6-1) and the twelve organizational areas required for true corporate transformation. As they reviewed the boxes in the diagram, EMC members agreed that those to the left—mission and strategy and structure—had all been addressed as part of the merger and integration process. They now had to address the right-hand side of the model—its so-called soft side—which was organizational culture and systems (policies and procedures). By using the accepted, proven model of change to frame SB's efforts, EMC members found the concept of designing a culture to deliver corporate strategy suddenly raised to a level they could address. Some of the skepticism started to disappear.

Before they looked forward, EMC members considered the past and the cultures of the two previous companies. They identified the attitudes they wanted to keep—such as being highly ethical—and those they wanted to eliminate—such as "we've always done it that way." But then they needed to look ahead: what were the values that would really drive SB's competitive advantage? It was then that the first part of the prework for the day's session was presented: four values that could, if every employee practiced them, make a difference in SB's performance. The four values proposed that morning had been inherent in all the work that had gone before and were entirely consistent with where they wanted to go in terms of the strategy outlined at Grosvenor House nine months earlier. While not unique in themselves, it would be how the EMC defined them and how employees executed them that would determine their success. The four outlined were performance, innovation, customers, and people.

Clearly, *performance* was a priority. SB needed to meet—if not exceed—shareholders' expectations if it were to continue improving shareholder value and become a winning, world-class company. It needed to grow sales and drive down costs and consistently challenge itself if it were serious about becoming the low-cost producer. SB's productivity per employee, for example, was the lowest in its peer group.

Greater *innovation* was fundamental, especially in the healthcare industry. SB needed a risk-free environment, compared with the risk-averse heritage of its parents; it must encourage employees to dare to think differently and creatively to generate the new products and realize the promised savings. At Grosvenor House the past October, for example, management had said that by 1994—five years after the merger—15 percent of sales would come from products that hadn't existed at the time of the merger. Everyone would have to work much harder at accelerating the flow of these new products if they were to achieve that goal.

Where science and the product had often been the driving force in their business, they now agreed that they had to be more *customer-oriented* and market-driven. In what was a revolutionary idea at the time, they suggested that customers were to be found both internally and externally. Identifying and meeting the requirements of coworkers was as important as understanding the needs of physicians, pharmacists, or consumers. Everyone, not just the few who dealt with people outside the company, had customers.

Achieving all this would require talented employees and high-quality management. Recruiting and keeping excellent *people* had to be another priority. SB wanted—and needed to be—the best-managed company in the industry if it were to achieve its goals.

After some debate (For example, was performance a value or an outcome of all the others?) the EMC agreed on the four.

The value that sparked the most debate was *integrity* (although, in hindsight today, everyone wonders why). Discussion began around the word "trust," which had been included in the old SmithKline Beckman mission statement. When the EMC realized it was actually going to use the values to drive behavior, "trust" became "integrity"—that is, employees would always be expected to act with integrity, generating trust. Trust was the result, not the driver, of their actions.

One side argued that integrity was so fundamental that it went without saying; so if the values were meant to help change behavior, then listing integrity would be unnecessary. Other EMC members, especially those involved with prescription medicines, wanted the value to be included to reinforce that no unethical behavior would ever be tolerated at SB.

Agreeing that too many values would diminish their importance, and that those selected had to combine to provide a real competitive advantage, the EMC finally agreed on some criteria:

❖ The Values would be called the "Core Values," to reinforce their fundamental nature to the company and role in guiding behavior.
❖ The Values would be few in number to ensure focus (no more than five).
❖ The Values would be qualities that in practice would provide the greatest leverage for realizing a competitive advantage and achieving the company's strategy.
❖ The Values would build on the heritage of both companies but be focused on addressing future needs.
❖ The Values would be simply stated to ensure clarity; they would be quantifiable so as to be measured.

In the end, five Values emerged: the original four plus *integrity*. While the wording that follows reflects subsequent editing, this is the order in which they came out of the meeting:

Performance: SB is performance-driven. We continuously aim to improve performance in all that we do.

Customers: SB is customer-oriented. We strive to provide products and services of superior value to meet the expectations of our internal and external customers.

Innovation: SB constantly strives to be creative and innovative in all its endeavors. All SB employees are encouraged to bring forth new and better ideas for improved performance, whatever their responsibilities.

People: SB employees are all partners, working together in the pursuit of the SB mission and strategy. We strongly value teamwork, and we want every employee to be motivated to succeed.

Integrity: SB demands openness and honesty throughout its operations to engender trust, and integrity underscores everything that we do. We believe that every activity must be able to pass the test of public and internal scrutiny at all times.

Figure 7-1 shows how the Values were linked with the strategy. Discussion of the Values continued longer than anyone expected, and it was now nearing time for dinner. Still, there was no sign of conclusion as EMC members continued to add refinements to the statements they had crafted. While prework had helped guide the session, there was no doubt that the Values as they were now crafted belonged to all of them. Just as they had known when they were devising the integration guidelines, they understood that this was another unique opportunity. The merger created the chance to start at the beginning, an opportunity to design an ideal culture that could deliver their strategic goals. They wanted to be sure they got it right.

Strategy		*Values*
Most effective marketers	⟹	Customer
Leader in new product discovery, development	⟹	Innovation
Most efficient producers	⟹	Performance
Best managed company	⟹	People Integrity

Figure 7-1 Linking Strategy with Values

When the session finally did break, it was for an informal evening. Dinner was leisurely, followed by a visit to a local pub and the English game of skittles (nine wooden pins knocked over with a wooden ball). Even during the game, the team-building activities continued—and the teams were a hybrid of Beecham and SmithKline, of British and Americans!

TURNING THE VALUES INTO PRACTICES

The next morning it was back to the Burke-Litwin model, this time with the Leadership and Management Practices boxes highlighted. As EMC members knew, the Values alone were not enough to distinguish SB from the competition—no matter how much they slaved over the words. What really counted was how employees brought the Values to life. What would each Value look like in action? For example, how would a "customer-oriented" employee behave? What would he or she do to meet customers' expectations? The EMC's goal for that day was to be certain that before the session was over everyone knew exactly how SB's desired culture looked in practice.

First they worked with some practical examples of how other companies had translated values into actionable statements. Then they tried to match each statement with each Value. The final test: could the statements be used to actually evaluate an employee's behavior—that is, measure behavior in a quantifiable way? This idea of measurement was critical: employees would focus only on what they knew would be rewarded. While the EMC learned a lot more about measurement later, even in these early days the power of keeping score was clear.

By the end of the session EMC members had narrowed a list of twenty statements down to twelve that reflected the kind of behavior they wanted from every employee. Their criteria:

❖ The Practices had to describe the Values in action.
❖ The Practices should be limited in number but broad in concept (e.g., two per Value).
❖ The Practices must allow for individual interpretation, creating accountability.
❖ The Practices must be specific enough to be measurable.

Since even twelve were too many statements, Peter took responsibility for reworking them with Joanne and Warner to clarify the message behind each and ensure they were measurable. The full committee would review them again before Values and Practices were made final.

The Chewton Glen retreat had been very successful. All had agreed that, to achieve its strategy of becoming an integrated healthcare company, SB was going to have *one* culture with *one* set of values. Significant progress had been made toward defining what that culture should be. As EMC members strove to create this one culture, they were also becoming more one team. Everyone felt positive about what they were saying and how they had worked through the issues.

It was soon after Chewton Glen that Bob began thinking through what would be required to design and implement the culture initiative. How would they first build awareness, then mobilize the organization? More important, how would they link and align all the activities that would be required to achieve the desired culture? Communications would be key.

Bob realized that Joanne brought to the task a unique set of skills that went beyond her professional ability as a communicator. Because she approached everything from a strategic and holistic viewpoint, she brought a consistency and focus to issues and ideas in ways that assured alignment both internally and externally. It was evident in the communications efforts behind the merger and the integration process. In each case communication strategy had helped create the alignment between what management was trying to achieve and the role each stakeholder had to play to achieve it.

The more Joanne learned about culture change the more intrigued she became. She had always believed that no matter what perception a company tried to create externally, it could not be sustained unless it was based on the internal reality. Advertising campaigns were not the key to company reputation; and shareholders were not the key to greater value; the employees were. She was steadfast in her belief in the need for strategically defining messages and getting them across with one consistent voice. From what she could see, culture change was all about working from the inside out: creating an environment where employees would actively and visibly be reinforced and supported in their efforts to realize business strategy. It meant communication, usually a staff role, was playing more of a line role—a role that could have a direct impact on long-term results. She was seconded to work with Bob, Peter, and Tom Kaney, head of human resource development, as part of the core team who would guide the design of the culture initiative.

Tom Kaney brought years of expertise and experience in organizational development to his current role. Coming from SKB originally, he had a deep understanding of the SmithKline Beckman culture. Combined with Peter's grasp of the old Beecham culture, the two had a clear picture of what lay ahead as the team tried to change what many perceived were two mediocre cultures into one that was dedicated to winning. (See figure 7.2.)

Following the Chewton Glen retreat, the output of the EMC's discussions was reviewed and reworked. The wording was still rather cumbersome. If the statements were to guide the behavior of every employee, they needed to be simplified and looked at from an employee's perspective. Each word was carefully chosen, each statement redrafted to be sure it was meaningful to the employees (but not so rewritten that the meaning originally intended by the EMC was diluted!).

Two Company Cultures Compared

SmithKline Beckman Culture (150 Years)	*Beecham Culture (150 Years)*
Scientific/Academic	Commercial/competitive
"Pharmaceutical"/Strategic	Brands/operational
Long product cycles and planning horizons	Short cycle, retail environment
Strategic/Visionary	Pragmatic/tactical
Traditional	Hierarchical chain of command
Multinational (country autonomy)	International (centrist/regional)
Improving mankind's quality of living	Bottom line and value added
People-oriented	Numbers-oriented
Technology/product orientation	Market orientation
Emphasis on scientific excellence	Emphasis on product development
Inertia/bureaucracy	Rigidity/formality

Both
Paternalistic
Disempowering
Creative dependency

SmithKline Beckman– ⇐ Risk averse ⇒ Beecham–"Don't make
"Don't look bad" a mistake"

"One-product companies" as viewed by the financial community

Figure 7-2 Two Company Cultures Compared
Source: Excerpt from *Corporate Identity Analysis,* interviews conducted by Landor Associates, 1989.

Later in July, in time for the next EMC meeting, the statements devised at Chewton Glen had developed into what became known as the nine Leadership Practices. There were two Practices per Value, except for Integrity, which had only one. The title, Leadership Practices, was deliberate: the Practices were meant to reflect the belief that everyone had responsibility, accountability, and the potential to play a leadership role.

The final copy of SB's nine Leadership Practices stated that at SmithKline Beecham, each employee is expected to:

1. Find opportunities for constantly challenging and improving his/her personal performance.

2. Work with his/her people individually and as a team to determine new targets, and to develop programs to achieve these higher standards of performance.

3. Identify and continuously implement improved ways to anticipate, serve and satisfy internal and external customer needs.

4. Stress the importance of developing and implementing more effective and efficient ways to improve SB procedures, products, and services through quality analysis.

5. Initiate and display a willingness to change in order to obtain and to sustain a competitive advantage.

6. Reward and celebrate significant and creative achievements.

7. Develop and appoint high-performing and high-potential people to key positions.

8. Help all employees to achieve their full potential by matching their talents with the jobs to be done and through quality performance feedback and coaching.

9. Communicate with all constituents openly, honestly, interactively, and on a timely basis.

The Leadership Practices were absolutely critical to the new culture; the Values would mean absolutely nothing if they weren't integrated into the way people worked day to day.

BALANCING LOOSE–TIGHT

The EMC debate about the Values and Leadership Practices and how to measure them was one of the most exhausting discussions any of them could remember. Although there had been little disagreement about the content of the culture, a lot of nervousness surrounded its move forward. Members knew that a "yes" meant they were committing not only themselves to this effort, but also every single person in every sector or function.

Without the EMC's personal belief in these bedrock Values and Leadership Practices, members would never be able to gain the commitment of each and every person in their own organizational divisions. The culture's entire success hinged on a universal buy-in. This point became more important in the months ahead, as Bob realized that while the EMC's minds supported the ideas behind the Values, their hearts—the emotional acceptance that created the inspiration for others—still had to be captured. They were not really convinced that the Values could actually influence results. That would take more time and more work.

In August, the EMC approved the statements for the five Values and nine Leadership Practices. All nine Leadership Practices, together with the five Values, would be core to the entire company. Not a single word could differ from one sector to the next. If SB was truly trying to become an integrated healthcare company, it was critical that everyone in every sector be working to the same standards. Because there might be some unique requirements in some sectors, a sector could add up to three Leadership Practices that would help it focus its organization on a particular need, but no sector could eliminate any of the nine.

In further discussion about what they would actually *do* to change the culture, they agreed that corporate would support the desired changes in behavior through human resource and performance management systems, extensive communication, and recognition programs. But each sector would be responsible for introducing the culture initiative within its own organization and devising ways to make the desired new behaviors a practical reality. This was a deliberate attempt on corporate's part to move accountability away from corporate and back into the sectors. Corporate would provide simple guidelines for designing the culture but, unlike the merger integration, would institute no rigorous development process or central corporate committee into which individual teams would have to report their implementation plans.

They were trying to tread a fine line between loose and tight, centralized and decentralized management; trying to limit corporate control to encourage local ownership, exerting just enough to maintain corporatewide consistency.

The final decision the EMC had made at Chewton Glen was that whatever it asked the organization to do, it would always do first, establishing itself as the pilot. This would give them a chance to see if the proposal would work with the company's senior management, and what improvements might have to be made. This principle would have some interesting ramifications for them personally later. But in terms of symbolizing commitment and giving the culture initiative credibility, it was one of the most important decisions they made.

THE GENESIS OF *SIMPLY BETTER*

As Joanne learned more about culture change, she looked to see the role communication had played, especially in mobilizing the workforce. She began to think of the need to market the new culture: to inspire and inform employees in a way that would persuade them to buy into what management wanted to achieve.

As she struggled with how to do this, Joanne kept rereading the statements, trying to get to the heart of what they were saying. Behind every statement was the desire to keep striving, to always do better than the day before. The goal was never really attained; it kept moving higher and higher, always just out of reach.

She decided to create a quality "brand" that would capture the essence of the culture "product" and present it in an imaginative way to focus employees' efforts. An added plus would be if she could make sure it was uniquely associated with SmithKline Beecham.

After considering, then discarding, a number of phrases, Joanne found that one that met her criteria kept playing over and over in her mind: *Simply Better.*[1] Striving to be *Simply Better.* It could fit. She tested the statement with the resident marketing experts in consumer brands management. All agreed it was the perfect umbrella, capturing the spirit of constantly striving, of embarking on a journey in search of a destination that could never be reached.

Simply Better was defined not as a slogan or a project, but as a sustainable effort to create a culture that would embody the five Values.

Packaged in the same white, gray, and teal green as the company name, its distinctive design—a hand-written signature—was intended to make the *Simply Better* message personal to every employee. So the phrase would not be trivialized, guidelines were deliberately provided to ensure employees understood the seriousness of what SB was about to undertake and would see the culture as something special and unique to SB. One of the most important: *Simply Better* could never be given as a statement of fact: it was an ongoing process, everyone was always striving to become *Simply Better*.

Having accepted *Simply Better* as the brand and agreed on the wording of the Values and Leadership Practices, the EMC now faced introducing them to the organization.

The data on efforts to change organizational behavior show that most do not succeed. The most common reason is that management, having developed the concepts, often takes implementation for granted and fails to develop a roadmap to help guide the organization. Given that the Myers-Briggs profile had revealed EMC's proclivity to do the same, *Simply Better* would go nowhere unless the top team shaped a plan for its implementation. The EMC needed to develop and agree on at least the introductory process, much as it had designed the principles for guiding the merger integration process. They now spent as much time thinking about, discussing, and working through exactly how they were going to get the organization to personally take on the culture as they had worked as a top team to own the Values and Leadership Practices.

The EMC now included some strong members. While Jan would not officially be joining SB until later that summer, he had attended the retreat at Chewton Glen. As an outsider his presence was clearly a benefit. He had no preconceived ideas nor any personal stake in the previous two companies. He was far more open to creating something new than any of the incumbents. The flip side of that was, of course, neither Jan nor any of the new team could appreciate the depth of the behavior change SB required nor how major a role they would be expected to play in its design and implementation.

HARDWIRING THE SOFT STUFF

By Autumn 1990 the EMC and a number of other people had put a tremendous amount of effort and energy into defining the Values and

Leadership Practices, working each phrase, debating each idea, and committing to their achievement. Still, they were only words. The real issue now was how to translate these words in a way that would impact every manager and eventually every employee throughout the organization. The transition from words to behavior would happen only if the Values and Leadership Practices touched every aspect of individual performance. They must become the primary basis on which employees would be measured: for hiring and firing, for developing, for evaluating and promoting, and for earning rewards. In other words: every human resource system—without exception—would be developed with the primary objective of supporting and reinforcing the culture of *Simply Better*. These systems would hardwire the soft stuff. By measuring behavior against the Leadership Practices, they would communicate in tangible terms that management was absolutely committed to developing the *Simply Better* culture.

At that point the major process by which managers were evaluated was the annual performance appraisal. The EMC agreed to move quickly and planned to incorporate the Leadership Practices into the performance evaluation of the top 250 executives during the following twelve months (1990–1991). Each person would be judged as to whether he or she behaved according to the nine Leadership Practices in day-to-day work. The Leadership Practices accounted for 50 percent of a manager's assessment. Company business and financial goals accounted for the other 50 percent. In reality, this meant that how these managers personally reflected the nine Leadership Practices would influence their opportunities for promotion and the amount of their merit awards.

In an effort to ensure *Simply Better* moved beyond the top management, the criteria for the management by objectives (MBO) reward system during that same twelve-month period would include all the usual financial performance objectives, plus an objective relating to implementing *Simply Better*. How well managers had implemented *Simply Better* in their particular organization would be reflected in the size of their bonus. The HR systems were starting to illustrate that while *what* was achieved was important, *how* it was achieved was as critical. (This point would resurface later, when SB learned about process management.)

The idea of hardwiring the soft stuff—changing the way managers would be rewarded based on *Simply Better*—would immediately attract the attention of senior and middle managers. The EMC would have the top 250 managers it needed to achieve critical mass *very* quickly!

Having agreed on the concept of the single culture and a centrally designed system, there were two implications that would affect the implementation of the new processes. Previously, performance appraisals were locally implemented against some general guidelines. Now the desire to create one culture implied that certain new human resource systems must be corporate driven and applied. First, human resources policies would have to be monitored from a corporate perspective and managers trained to implement them consistently throughout the company. Detailed guidelines were developed for the new appraisal system, including a training program and standard booklet on how to implement it. Specific examples were given of what a Practice would look like in action to be sure everyone had the same picture. For example, against the customer-related practice, the question to ask was: "When did you last sit down with a customer to find out what his needs were?" The form, the guidelines, the process, and the timing for every performance appraisal would be the same in every sector; it was essential to move forward in a corporatewide disciplined and planned manner. Second, to give credibility to the new approach, the process would have to start at the top of the organization.

The EMC became the first group at SB to be evaluated against how well its behavior reflected the Values and Leadership Practices. Using a process called "360-degree feedback" through which individuals are evaluated by their boss, their peers, and their subordinates, each EMC member would provide his peers (other EMC members) and those who reported to him directly with questionnaires to be completed anonymously and submitted to Warner Burke's team for evaluation.

While the idea of piloting was entirely consistent with the process they had agreed on, the use of 360-degree feedback was not common practice, and some EMC members approached it with apprehension.

The idea of 360-degree feedback was very powerful not only for what managers could learn personally, but also because of the process itself. By asking others for feedback, the EMC was practicing openness. By seeking their peers' opinions, they were building trust as a team. Even more important, by asking those reporting to them to grade them, they were starting to send out a message that they were personally committed to the Values and Leadership Practices.

That's the way Bob learned that he scored very poorly against Leadership Practice number 6, Reward and celebrate achievements. He would say "thank-you," or "well-done," usually adding "but . . .", either implying what had been done was not quite good enough or setting out the next challenge before a person had a chance to savor conquering the current one. To exemplify the spirit of *Simply Better* in action, he shared what he learned about himself with EMC members, telling them he needed to change his behavior and wanted them to help him. From that day forward, any time they caught him saying "but . . .," he would pay them £5 or $10.

Bob took that same challenge out to the organization at the management conference that autumn. For a few months, he couldn't keep enough bills in his wallet to pay those who caught him!

THE CHALLENGE TO BECOME AN INDUSTRY LEADER

In less than six weeks, the next Senior Management Conference was scheduled—November 4–5 1990 at Eastbourne on England's south coast. This year's conference would be about moving the company forward. During the past six months, even as all had worked on the myriad integration and culture issues, an effort to create the company's first five-year strategic plan had been under way in each of the sectors. The results of that work would be presented at Eastbourne, officially closing the past by providing a window to the future. Those in strategic planning had been relentless in gathering as much detail about the competition as possible. The information would be used to show SB's position versus the competition's and the gap that must be filled for SB to become an industry leader, thereby establishing the need for SB to change.

The EMC would also introduce *Simply Better*, the culture that would help SB meet its strategic goals. The conference theme, "From Promise to Performance," was intended to get everyone focused on the future. Managers who were invited clearly were those the EMC expected to become champions of the new SB.

It was a rainy Sunday afternoon, just hours before the conference. A number of people had already arrived at the large Victorian hotel. There was less tension than there had been at Grosvenor House but the tiredness lingered. It had been a year of hard work and tough decisions.

The official kick-off was scheduled for 8:30 Monday morning. The Grand Hotel had been booked months before, when fewer attendees were expected. By 8:25 A.M. stragglers had to clamber over rows of filled seats to find one of the few places remaining in the crowded amphitheater.

The meeting began with a review of SB's first 500 days as SmithKline Beecham. It was an impressive list of achievements: integrated in more than fifty countries, financial objectives met, major disposals completed, debt substantially reduced, and a targeted debt-equity ratio of 1:1 that would be achieved by year's end. A great job had been done in very demanding times under ambitious expectations. The momentum of the business was being maintained, the integration phase for building the new and better company had been completed, and all the work plans were being executed. One key message Bob hoped to convey was "thank you" to everyone for everything they had done to get the company where it was.

Against a challenging industry backdrop, the company's first five-year strategic plan, covering 1990 through 1994, was then presented. The strategic plan expectations were compared with the expected performance of the twenty European and American companies SB had identified as its reference peer group at the time of the merger. The company's strategic aspiration was then put forth:

SB intends to be a leader in this peer group.

Even with all the integration efforts and hard work, the peer group was still well ahead of SB's expected growth over the next five years in sales, earnings per share (EPS), and return on trading assets (ROTA). Where the new company was off to a good start, what was being done was not going to be enough to make SB win. To achieve that goal meant SB would have to perform as well as those at the very top of the list (Merck, Glaxo, and Bristol-Myers Squibb). That meant achieving some very specific and ambitious targets every year:

- ❖ Sales growth of 10 percent
- ❖ Earnings per share growth of at least 15 percent
- ❖ Return on trading assets of over 50 percent.

All the objectives were aggressive and particularly ambitious in light of the rapidly changing industry environment and the knowledge that Tagamet would come off patent in 1994. SB would have to make some dramatic changes just to catch up with the top five companies, let alone pass any one of them. As the sectors put forward their plans for delivering these objectives, Jan set the stage for the discussion that would follow. "How we manage our resources will be the difference between a good company and a great company," he told the audience. For him, the issue was sales: applying their collective energy and ideas to offset mature products by developing new ones, maximizing sales of existing products, and getting those in development through the pipeline and into the marketplace faster.

The audience was silent. This was bigger than a "new and better healthcare company." This was setting out a hard and quantifiable vision—to truly be an industry leader—and a shareholder value goal that had a time frame around it: among the top five by 1994. How were they going to do it?

CULTURE BY DELIBERATE DESIGN

Bob introduced the next agenda item with a definition, "Culture," he said, "is an accepted way of doing things around a company." "Every organization has a culture," he explained. "A culture happens either by design or default . . . and we are going to design ours!"

He then presented the work the EMC had done at Chewton Glen.

"For us to become a 'new and better' SmithKline Beecham, we need to have *one* overriding culture, *one* set of values that will drive the behaviors that are needed to accomplish our strategy. If we are going to continue to develop SB as a new and better company, it is important that we consciously create an SB culture to support that goal, and not just let any culture happen," he told them.

As he concluded, members of the audience were reminded that developing their own SB culture was a long-term effort that would take at least three to five years but would actually become a way of life and affect all employees. In line with the EMC's belief that ownership starts at the top, the Leadership Practices would be incorporated into the EMC's performance Appraisals that very year, and every one of the managers in the audience would be evaluated on these nine Leadership Practices in the next performance appraisal. The new appraisal system would move out to the next level of management—5,000—the following year.

Members of the audience were reeling from the amount of information they had received. Then Peter stood up. He approached the stage with apprehension: his job was to tell them how this new culture was going to happen.

The corporate division and the sectors each would play a role in developing and implementing this culture. Each sector was to prepare a plan that would address the following questions:

❖ What other Leadership Practices, if any, will their sector add to the core nine?

❖ How will the Values and Leadership Practices be instilled in their sector?

❖ Who will be involved? How?

❖ How will successful implementation in their sector be measured?

These implementation plans were due January-February 1991—less than three months away, *including* the Christmas break.

With that the break-out session was announced—just in time. Having sat through a morning of strategy and an afternoon of espousing a new corporate culture, the participants had grown restless. They needed to get out of the room and start talking.

The break-out sessions were designed to build understanding of the company's strategic aspirations plus the Values and Leadership Practices and seek feedback on ways that they might be improved. It was all part of creating a dialogue with these important managers and through that face-to-face involvement begin to gain their personal commitment to the new business goals and culture.

The next morning, as the groups' results were fed back to the whole, some consistent themes emerged as organizational concerns. Predictably, the groups were not convinced the stretch corporate targets were achievable in the time scale defined (i.e., by 1994), and they certainly could not see how they were expected to generate the desired financial results if they were also to meet the substantial target headcount reductions they had agreed on as part of the integration.

On *Simply Better,* there was less controversy. They agreed with the Values and Leadership Practices but were concerned with how they would be implemented throughout the organization, especially since each sector was still at a different stage of the merger integration process.

Following this session, the last formal presentation was made and the financial objectives for 1991 were presented. Along with beating targeted product registration dates, achieving 15 percent growth in earnings per share, and executing all the SB integration plans, they had to develop and implement the *Simply Better* initiative, including the nine Leadership Practices.

The audience listened intently. Then the floor was opened for questions.

One by one the hands rose. The questions began rather quietly, focusing on the business and several personnel issues. Then the frustration, the exhaustion, all the emotions that had been festering beneath the surface for the past fourteen months erupted.

One participant, a doctor, got to his feet: "At the beginning of this merger you guys told us 'no divorces, no heart attacks.' But you have *no* idea of the stress you have put this organization under." Citing a number of illnesses and divorces caused, he believed, by the strain of the past year and a half, he challenged Bob: "What are you going to do about it?"

Another member said, incredulously, "We've just managed to get our operations merged, meet some pretty tough financial targets, and lay off a huge number of people. We are all exhausted—and *now* you want us to *develop a new culture?!*"[2]

He was aghast that, with all the work they had done and done well, Bob could really be serious about going deep into the company to try and change the behavior of the very people who had delivered that accomplishment.

While those in the hushed room understood the reasons for the new financial and business objectives, and accepted the idea behind the *Simply Better* initiative, there was utter disbelief at the timing. The question-and-answer session, originally scheduled to last one hour, lasted nearly two, as managers vented their frustrations, Trying to model the behavior he was encouraging others to practice—that is, to face conflict rather than avoid it—Bob stayed on the stage alone until every question from the audience had been answered.

While he tried to sympathize, he also told them that if SB didn't sustain the momentum of the merger, it was in danger of losing what it had gained. They *had* to keep going. And when they said they'd need more people to do everything he was demanding, he unabashedly reminded them of the headcount targets they had agreed for each business. There just wasn't any choice: SB would never reach its goal of becoming a leader in the industry if they didn't do all of it, and do it now.

It *had* been a difficult year—and the EMC had set an incredible pace. The closing Q&A session at Eastbourne became another symbolic watershed as it showed the EMC, and Bob in particular, just how far top management was from the reality of the organization at that point. The EMC had to back off and make some choices about priorities. The organization was saying it couldn't do it all—at least not now. Still, Bob firmly believed the priority was that SB had to keep pushing toward its aspiration. Changes might be made in timing, but not on the agenda.

The discussion turned to working more effectively and efficiently, which only added to the manager's frustration, since most of them felt they already were. They were working hard, Bob agreed, but were they working on the right things? The response: most of the work was generated by multiple corporate requests. Bob suggested that in future corporate staff would look to one another for information before demanding it of the organization. Disbelieving, but hopeful, the audience accepted with a sigh the minor concession to their plight.

The lesson everyone learned at Eastbourne was the importance of feedback. From then on more effort was made to learn what managers were thinking and feeling. Where the conference had been intended to share information, the EMC now learned that a far more important role was the dialogue it had created among the company's managers. Reinforcing the importance of this discussion upon their return, meeting attendees were encouraged to debate the Values and Practices with their direct reports, asking themselves how they could all work differently to put them into action. The EMC hoped initiating this systematic dialogue would eventually lead to the organization's alignment with the company's new goals and values.

ROLLING OUT *SIMPLY BETTER*

The events at Eastbourne made it very clear that each sector was in a different state of readiness for *Simply Better*. In Consumer Brands and Clinical Laboratories, sectors that had hardly been touched by the merger, enthusiasm was high. In Pharmaceuticals, the sector most affected by the merger, some kind of reorganization had occurred every year since 1985; now an entirely new management team was putting them through it all yet again. This difference made it important that each sector develop a plan for instituting *Simply Better* at its own speed. While they didn't all have to be traveling on the same freeway at the same speed, they were all going to the same destination. They just had to get there within a reasonable time and all in one piece.

The idea of deliberately designing a culture was new to nearly everyone at SB in 1990. With the clock ticking toward the due date for *Simply Better* implementation, lack of understanding meant a lot of floundering.

Throughout the next few months as the sectors wrestled with the concept of *Simply Better,* resources remained a consistent concern. Bob had insisted that no new positions be dedicated to *Simply Better* beyond those few on the core team. He feared that if created positions were dedicated to *Simply Better,* its principles would be seen as separate from, versus integral to, the business. Responsibility and accountability would be abdicated to a separate department rather than become part of the way the business was managed.

In their existing cultures the natural tendency was to approach everything as a task. Each sector began to plan its own launch to communicate and explain what *Simply Better* was, taking the material provided after the Eastbourne conference and adding its own sector stamp. Consumer Brands, for example, invited its senior management from around the world to convene in Italy that February, where they launched *Simply Better* like a new consumer product. For the ever margin-conscious Consumer Brands people who rarely held such gatherings, this act alone underscored the significance of *Simply Better.*

The *Simply Better* launch meetings continued through the first quarter of 1991, with individual EMC members attending as many as possible to underscore their personal commitment and that of the entire EMC to the Values and Practices. The only way to diffuse the organization from thinking this was a one-off program or "flavor of the month" would be to demonstrate consistently that senior management was willing to commit time to the effort. Words were not enough; the senior team needed to participate and demonstrate the Leadership Practices in action to build credibility. To get employees thinking about the implications of *Simply Better* for their personal behavior, the launch process encouraged two-way dialogue. To begin their involvement, it required some follow-up action steps.

For the most part, these efforts went well, but the reactions were still somewhat mixed. There were many who remained skeptical about what values had to do with running the business. This skepticism seemed to vary across the businesses and the national cultures. At the Consumer Brands and corporate U.S. launch meetings, for example, response to *Simply Better* was enthusiastic, as participants saw the potential effectiveness of having one corporate-wide mindset. On the other hand, those in

R&D or who attended the U.K. corporate session saw the concept of creating a single culture as a threat to the right to think independently.

The *Simply Better* signature was gaining greater visibility, appearing in more and more local employee publications all over the world. No matter which sector or what language, its appearance was consistent, helping to tie the sectors together and reinforcing the feeling of oneness that was so important to the still-new company.

That winter those editing the company publication *Communiqué,* which went to 5,000 SB middle managers around the world, offered a series of bimonthly issues, each focused on one of the five Values. For example, the September–October issue raised the question "What does integrity mean at SmithKline Beecham?" and included discussions with the EMC, managers, employees, and the company's recruitment professionals, all of whom interpreted the Value in a way that made it personal and brought it to life. Later issues shared some of the sector activities that showed the Values in action and started to build a data base of internal best practices. *Simply Better* was beginning to gain some notoriety, but not everywhere, and not always positively. And it still had a way to go before it penetrated the depths of the organization.

Externally, *Simply Better* and the five Values were introduced to shareholders in the 1990 Annual Report (published in April 1991) along with the company's commitment to deliver its promised performance targets. The annual report was the only place *Simply Better* appeared externally, and it was referenced there to help analysts and shareholders understand how SB was trying to make its strategic and financial goals a reality. Any other external mention was discouraged; until *Simply Better* was a fact, it was not to be promoted outside SB.

SIMPLY BETTER LOSES MOMENTUM

In the spring of 1991, the *Simply Better* initiative began to run into some serious problems.

Until then, everyone had been very active in the *Simply Better* launch efforts: it was still very much a hands-on, task-driven activity. People were comfortable with the tangible side of pushing *Simply Better* Values and Leadership Practices through their organization with the communication cascade and good at working through the ideas with their managers. But as the official launch activities worked down through the second and into the third management levels, questions started to surface about turning the nice words and good ideas into practice.

The problem wasn't commitment: the good news was, the organization wanted to do more. The problem was lack of an overall structure for change, which was not something corporate had planned to provide. The only support activities they had identified were extensive communication, human resources reward systems, and a preliminary recognition program. What they hadn't realized—until almost too late—was that the missing link, the vital flaw in the *Simply Better* initiative, was the lack of a disciplined process for implementing behavioral change.

As so many others before them had done, members of the EMC erroneously assumed that good managers have the necessary skills to develop plans for serious cultural change initiatives. Rarely is this the case, and SB was no exception. Yet in rolling out *Simply Better* no thought had been given to building this competence. It was a lack of investment that now threatened to bring *Simply Better* to a shuddering halt.

So while the Values were promoting "work better," by and large the organization didn't know how to work any differently than it was. "Better" was not defined, nor were employees offered any guidelines or skill-building devices for improving their performance. Eventually the EMC would realize that the training to help employees work more effectively was really what *Simply Better* was all about. At this stage telling them to behave *Simply Better* without actually showing them how was only adding to everyone's frustration.

In the vacuum left by the EMC, the sectors each started to do their own thing, often using broad-based total quality management (TQM) principles. While these were good efforts done in the right spirit, they undermined the single culture needed to deliver the integrated healthcare company strategy. Reaping the benefits of the combined businesses would require working across sectors and functions. They needed a common way of working companywide. But instead of one language and one set of behaviors, multiple interpretations of *Simply Better* were springing up in different parts of the company depending upon which training advisor a sector, function, or country manager consulted. To add to the frustration, some parts of the organization started working at a much faster pace. Without a specific process, there was no systematic way to learn from one another or share best practices.

The failure to plan and provide any training was a major issue indicative of a much greater problem. The EMC had decided at Chewton Glen to have only the most basic guidelines for implementing the culture, and its view was reinforced at Eastbourne. In agreeing to move away from the controlling, centralized posture taken during the merger integration phase management was advocating that the individual sectors assume a much larger role. For the culture to really take hold, the EMC believed it was important for each sector to feel it was their plan, thus some of the confusion resulted from the EMC's dramatic departure from its role of controlling agent. For example, in deference to the pressures and the amount of work involved in implementing *Simply Better,* managers were given as much time as they thought necessary to work on *Simply Better* and as much room as they requested to do it their own way. The time frame was not rigid, as it had been during merger integration. The process was far less demanding. Without the discipline and rigor, *Simply Better* had started to drift and was losing momentum.

The organization had not been prepared for this change in corporate's role. From the manager's view, the planning responsibility for *Simply Better* had been "dumped" on them with no real explanation as to what an ideal plan would look like, what type of activities it would generate, or what its success would mean for them. The EMC had gone from being too prescriptive to not being prescriptive enough. They also were concerned that some parts of the organization were moving along faster than others.

Still, managers had been told at Eastbourne that the implementation of *Simply Better* was one of their performance objectives and that they would be evaluated against the Leadership Practices that very year. Without consciously realizing it, and with all the best intentions, members of the EMC had created anxiety on one level and confusion on the other. Rather than reducing the level of stress throughout the organization, they had increased it.

To add to the problem, the economic environment in 1991 was extremely difficult, with some countries claiming it as the worst in fifteen years.

GETTING BACK ON TRACK

Despite the difficulties, the EMC continued to work on *Simply Better,* even as it oversaw the launch of Kytril for chemotherapy, the antidepressant Seroxat/Paxil, and Kredex for treating high blood pressure—plus the U.S. approvals of Havrix, the world's first hepatitis-A vaccine, and Relafen/Relifex, an antiinflammatory drug for treating arthritis. Twelve new products were brought into the development portfolio, and there were twenty-four new registration filings. Pharmaceuticals' sales passed £1/$1.9 billion in the United States. Consumer Brands refocused its R&D and launched several of its well-known U.K. cold and flu remedies in Germany and America.

By year's end, results would show SB's market capitalization had grown 46 percent in 1991, and that the company had outperformed the FT-SE 100 Index by more than 20 percent and the S&P 500 by 15.4 percent.[3]

Confusion and frustration still surrounded *Simply Better.* Compounding it, or maybe even causing it, was the difference in the EMC's own understanding of what *Simply Better* was all about. While Bob insisted that *Simply Better* be first on the agenda at every EMC meeting, it was clearly not a priority for many of the company's most influential managers. There was a feeling among some that they had done their part once the launch was accomplished, or "I know all about this culture stuff." For them, the growing business pressures required the cultural change issues to be put on the back burner for the time being (i.e., not to be revisited). While the EMC had gone along with Bob, many members were not quite as committed to *Simply Better,* nor as appreciative of its potential benefits, as he was. Reflecting the EMC comfort level, the organization was growing complacent. The EMC needed a jolt that would make it realize it was still far from the company's goal. As far as Bob was concerned, SB would never achieve the goal of becoming a world-class organization if *Simply Better* didn't succeed.

It was at this point, around June 1991, that a few managers familiar with world-class continuous improvement efforts began to realize SB's initiative did not have enough discipline to make *Simply Better* a reality. As these few saw it, managers who had always valued intuition over analysis, delegation over coaching, and risk avoidance over risk taking and innovation were not going to find behaving according to the Leadership Practices an easy task. They brought this fact to the EMC's attention.

While *Simply Better* was actually about a complete culture change, its underlying principle was the incremental or continuous improvement of every activity by every employee—50,000 ideas. To achieve it required a shared vision of what such an organization looked like. No one in SB, including all the EMC members, had really seen anything with enough depth and understanding to guide them.

Unfortunately, no one knew exactly what the next step should be. Reflecting the fact that external benchmarking had become something of a way of life in SB, once again they sought best practice and a model culture for SB to emulate.

In his experience Bob had found that those who were most disciplined and most effective at generating continuous improvement by tapping the hidden talent and ideas of employees had been the Japanese. In the early 1980s he had taken his top fifteen senior managers at Avco to Japan to study and learn from their success. They went as disbelievers but returned as disciples, having gained a fundamental understanding and appreciation for the Japanese improvement process. Bob also believed that having the EMC benchmark the Japanese companies as a group would give them a shared experience and common knowledge base on which they could build. Both would help to bring the EMC members closer together.

At Bob's instigation Joanne had started to investigate firms specializing in continuous improvement education. Her major criteria: the courses had to have substance and the consultants enough of an in-depth understanding of total quality management to be able to illustrate that TQM principles were applicable beyond manufacturing, their typical domain. Otherwise, she feared the EMC would remain unconvinced that any of these principles would be applicable to a science-based organization.

She identified and interviewed three consultancies. In June she invited one of them—Deltapoint—to make a presentation that showed clearly it could meet the criteria. Given just enough information about Japanese management techniques to whet their appetites, by evening's end the SB people were hooked. Joanne knew they had found the firm that would take the EMC to Japan.

The trouble was—the EMC didn't know it was going.

WINNING ATTITUDE   Employees were beginning to feel like winners as the company consistently met the targets for merger implementation and financial performance. Some were feeling comfortable enough to revert back to the old ways. But winning is about never being satisfied with current performance. If one goal has been reached, then a higher one must be set to maintain momentum. Thus SB's vision of becoming a "new and better healthcare company" was redefined to become a "leader in its peer group." The goal of closing the enormous gap between SB and its U.S. and European peers awakened in some the competitive spirit. The next challenge—creating the new culture that would help fill the gap—was introduced, and new milestones were set.

ORGANIZATION AS HERO   The process of involvement again started with the top team as it struggled to define first the Values, then the Leadership Practices. Those who would champion them were asked to provide feedback. If time had not been a constraint, it would have been better to involve more people in their actual development, thereby gaining more ownership. If a group beyond the 15 EMC members had been committed to their success, the managers responsible for introducing them to the entire organization might have been more inspiring.

CUMULATIVE LEARNING   Rather than build on what had been learned in planning the integration process (i.e., overly manage the process but not the content), corporate loosened its control, leaving implementation of *Simply Better* up to each sector. There were several problems with this: (1) the organization wasn't prepared for the shift in corporate's role; (2) no one had training in how to lead behavioral change; and (3) without a central plan SB could not achieve the one-culture goal so critical to delivering the strategy of an integrated healthcare company. It was not until *Simply Better* began to run out of momentum that management realized it had failed to incorporate into planning *Simply Better* much of what they had learned from the merger integration process.

STRATEGIC COMMUNICATION   Creating the *Simply Better* brand and giving it a very specific definition and application positioned the new culture for employees and initiated a common language that was spoken through one voice, other than the sectors. There was also a growing focus on communication as a process. Encouraging discussion around the new Values and Leadership Practices at Eastbourne was a first step in involving managers, getting them to buy in to the underlying concepts. Finally, the Q&A session taught everyone the importance of feedback. The company's first cascade kit, illustrating the Values and Practices, was also created to encourage meeting attendees to debate the Values and Practices with their own direct reports and ensure consistency in message delivery.

ALIGNMENT OF BEHAVIOR AND SYSTEMS When the managers heard SB's new vision—to become a leader in its peer group—and saw the enormous gap they would need to fill to achieve it, they recognized that a sound business strategy alone would not be enough. Everyone must behave differently from the past. For these desired behaviors—the Values and Leadership Practices—to become part of day-to-day work, they were deliberately written so they could be measured. Business and behavior were tied together in the performance appraisal process and aligned toward the same vision, equally weighted so a manager would have no doubt about the importance of both.

Developing the Road Map for the *Simply Better* Way

T HE COFFEEPOT IN THE NEW
York hotel room had long been empty, and the half-filled, forgotten cups languished on the silver tray. It was June 1991, and Bob, Warner, Peter, and Joanne were studying the sheaves of paper that represented SB's first management survey.

The survey was going to set an important baseline in the development of the new culture. It would help them assess how successfully they had instilled the Values and the Leadership Practices into the organization and as much as possible, also help to identify where they needed to focus their improvement efforts.

The goal was to have the questionnaire ready for final distribution in June so results could be ready by autumn—a year after the Eastbourne conference—providing an important benchmark against which to measure their progress. The second half of the process—how to handle dissemination of the results once they came in—was an issue they decided to save for another day.

PREPARING FOR JAPAN

With the survey in progress, Joanne had been working with Deltapoint to develop the preparation process for the EMC's trip to Japan. One of Deltapoint's attractions was the absolute insistence its consultants placed on educating senior managers before a trip to be certain that they derived greatest benefit from it. Having experienced one trip where that had not been the case, Joanne could not have agreed more. If SB was going to do this, it should be done right, and that meant a lot of advance preparation by the participants.

The agenda for the EMC meeting that Wednesday in June listed a number of items, half of which could warrant a day's discussion each. (For example, the half year's earnings results had to be reviewed and the final guidelines for the 1992 strategic planning process were due for distribution.) As had been the case since it was launched, however, first on the agenda was *Simply Better.*

Bob started out slowly, suggesting to EMC members that he thought *Simply Better* was losing steam, that perhaps it had to be rethought. As they had always done, he thought it might be time to look at best practice and see if perhaps there wasn't more to learn.

Because of Bob's previous efforts with employee-driven change, his expectations for *Simply Better* were probably much higher than those of the other EMC members, who seemed to be far less critical of how it was going. Nonetheless, they nodded in agreement with the suggestion to seek best practice; no one, after all, was against learning something new.

In his experience, Bob explained, the companies that seemed best at instilling disciplined, all-engaging improvement efforts were Japanese. Again the EMC members nodded.

"So, I propose that we visit Japan, and see firsthand how these companies do it," he concluded.

The uproar was immediate. Go to Japan? Now? There was no time in the diary as it was. He couldn't possibly be serious. There were plenty of excellent U.S. companies they could visit in locations that were a lot more convenient. Couldn't they learn about Japanese management techniques without actually going to Japan?

For some this was Eastbourne all over again: Bob was telling everyone "performance, performance, performance," the organization was still try-ing to get *Simply Better* going . . . and now he wanted them to do yet another thing.

Bob acknowledged their points, but then came back to two. First, the U.S. companies were employing techniques that started in Japan, so why not go to the origin? Second, going to Japan was actually more efficient because they could visit a number of companies all at once. As members realized that this was something Bob really believed in and that he would not change his mind, the objections gradually stopped. It was Jan who finally said, "So, Bob, when are we going?"

Bob knew that while the EMC as a group believed in the Values and Leadership Practices, as individuals they had not worked through the real implications of *Simply Better* for the organization or for themselves. They needed to feel more of a personal stake in *Simply Better,* and that meant having a deeper understanding of what was involved for themselves and as a team. They were on the right road but had taken only the first few steps in what Bob had said at Eastbourne was at least a five-year journey.

Bob also had a huge advantage over the others in that room. He knew the power of a study trip like this. Even as he tried to explain about his Avco trip ten years earlier, he knew that EMC members would not be able to understand until they had gone themselves. Seeing truly was believing; the direct exposure worked. It gave him the confidence to remain resolute in his determination that the SB team would go.

Following that meeting, the education process began in earnest. Deltapoint rejected the EMC's proposal to go to Japan in September. There was just too much to learn. After much debate and disagreement about the amount of study the consultants demanded, the EMC conceded to the complete educational process with some modifications. Members agreed more out of compliance than conviction, however; they were not really certain it was all actually necessary.

A new date for the trip was set: January 18–26, 1992. This would squeeze the trip in between Christmas and the next management confer- ence, which was scheduled for early February in Rome. This conference would be a key milestone as the organization, growing frustrated with *Simply Better,* would need something to sustain its enthusiasm and the initiative's momentum.

At this point the question of SB's management for the long term arose again. If the trip's key objective was to build a shared understanding as to what *Simply Better* could look like, and if *Simply Better* was at least a five-year effort, shouldn't those going be those who would be the ones to lead its implementation? To ensure the lessons learned would not be lost at Consumer Brands and Animal Health, a manager from each of those sectors was selected to join the EMC in place of their retiring chairmen. Along with Tom Kaney and Joanne, it brought the number in the Japan entourage to fifteen.

The learning process—dubbed the Japan Study Mission Preparation Seminars—would be very disciplined: a book was assigned (but not always read!) each month to be discussed over dinner before the EMC meeting; a day was set aside before (or after) each EMC meeting when they would be introduced to some of the key Japanese management learnings; and homework was assigned to be sure the key lessons weren't lost. The first preparation seminar was held in August; the last was a three-day marathon meeting in early January. In between, EMC members spent a minimum one and a half days per month learning together. If anyone said they wouldn't be able to attend a workshop, Bob would telephone to find out why. This course was not elective.

INVOLVING THE BOARD

While the EMC acknowledged it needed more education to lead *Simply Better,* it also recognized that the board needed some understanding of the initiative. That summer, a presentation was made to the board on *Simply Better.* The goal: to give the nonexecutive directors an overview of what it was and why it was important to SB's long-term future so they could participate in its progress. The hope was that the directors would understand it well enough to actively challenge and support those in their assigned sector, illustrating further that commitment to *Simply Better* started at the very top, with the board.

Each nonexecutive board member had been assigned one of the major business units, including R&D, at the suggestion made by one of them soon after the merger. The directors were expected to spend a few days a year with the sector management team to get a close look and gain better insight into the specific sector, including its business issues, progress against major corporate goals such as *Simply Better,* and employee morale. The board visits were often built around the sector's strategic reviews and included site visits. The benefit to sector management was that it made the board much more visible and allowed the SB managers the chance to share ideas; the benefit to SB was that it helped the nonexecutive directors gain a greater insight into the company's management, providing them with valuable input when it came to succession planning.

At the end of that particular meeting, Henry met privately with the nonexecutive directors. He had been invited to become more involved in industrywide issues such as defining government healthcare policy. With SB's management now in very good hands, he felt it was time he reduced his day-to-day management involvement and moved more toward the role of a nonexecutive chairman. As the board evaluated Henry's request, they recognized that his assuming this vital role externally would give SB a prominent position as a leader in helping to shape healthcare decisions rather than simply responding to them.

They agreed he would move to more of a part-time, nonexecutive role at the end of the year.

RAISING THE GOALPOSTS

One Japan study session was held in October as part of the annual three-day strategic planning meeting. Jan had been on the EMC for two months, JP Garnier for one, and George Poste, the new head of R&D, would be joining shortly. The management survey and the Japan trip were both on the agenda, but the real focus for this meeting was team building and strategy: what would define winning in the longer term, and how would SmithKline Beecham get there?

As the senior managers considered the industry prospects, they acknowledged that overnight the balance of "price power" had shifted from the sellers of medicines to the buyers. Only the unique, truly beneficial products would continue to demand premium prices. Seeking to reduce costs and broaden its base in OTC medicines, the industry was building greater scale through mergers, acquisitions, and strategic alliances. (Since SB's merger a little more than two years before, Bristol-Myers Squibb (BMS), Rhone-Poulenc Roher, American Home Products, A. Robbins, and Marion Merrell Dow had been created as healthcare versus pure pharmaceutical companies. Major alliances also existed between Merck and Johnson & Johnson, Sanofi and Sterling, and Merck and Du Pont.) The constant changes in technology and science added more pressure; biotechnology and gene therapy were the competencies they would all need for tomorrow. Against this background began a discussion later viewed as a turning point in the transformation of SB, as the EMC started to think much more about what "being the best" actually meant.

It was at this meeting that "To Be a Leader in its Peer Group"—the aspirational phrase that had helped launch *Simply Better* and guided SB's financial goals and business strategy to this point—was redefined and the goalpost for winning raised. To become "The World's Leading Healthcare Company" was SB's new and higher aspiration, setting out the next milestone in its journey. What the EMC still didn't realize was what it would take to get there.

Since 1989, SB's share price had moved from its opening price of £5.38 to £9.77. Yet compared to the competition, SB's shareholder return of 19.8 percent was still below its peer group average and well below industry leaders Merck and Glaxo. In analyzing the source of SB's valuation, it was estimated that roughly half had been based on reducing expenses, primarily as a result of the merger integration. Little had been attributable to increased sales from new products.

As the EMC set out the financial objectives for sales, profits, and ROTA for 1991–1996, they could see that they were far more ambitious than SB's current performance. But even where it looked like SB would do well, the competition was projected to do even better. Even if SB could achieve the aggressive sales and profit targets (and that was suspect, since many of the new products were not expected to come on stream until 1996–1997), it would place SB in the bottom ten out of its twenty competitors in 1996. Unless it did something, the gap between SB and the industry leaders would increase, not decrease, over the next five years.

EMC members began a debate around which financial yardstick defined winning. What did they want to be "leading" in? The discussion followed familiar lines. One group believed that winning meant profits, so SB should focus on reducing costs and boosting employee productivity. Others argued winning was sales, therefore having a strong pipeline from which would emerge the next blockbuster product was the real key. Finally, they agreed: the ultimate way of measuring winning was growth in shareholder value. And by that measure a gap of £3/$5.6 billion would separate SB and its competitors by 1995.

As they considered the size of this stretch goal, the magnitude of what would be required to fill it gradually dawned on them. To become The Leading Healthcare Company and increase shareholder value as dramatically as it wanted to, SB was going to have to break its paradigm. As managers, they would need to think radically differently about the industry and its needs, about SB's present strengths, and about how to bridge the gap between the two.

It was going to require dramatic actions that would affect both what SB did in terms of business strategy and how SB did it, which the managers were trying to address through the five Values. For example, the Customer Value drove sales and marketing, Innovation the R&D efforts, and costs were tackled through the Performance Value. Nothing could be taken for granted: they needed to focus on *everything* within their control to fill the gap.

Addressing strategy issues such as what businesses and product lines they were in was not an easy task. The merger was still relatively new, and all the businesses were sensitive to potential sell-offs as they realized that some did not fit the vision of an integrated healthcare company. But the more EMC members focused on what it would take to improve SB's shareholder value, the more they moved beyond thinking of their individual function or business to thinking what was best for SB. By the end of the meeting, they had made some major portfolio decisions that—most important—had been made together. It was a major step forward in creating an SB frame of mind.

As they considered the enormity of the challenge remaining, they started to look at potential levers beyond restructuring the businesses and what improvement would be required in each to make the necessary leap forward. They addressed sales and the new product potential. They considered administrative expenses and set aggressive reduction targets. They looked at free cash flow and debated its meaning and impact. And then they got to productivity, where the gap between SB and the leaders would grow, not close, over the five-year period based on current projections for new hires. The conclusion after that meeting: costs had to halve, and productivity had to double.

That was when they realized the real answer would lie somewhere within *Simply Better.* They would need the entire organization to participate in a way it never had before. *Simply Better,* with its Leadership Practices focused on the customer, innovation, and performance, would be key.

But as EMC members finally concluded that a motivated, mobilized workforce could be a primary driver of SB's future competitive advantage, they suddenly realized they had no idea how to actually create one. In recognizing their own fallibility in the face of a potentially ever-widening gap between SB and its competitors, they changed their attitude about the Japan study trip from one of compliance and "because Bob says so" to one of genuine desire to learn more from those acknowledged to be experts in involving people.

W.E. Deming, the expert who introduced total quality management to Japan and to which much of that country's post–World War II economic success has been attributed, once said that, to truly understand TQM required humility, discipline, study, and a shift in leadership values. It was only then, he said, that a manager could move beyond superficial concepts and make continuous improvement a way of life.

At SB, the humbling of the EMC had begun.

ESTABLISHING THE BASELINE

Following the strategy discussion, the EMC broke for the day. On the agenda first the next morning was the initial results from the employee survey that had been sent that June to 5,000 managers around the world.

According to the results, managers liked their work, were highly motivated, and set high performance standards. In fact, the Value against which the employees felt the company performed the best: *performance.* Table 8.1 summarizes the survey findings.

Table 8-1. Basic Findings of SB's First Employee Survey, 1991	
Positives	*Negatives*
• SB is a good company.	• SB is not customer driven.
• I like my work.	• Employees are underutilized.
• SB has high performance standards.	• There is a lot of waste, inefficiency, and bureaucracy.
• SB managers are motivated.	• SB people need more training/ development.
• SB people are ethical.	• SB doesn't allow for feedback.
(Based on 4,900 employees surveyed in 10 countries—73% response rate)	

The Values and Leadership Practices rated least present in the organization reinforced the EMC's worst suspicions about waste: managers said there was too much inefficiency and bureaucracy, and that employees were underutilized. They said there was a need for more training and development, and the company needed to become much more customer-oriented. The Practice that scored the lowest was number 9: communicate with all constituents openly, honestly, interactively, and on a timely basis. While employees did think management was honest, they did not feel that any real dialogue was going on; there were few opportunities for employees to feed back their thinking on issues important to them. The conclusion: *Simply Better* still had a long way to go.

While the survey provided the baseline, its full potential was never realized because those whose responsibility it should have been to discuss the data remained preoccupied and either unaware or unconvinced that it was their responsibility to share it. With integration still occurring in some parts of the organization, the tough business climate, and launches of *Simply Better* still under way, the EMC never established clear guidelines on how managers could use the data for real problem solving at a local, personal level. Without giving this guidance, management missed a chance to ask employees personally to address the gap they saw between the reality and vision of *Simply Better* and to suggest improvements. In the end those closest to the work would have the answers; given the opportunity, the employees could have helped design some meaningful action plans. Managers kept deferring the survey discussion because they said they were too busy, failing to see that by discussing the results with their staffs, they could actually help alleviate some of the problems that were keeping them so busy. There never was a right time because they did not make it, and the EMC never insisted that they did. As a result, the power of this first survey as a tool to engage the organization more fully in *Simply Better* was never realized.

PROFITS PASS A BILLION

While the October planning meeting opened the EMC's eyes to the reality of the challenge it faced in pursuit of its new stretch goal, the sectors were making steady progress against the business objectives already set, particularly 15 percent sales from new products by 1994.

Between 1989 and 1991, SB had launched four major new products in four therapeutic categories. In 1991 alone there were twenty-four new registration filings around the world, and twelve new products were brought into the development portfolio. The increased number of alliances and licensing agreements demonstrated SB's attractiveness as a scientific and marketing partner.

Each sector continued to progress against the strategic objective of best marketers: SB Pharmaceuticals passed £1/$1.9 billion in sales in the United States, while it managed to maintain Tagamet's £600 million/$1 billion sales level for the sixth year running, and the U.S. sales force was rated second only to Merck for excellence. (It was the first time either SmithKline or Beecham had ever made it to the top five.)[1]

Like SB Pharmaceuticals before, SB Consumer Brands refocused its R&D efforts and agreed on five key healthcare areas. It also created a special market development team to start looking at opportunities for switching prescription medicine to OTC medicines. First on its list: Tagamet or OTC Cimetidine. SB Clinical Laboratories (SBCL) reached its $1 billion sales goal and was rated number 5 by physicians and hospitals, and first over every other laboratory in the country. SBCL Scan, a system linking customers—the physicians' offices and hospital laboratories—to SBCL was launched, promising an even better service.[2]

One step at a time, each sector was establishing the linkages between businesses that would make the concept of an integrated healthcare company an eventuality. This was further supported by more travel and interchange between the people across the sectors and across the countries. In a determined attempt to create a one-company culture, SB started transferring people more often, especially between the United States and the United Kingdom. It was a deliberate effort to help employees learn more about each country's perspective and how it influenced the way they approached their work.

To become best managed was an ongoing process as the EMC strove first to strengthen the senior team, then to address a leadership development plan that would reflect the *Simply Better* values.

By the end of 1991, SB would exceed £1/$1.9 billion in trading profits—breaking that barrier for the first time—up 13 percent from 1990. Of the trading profit, SB Pharmaceuticals accounted for close to £700 million/$1.3 billion. Cash flow had improved, and return on trading assets was almost 50 percent. With debt now at £502/$933 million, interest expense had been cut almost in half, to £59/$110 million. The debt equity ratio was now 42 percent.[3] With the share price around £9, SB started to think about splitting the shares.

Finally, taking one more step away from the past, in December 1991 the 1,500 employees of SB House moved down the road to a brand new headquarters that they christened New Horizons. With its open space and glass walls, the new facility reinforced open communication, while its art by artists with mental disabilities from thirty different countries reflected SB's Promise to make people's lives better. More than anything, the new building symbolized 'one integrated company: SB could now physically manage all the major businesses from one location.

For some companies, such a move would be a major event in itself; for the new SB it was just one of many things the company was doing to become *Simply Better.*

OFF TO JAPAN

The move to New Horizons over Christmas came and went in a flurry. The EMC gathered in Philadelphia in early January 1992 for its last session before departing for Japan. Business cards had been printed with Japanese characters on the opposite side; members had studied tapes of key Japanese phrases and reviewed books outlining local customs, foods, and the "salarymen's" (white-collar workers) lifestyles. Brief biographies with photographs had been prepared and sent to each of the companies they would be visiting. No detail, it seemed, had been forgotten. There came a point, however, when EMC members had had enough and their patience had run out. They were definitely ready to go.

The organization, meanwhile, wasn't sure what to make of the trip. Here they were, being told to perform, perform, perform, and senior management was going off to Japan. They held their breath: the EMC is going away together for two weeks; *what* will they come back with?

The first meeting in Tokyo was on a Sunday afternoon in the hotel conference room. It was a gray day, colder than both London and Philadelphia had been. That afternoon a test on the key concepts behind Japanese total quality management was given. All were pleasantly surprised at how much they remembered; it helped them to refocus their thinking for the visits ahead.

Deltapoint believed that it was important that the trip be highly structured and disciplined if the EMC was to gain the maximum learning. (Practicing their own TQM, Deltapoint had created a "standardized process" for educating senior management.) So each day had a routine: preparation the night before, question teams assigned per company, debriefs in the coach ride home. The managers would be visiting five companies—Fuji Xerox, Canon, NEC, Esai, and Nissan—and were expected to know enough to ask specific questions about what they were seeing. As they grew more familiar with watching the concepts in action, their questions became more pointed. In particular, they wanted to know more about *how*: how to get employees to assume responsibility, how to generate ideas, how to implement them. . . .

After each visit EMC members would sit quietly on the coach and reflect on what they had just seen and heard, trying to put it against the complete framework of what they were learning. As the trip continued, their sense of wonderment and appreciation for what had been achieved grew: they were seeing firsthand the painstaking work and deliberate thinking that had changed the meaning of Made in Japan from "junk" to "world class" in just one generation. Gradually it dawned on them that they were witnessing *entire* management systems designed to sustain continuous improvement. Whereas they had understood the importance of each component, now they were beginning to see how they could all come together in a way that systematically ensured continuous improvement through the involvement of everyone at every level of the organization. Nothing was left to chance. Little by little the EMC began placing its learnings within the context of SB and how it could create a management system that would support an environment of constant self-renewal.

After eight days of visits, the penultimate day arrived. The group was divided into four teams, with each member deliberately chosen to advance the trip's goal of strengthening the overall EMC. Each group was assigned a topic around which it was to share its key learnings.

That evening the hotel atmosphere was a little like a college dormitory as the teams huddled in their assigned workrooms, scrambling for posters and overheads. At 8:00 the next morning, they reassembled in the large hotel conference room for their last session.

By now they all understood the importance of leadership and the need for personal commitment. Whatever change was undertaken, it had to start at the top and be executed consistently there first. But what had been clarified was the need for well-defined, articulated principles of how the leaders would manage the company. The underlying objective was to create a continuous wave of renewal and constant regeneration. It would require managers to manage in ways fundamentally different from those of the past.

The paradigm shift that they learned in Japan—the new management concept that really was a leap forward—was the power of process management, which defined all work from the perspective of what it ultimately delivered to the customer—both internally (the next person in the process) and externally. Rather than by a traditional hierarchy of "stovepipe" functions and delegation, they managed across functions, in small groups, engaging everyone everywhere in the company. Employees followed a prescribed, step-by-step process that had been designed around data gathered and analyzed on the basis of customer needs. Through constant analysis and improvement, the process had been standardized and made reliable to produce the same excellent results time after time. If things went wrong, it was the fault of the process, not of an individual. The result was a much more open, risk-free environment where new ideas were encouraged and considered against the needs of the customer and steps in a process, rather than disparaged and discouraged based on individuals or hierarchy. Employees were less likely to feel threatened for making suggestions or trying to change things they felt didn't serve the customer. In an industry like pharmaceuticals, where product-push had been the rule, there was enormous power in a mindset that forced every employee to ask what value he or she was adding to the customer.

Employees were respected for their ability to contribute and were heavily supported in their efforts to do so. They were trained in common methods to help them analyze their work, gather relevant data, and organize information in a way that led not only to recommendations, but to actual implementation. Simple but continuous communication (they met every morning in work teams) was fundamental to how they managed: employees understood what they were doing and why, how their team was progressing against the company's goals, and how they were doing in their personal efforts to improve. Team recognition and sharing success were regular events designed to reinforce employee efforts and at the same time build a common knowledge base across the company.

The more EMC members had seen process management practiced, the more convinced they were that managing *across* the organization, with employee involvement at every level, was the most effective way of ensuring customer focus and increased productivity. To their list of required practices at SB they added introducing a common way of working and process thinking, along with standardization and continuous improvement.

The principles inherent in total quality and process management were absolutely consistent with the Values and Leadership Practices. Some were exactly the same: the importance of using fact-based and data-driven analysis, focusing on the customer, and rewarding and celebrating achievements. Through education and training in all these concepts, SB employees would be able to turn the still fuzzy beliefs and concepts behind the Values and Leadership Practices into reality. The importance of building these skills through education and training had been a consistent message in all that they heard during their visit.

For SB, this link between the Japanese principles and the Leadership Practices was key. It was critical that the organization understand that what the EMC had learned in Japan was building on *Simply Better*, not replacing it. Nor was it a wholesale adoption of Japanese techniques. Employees must not mistake *Simply Better* for a "flavor of the month" when it was in fact the bedrock for SB's culture.

By the end of the session one more new concept for managing SB was put on the table. The idea of planning over a 10>3/1 year time span, versus the traditional five- and one-year time frames, had enormous validity in an industry where products took ten to twelve years to develop, and horizons were all so long term.

While the participants now acknowledged the huge amount of hard work that lay before them, their competitive spirit to win was stronger than their fear of the challenge. The idea of creating an entire management system designed to sustain an environment of self-renewal was—in their minds—revolutionary. It was an opportunity to gain a real competitive advantage.

As they convened for the last time the next morning, each person was asked to consider two final questions:

❖ What was the most significant learning for you?
❖ What will you do when you return to your office?

The consistency in their responses was even more telling than the content. They felt that the trip had contributed significantly toward the dream of SB having a different style of management, and they learned that, despite their different perspectives, they all had the same aspiration: to make SB the best.

Before they left for Japan they had agreed they would return knowing where to go next with *Simply Better*. After all, they still had the senior management conference scheduled for February. Now, from around the room, there emerged what became a list of EMC agreements around what it would take to change employee behavior and the way people worked at SB:

Discipline and planning
Customer focus
Disciplined use of methods and tools
An open environment
Commitment
Investment in training
A common language
Years!

Finally, in a comment that surprised them all, they all agreed it must be *corporate led* and *corporatewide.* If they had gone to Japan as functional and sector heads, they were leaving as **SB leaders.** Another objective for the trip—to get the team thinking for SB—had been met.

What all these lessons had taught them was that what they really needed was a master plan: a well-structured, comprehensive approach to coordinate, then implement, these ideas at SB. Designing such a plan would require time, discipline, and most important, more education. If they had gone to Japan thinking that country's phenomenal success was based on government intervention or that employee involvement was something specific to Far Eastern culture, they left knowing that the principles they had witnessed in action at company after company were just good sense. Japanese management had simply recognized that people, given the respect and opportunity to do so, want to contribute to making their organization a success. All the principles had been embodied in the Leadership Practices. As far the EMC could determine, where the Japanese differed from their Western counterparts was in the enormous discipline and rigor they applied in analyzing data and managing by process rather than by function. With this same work, all could be successfully applied to SB.

As they started to disperse from the hotel to pick up luggage and meet their planes, members grabbed the faxes that had been awaiting them at the cashier's desk. Even these lacked the sense of urgency they once might have held as individuals recognized another important lesson: their roles as leaders would have to be different in the future. For them to truly implement the lessons they had learned in Japan, they would have to be more coaches and planners than controllers and implementers: some of their business responsibilities would have to be delegated.

PERFORMANCE THROUGH PEOPLE

A few days later, the EMC met in London. The Rome conference at which 200 managers expected to hear about the next steps in *Simply Better* was less than two weeks away. Some agenda items such as strategy definition, setting shareholder value targets, and sharing the survey results remained fixed, but the rest of the agenda was tossed away. EMC members had learned too much in Japan to go to the organization with their original plans for *Simply Better.* Although they now had visions of what could be, the organization was still living with what was and, in some places, what used to be. The conference would have to bridge that gap and help transition to what was possible by sharing what the EMC members had learned in Japan and reflecting their personal commitment to *Simply Better.* For the first time, the entire EMC would share the stage.

In the huge hall that February morning, the audience was still. As the managers listened to each man speak, they realized that what they were hearing were not conventional presentations. These men were sharing what had been personal learnings with passion, the freshness of their understanding and wonder at what they had experienced in Japan still very much apparent. Most important, they were doing it as a team, speaking with one voice for SB and not as individual sector or functional heads. It was a strong message to the audience—they were all pulling for SB.

At the end Bob stood up. The biggest learning, he told them, was that there was more to learn. The EMC had no prescriptions for the organization: only an aspiration and an appreciation for the hard work it would take to achieve. They were all committed to continuing their education. Then he shared the agreements they had made at the end of their trip and showed how the agreements had been integrated into what they called the Ten Building Blocks (see figure 8-1).

Over the next year, the managers would continue to learn more about each of these elements, replacing some and refining others, working their development into an overall master plan. This master plan would lay out all the activities that would have to be done against each building

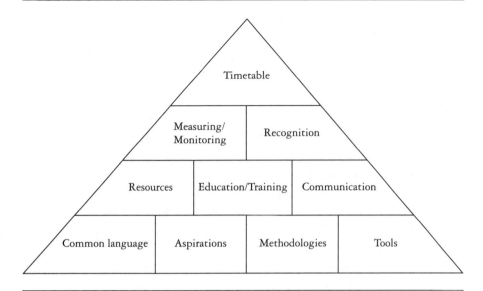

Figure 8-1   The Ten Building Blocks
Source: SB Presentation—1992 Management Conference, Rome

block and, eventually, how they might come together to support the achievement of SB's desire to be The Leading Healthcare Company.

But the EMC needed time to learn more about how all these pieces came together. Bob asked members of the Rome conference to have patience. He didn't want them to stop doing what they were doing in the spirit of *Simply Better,* but he did ask them to not start anything new. Those in the audience who had taken significant steps toward developing their own *Simply Better* education and were now ready to move forward could not help but feel frustrated and disappointed. They wanted to move ahead, yet instinctively understood that they needed to move *together* for *Simply Better's* true potential to be realized. During the subsequent Q&A session they grew aware that they needed more disciplined, companywide processes to move forward as one. They suggested the ad hoc systems that existed presently between the sectors be made systematic to encourage more collaborative efforts and learning of best practices from one another.

The EMC would try to get the right balance between allowing sectors to do their own thing and the need to work as one: between moving too fast, without adequate plans, and moving so slow that *Simply Better* lost momentum. But it wasn't going to be easy.

They were going to take the next steps and work together on completing this master plan (to cover from two to five years), developing an interim (one-year) plan in parallel. Teams would be assigned to work on designing the various elements, and many of those in the audience would be asked to help.

To create the bridge that would enable the organization to see that what SB was doing now was clearly building on all that had gone before, Joanne had suggested they use the phrase *"Simply Better* Way" to define this next phase (see figure 8-2). She had drafted two working definitions that Bob now shared with the audience. As he introduced the new phrase, he explained: *"Simply Better* is the way we live and the values we hold; *Simply Better* Way is the way we work, it's the methods and tools that help us to realize the Values." The *Simply Better* Way would give them the methods and tools to do the right things in the right way.

All of the principles they had learned were absolutely consistent with the five Values and nine Leadership Practices, he told them. What was different were the methods they had studied, which would help SB to put the Values and Practices into action. For that to happen, SB would invest the time and money necessary to train people in the skills they needed to make the Leadership Practices an instinctive way of working throughout SB. For this was one of the greatest lessons the EMC had learned: to see people as an investment, not just a cost, and that meant giving greater focus to their education and training.

Strategy	⟹	Culture	⟹	System
Peer group leader		*Simply Better*		*Simply Better* Way
Most effective marketer		Customer		Customer-driven processes
Leader in new product development		Innovation		Continuous improvement
Most efficient producer		Performance		Eliminate waste, use data
Best managed		People Integrity		Training Communication
Cross-sector linkages				Teamwork

Figure 8-2   Culture to Management Systems

As the EMC and the new design teams undertook the work outlined in the ten blocks, Bob promised to keep the audience informed of their progress through regular updates. Within six months, the EMC and the teams would be back with the interim plan.

Until now, SB had been very good at informing everyone, and getting them on board with the ideas behind *Simply Better.* But they hadn't yet inspired them to **feel** *Simply Better.* The emotional element—the spirit that would make *Simply Better* self-sustaining—was still missing. Capturing hearts and minds—the key to sustainable success, according to the experts—was not going to be easy. By the end of this meeting, however, those present felt they had made more of a start. In witnessing the EMC's visible humility and absolute commitment to learning how SB could become an industry leader, the management group in the audience realized that they really were part of one team. Suddenly, the group of fifteen champions had become closer to 200. It would be through their inspirational leadership that the organization would develop the real will for SB to win.

At that moment, as they were all asked to be patient until the teams had done their work, the audience may have wondered if *Simply Better* and SB might be taking two steps backwards to take one step forward.

SB was embarking on a road many had dared to take, but few had traveled successfully.

WINNING ATTITUDE   The goalposts for winning is once again raised as the EMC redefines SB's aspiration from "leader in its peer group" to "The Leading Healthcare Company" in terms of shareholder value. As the implications of the new aspiration and what it will take to fill the gap between SB and its competitors gradually dawn on EMC members, they realize that *Simply Better* holds one of the keys to achieving their strategic goals.

Meanwhile, as SB continues to communicate its business successes against its own targets as well as the results of its rivals, the feeling of winning is constantly reinforced among the employees, with the organization gradually beginning to grow more confident of its potential to be winners.

ORGANIZATION AS HERO   While the organization is participating in *Simply Better*-related activities, several managers realize that their level of involvement and degree of improvement is not enough to make a real difference. Some begin to seek training their employees in continuous improvement techniques. At the same time, the EMC learns in Japan that investing in people by training and developing them is one of the most significant drivers of continuous success. In order to create a single culture, they commit to developing a common set of skills that will help employees to put the Leadership Practices into action and allow them to be more actively involved in achieving the company's goals. This involvement would start immediately with the naming of teams to help define each element of the *Simply Better* Way.

CUMULATIVE LEARNING   The Japan trip was a turning point for the EMC in terms of its own learning process. Where members had instinctively supported the concept of teamwork and involving people in the integration process as well as that of having defined, rigorous processes to guide that effort, they realized they had only touched the surface in terms of the real power of both. They left Japan with an appreciation of managing by customer-driven processes rather than company-derived functions, an in-depth understanding of the need for widespread employee education and training in standard methodologies, and the importance of having a well-defined master plan that would allow them to systematically plan how all of these ideas could be introduced and integrated into SB. But, by far, the most powerful lesson of all was the realization of how much more they had to learn. That was the lesson gleaned by the organization: to take these next steps, they would all be learning together as part of the *"Simply Better"* Way.

STRATEGIC COMMUNICATION   By using the phrase *"Simply Better* Way,"* and defining it as "the way we work," which clearly illustrated the link with *Simply Better* ("the way we live"), communication helped to position what was learned in Japan as a continuum rather than a new program. This link was important to make sure employees did not see what would happen next as a change in direction or a new fad, but a step forward in making the Values a reality. The marketing of the *Simply Better* Way would connect what had been learned in Japan to SB's Leadership Practices and the benefit standardized processes would provide employees: i.e. a new way of working that would free them from day-to-day firefighting and create more of a risk-free environment that would encourage greater innovation.

ALIGNMENT OF BEHAVIOR AND STRATEGY   The importance of culture in delivering strategy is finally internalized by the EMC as it recognizes how *Simply Better,* through encouraging employees to constantly strive to do better every day, in everything they do, could help fill the £3/$5.6 billion gap between SB's present performance and future aspiration. Agreeing to change from the standard five-year plan to institute a rolling 10>3/1 planning process that would better align planning with their long-term industry reality was another critical step. But the real leap forward was recognizing the potential of how both could come together to create an entire management system dedicated to continuous self-renewal. It was the EMC's first step in what would it would later agree was a breakthrough in how to systematize change to achieve strategy.

CHAPTER NINE

Making Change the Strategy

IN THE WINTER OF 1992 DEMO-cratic front-runner Bill Clinton was promising major healthcare reform as a first-order priority in his campaign for the U.S. presidency, accelerating the U.S. trend toward managed care and cost containment. Suddenly medicines had to be economically as well as therapeutically beneficial. The growing pressure sent shock waves through the financial markets, depressing share prices of all the major pharmaceutical companies. SB's price was particularly hard hit, as concern continued to grow over the expiration of Tagamet's U.S. patent, now only two years away.

The EMC, fresh from Japan and the Rome management conference, wanted to focus on applying its learnings as soon as possible to move *Simply Better* forward. But implications of the proposed U.S. changes along with many other issues that had arisen while members were away now appeared as mountainous stacks of paper atop their desks.

Although frustrated by the delay, they soon realized that insights gained in Japan would prove helpful in addressing the industry changes they now all accepted as imminent. In their efforts to identify every possible lever that could drive the business in this new, highly competitive environment, the EMC now added examining SB's major processes to restructuring the business portfolio and implementing continuous improvement.

At the senior management level they continued to pursue the strategic initiatives they had previously identified, including disposing of noncore businesses such as personal care and toiletries and seeking key technical competencies such as gene technology. They had become very aggressive about strategic alliances and had signed a large number of agreements to comarket products, license in others, and, through partners, broaden their presence in key geographic markets.

To tackle the threat to the industry's margins, teams of managers had been trying to see how they could increase both efficiency and effectiveness. They considered certain key processes, trying to understand how the work was organized and approached, assessing how each step added value from the customer's perspective. Pharmaceuticals focused on getting products into the marketplace faster and began to analyze its clinical development and new product registration processes. Consumer Brands had begun to address how the product went from factory to market shelf and was reviewing every step in the supply chain. A few cross-functional teams were set up to evaluate how they could better exploit the market benefits of being an integrated healthcare company.

The more they considered the changes to the industry, however, the more the managers realized that being integrated was not only about products and markets, but just as much about processes and how they might uniquely combine them to create a competitive advantage. By expanding their definition of "integrated" to include processes within and across the four business sectors, they realized that they had only begun to exploit the potential of their real business linkages.

While senior managers were focusing on strategic initiatives and rethinking the way they performed some major tasks, *Simply Better* was still aimed at involving 50,000 employees in incremental improvement. As it had cascaded through the sector-driven programs during the past two years, close to 34,000 employees had been introduced to the five Values and nine Leadership Practices, and by mid-1992 *Simply Better* was starting to generate some tangible results. Improvements ranged from reducing time to issue a certificate by 80 percent to streamlining a paperwork process and saving $30,000 annually to a performance enhancement process at the Worthing antibiotic plant that lowered costs by £3.6 million per annum. Through a grassroots effort, this plant had dramatically reduced lead times, quality costs, and inventory control, significantly contributing to SB's target for better returns on its assets. In total an estimated 250 work teams had been initiated over the last twelve months. Their combined efforts were estimated to reduce SB's costs by around £100 million per year.[1]

Employees were doing a lot, but still it wasn't enough. They were addressing the obvious, the "easy pickings," and not challenging the tough things that could really make a difference. The £3/$5.6 billion shareholder value gap remained between where SB was and where it must go to become the true industry leader. What would it take to get there?

INVOLVING EVERYONE

The EMC knew that a large part of the answer to closing the gap was within *Simply Better:* that by getting employees to think differently about their work and making sure their efforts were focused on SB's overall strategic goals, SB could significantly improve sales and profitability along with its employee productivity record (currently lower than the competition in terms of sales and trading profit per employee) at the same time it improved customer satisfaction. This deliberate and system-atic effort to motivate, involve, and align all employees in the company's overall purpose was what the EMC had seen in Japan as one of the significant drivers to success. Through engaging and aligning *everyone,* from the chief executive to the production worker, from the salesman to the scientist, the Japanese companies had generated customer improve-ments and cost savings that the EMC would not have dreamed attainable. But how could SB mobilize the efforts of a global workforce into the single-minded power necessary to achieve its overriding goal—to be the best?

Given that the individual components such as those that drove behavior (the Values) and those that drove the company and business (strategic initiatives and processes) were equally important, what would really make the difference would be bringing them together, linking them to create one integrated whole. The optimal system would somehow connect an employee's day-to-day task with the company's long-term direction and ensure that the way the task was executed meant it was constantly improving. Yes, bringing these two elements—business and behavior—systematically together could be potentially all powerful, thought the EMC.

Such a comprehensive system would help set business priorities and establish a logical order for developing and introducing the various components to the organization. As an all-encompassing system, it would create a shared understanding of where the business was going and communicate the actual steps necessary for management and the whole organization to get there.

But knowing what it wanted was just the first step; determining how it would design such a system was another issue. The EMC needed to understand what the system might look like before it could even begin to address developing the individual components. And, just as it had seen in the Burke-Litwin model, the EMC recognized that the links were *as* important—if not *more* important—than each of the pieces.

The EMC had promised to provide the Rome conference participants with some details behind the *Simply Better* Way by June. The self-imposed deadline had been intended to sustain the positive momentum as well as build on the EMC's collective enthusiasm from the Japan trip. But it now created a good deal of pressure and frustration within the EMC as members struggled to understand all the issues and implications they would need to resolve in order to meet the deadline. At the same time, increasingly acute business issues were demanding more and more management attention.

PUTTING IT TOGETHER

As the weeks wore on, EMC members struggled with their commitment to the Rome conference participants. In raising the goalposts from implementing continuous improvement under *Simply Better* to creating an entire management system designed to deliver world-class excellence through the *Simply Better* Way, they had made their task that much more complex. The problem was that none of the EMC members had a clear picture of how all the components were supposed to come together to create this management system. What was it supposed to look like?

Members pondered the various components they already had—the Promise, the Values, the Leadership Practices—and the new pieces such as the 10>3/1 planning process on which they had agreed after the Japan study, and put them together against the background of everything else they had learned. The merger integration had taught them how important a disciplined planning process was, while the failure to reach out beyond the EMC in defining the Values and planning *Simply Better* had taught them that involving as many people as possible as early as possible was critical to gaining commitment.

From these discussions, EMC members determined that any next steps would need to include the following:

1. A way to integrate the so-called soft stuff—that is, the Promise, the Values, and the Leadership Practices—with the so-called hard stuff—that is, strategic goals, business restructuring, and major processes—to form an entire management system.

2. A way of coordinating and aligning all the strategic initiatives such as acquisitions and alliances and the process improvement efforts—big and small—across the different sectors and functions so that they would eventually deliver the "strategic intent," the phrase SB was using to capture its ten-year aspirational goal. The mechanism to link employees' day-to-day work with SB's long-term aspirations could be the 10>3/1 planning process.

3. A means of instilling within the entire company the concept they had witnessed repeatedly in Japan: managing by process rather than by function to meet customer needs and continuously improving every process so that it consistently delivered excellent results. Introducing this concept had several implications. Employees would need to be trained to think of their work as a series of steps that moved across as well as down functional areas, changing the way they executed their day-to-day tasks. This implied a need for a new methodology and a common way of working that would allow them to interact with others outside their functional discipline or business sector.

   Employees would need to learn first to standardize, then to improve these processes as a fundamental part of their day-to-day work. This would require using the methodology consistently, incorporating far more analysis, rigor, and discipline than they were accustomed to. The methodology would apply at the levels of both incremental and radical redesign improvement and involve a substantial investment in education and training.

4. Identification of (and agreement on) what they believed were SB's "core capabilities"—the name they had assigned to those processes fundamental to SB that could provide SB with a truly competitive advantage. Depending on whether core capabilities were business specific or crossed the company, their development would be the

responsibility of the business sectors or the corporate staff. Improvement efforts should be focused first on developing these core capabilities.

5. Establishment of well-defined support systems, including human resources, communication, and recognition, that would motivate, inform, and involve employees and help integrate their efforts into a well-aligned whole, as well as a means of monitoring and measuring that would ensure organizational focus and constant progress against 10>3/1 overall goals.

6. A well-defined master plan for developing, introducing, and implementing all these components that would involve people from across the entire company.

They took this final requirement very seriously. The effort they were talking about eventually had to engage and align a global organization of 50,000 people working in different businesses at different levels and having different needs and aspirations. It was going to require enormous coordination to get it right. The need for a master plan to help manage implementation had been one of the key lessons learned in Japan. The absence of this detailed, disciplined mechanism to coordinate the many required activities had been cited again and again as the reason why most (some say 70 percent) initiatives similar to *Simply Better* fail.

Some of the frustration eased at last as the EMC understood what it wanted: a strategic management system that started with the Promise—the company's overarching statement of purpose—and set its direction and remained constant for a long period of time but then, through a series of steps and actions that would be decided through the 10>3/1 planning process, would bring the long-term future to the present through the development of core capabilities and the improvement and standardization of every process at every level of the company.

DEFINING THE ARCHITECTURE

From their benchmarking, EMC members had learned that entire management systems built around sustaining continuous improvement as a competitive advantage were rare. Most were limited systems that had focused on incremental improvement activities alone.

Many companies operate under management systems that have been tacked together over the years, bolting new ideas onto old ones rather than rethinking and redesigning the systems to integrate them. The result is often a series of stand-alones, seemingly unrelated and often needlessly complex systems that ignore employees' day-to-day work, as if employees had nothing, versus everything, to do with strategy.

What the EMC was trying to do was begin with a clean piece of paper and design a system that showed what they now knew to be true: aligning *everyone's* day-to-day work and behavior with SB's long-term goals and company purpose was critical to the company's long-term success.

First they tried to imagine how all the pieces might fit together. That is when they realized they needed something visual, a simple diagram that would illustrate the linkages so both managers and employees could see where their work fit within SB's overall strategy. This framework would be the way they communicated the company's priorities and helped employees understand how important their day-to-day improvement efforts were to SB's overall success. This graphic road map would have to be as clear as possible so employees could not only comprehend the linkages between their work and those of the senior team, but also realize what was expected of them for SB to reach its destination.

Just as they had for each step, the EMC would have to develop this picture, or "architecture," itself. Both McKinsey and Deltapoint presented some ideas, only to have them rejected as too complicated, not meaningful, or too limited. Finally, at their *Simply Better* workshop in March, EMC members reviewed a diagram that captured some of the concepts they now considered fundamental to creating SB's strategic management system.

BIRTH OF THE ARCHITECTURE

EMC members reviewed the schematic in front of them. They noted that the most critical pieces to the puzzle appeared to be there, but the Values and the planning time horizons—the 10>3/1 they had agreed on—were still missing. They continued to rework the diagram until finally, on May 11, 1992, three months after the Rome conference and one month before their projected deadline, they held a *Simply Better* workshop via videoconference. They were going through a black plastic bound document, and they had reached page 24, *Simply Better* Way Architecture. What EMC members were working at appears in figure 9-1.

Starting with the company's long-term (say twenty-five years) goal of the Promise at the top, the diagram laid out very clearly how achievement of the strategic intent (later defined as achieving a sustainable competitive advantage in each of the five Values) would be the culmination of all the actions occurring over the 10>3/1 planning time frame. Some of these would be activities such as strategic initiatives, typically the

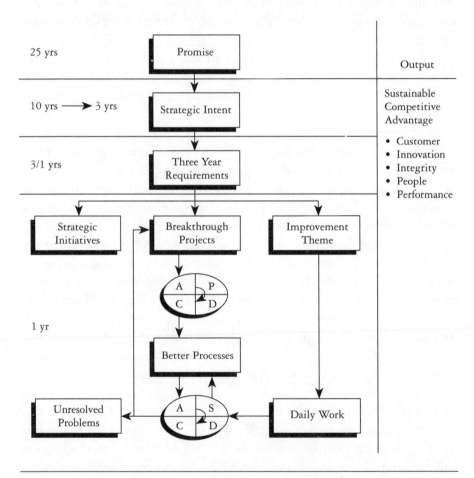

Figure 9-1   The Simply Better *Way Architecture*

domain of senior management. But the majority would depend on the development and improvement of the core capabilities, either as break-through projects involving middle managers (reengineering) or through the improvement theme engaging all employees (incremental improve-ment). Linking all these improvement activities was the well-known Deming wheel Plan-Do-Check-Act (P-D-C-A), which implied planning for every process to constantly improve, every day, creating the better processes that would become SB's new standard of excellence.

By linking the top half of the diagram (*what* had to be done) with the bottom half (*how* it would be done) through P-D-C-A, the architecture was making continuous change a fundamental part of SB's long-term strategy.

Recognizing its potential and appreciating the power of its simplicity as both a management and communication tool, Jan championed the architecture as a means of managing SB. His excitement was contagious as EMC members considered their morning's work. After three months of steady effort, of working with one another and challenging each compo-nent and how it came together, all the thinking that lay behind the architecture had now become part of them. They knew they had achieved a major breakthrough.

With only minor adjustments over the next few months, the sche-matic agreed on that day by the EMC became the *Simply Better* Way architecture, a visual representation of what SB's management system looked like. In showing how the pieces came together it also provided a road map for determining all the work that would take place over the remainder of 1992.

DEFINING STRATEGIC INTENT

Starting with the top of the architecture, the EMC's first assignment was to tackle development of the 10>3/1 planning process, which would require a fundamental rethinking of the very traditional five-year planning system the company had in place.

The new planning process would begin with defining strategic intent, a stretch goal that was just out of reach but still seen by the organization as realistic and achievable within ten years. It needed to be quantifiable but expressed in a way that was both aspirational and inspirational. The statement SB had been using since the October 1991 meeting was "To Be the World's Leading Healthcare Company."

But it wasn't specific enough. While EMC members had quantified "leading" in terms of shareholder value, they had not described what "leading" actually looked like, which was the only way they would be able to make the goal relevant to all employees. More motivational statements were proposed, including phrases like "better than the best" and "first in healthcare." But somehow the EMC was struggling. None of the slogans was unique, and none captured what they thought SB was actually striving for. That's when the debate around the definition of "best" began.

Until now, the Values had been viewed as fundamental to achieving SB's competitive advantage, which is why they appeared under Output on the architecture. If the Values reflected the kind of behavior SB needed to win, then it made sense that they be used to define what winning looked like and be used as the measures by which SB would evaluate its success. But being the best implies a comparison. Unless other companies and the financial analysts used something similar to the Values as measures of success, it would be difficult for SB to evaluate how well it was doing relative to its competitors.

(If one really thought about it, however, the primary criterion by which analysts judged any company was the strength of its management team; for pharmaceutical companies, products in the pipeline constituted another. At SB, these areas were being addressed under the people and innovation Values. From that perspective, SB was actually focusing on the two most critical qualitative measures by which analysts projected the company's future performance!)

The EMC debate about the relevance of measuring by Values continued until finally the members considered some criteria that might help them to identify potential measures. Each measure, they said, would need to satisfy the following:

❖ Be a measure of output
❖ Drive the desired behavior
❖ Be easily measurable
❖ Be relevant across the corporation
❖ Remain meaningful over time

Defining the criteria actually made their task harder, as EMC members found it exceedingly difficult to suggest measures that could actually meet all the standards they listed. One of the toughest: Be easily measurable. How, for example, would they be able to identify a measure and target that (1) was applicable at both a corporate and local level, and (2) generated a meaningful corporate number that resulted from consolidating locally derived data? From that day onward, EMC discussions on the topic of measurement would always be lengthy ones. They would continue for months, never culminating in any conclusion that was satisfactory to all.

Still, at the end of this particular meeting, they did reach some agreement: their long-term sustainable success depended on how well employees practiced the Values and Leadership Practices. Measuring against the Values would be a useful way of evaluating how they were doing in beating their own best and attaining the aspirational goals they would set against each. At the very least, they could use employee surveys to evaluate how well they were doing against the Value-driven Leadership Practices internally, and commission external surveys to monitor SB's performance relative to achieving customer satisfaction and integrity.

They suggested that a minimum number of measures per Value (two or three) be applied corporatewide and that the process for setting the targets against each measure fall within each sector's 10>3/1 planning process, ensuring local ownership. Some of the suggestions they made for SB corporatewide that day were the following:

Customer	Customer satisfaction (all the businesses)
Innovation	Total new products as a percent of sales
Integrity	Most admired by three key groups: customers/shareholders/employees
People	Turnover and retention of best people
Performance	Shareholder value, sales, profits, return on assets

For example, a potential measure for the customer value could be customer satisfaction, while the ten-year target might be to become two times better than the nearest competitor. The measure—customer satisfaction—would be used across the company. The timetable for achieving the target would be determined by the sector, then refined further for the three- and one-year periods by the local business.

While still uncomfortable with the novelty of measuring things as soft as Values, the EMC was now able to move on.

Having determined SB's true source of competitive advantage lay in the five Values, the EMC agreed that any statement of SB's strategic intent needed to capture that belief. That meant that *Simply Better*—as something unique to SB—had to be part of the phrase. Later that year, after considering further suggestions made by the top four hundred managers, it was Jan who proposed they select "To become **The** *Simply Better* Healthcare Company" as their strategic intent.

Striving for this strategic intent would drive all SB's future actions, focusing and aligning the entire organization over the ten-, three-, and one-year time frames.

ACHIEVING STRATEGIC INTENT

The EMC now turned its attention to the three ways the strategic intent could be achieved as identified in the architecture: strategic initiatives, breakthrough projects, and the improvement theme. SB would have to address all three almost simultaneously if it was to meet the challenges of an industry in the turbulent throes of redefining itself.

The Role of Strategic Initiatives and Breakthroughs

Strategic initiatives such as acquisitions, alliances, and comarketing agreements could help SB to take quantum leaps in size and scope, as well as provide it with technical competencies it might be lacking. Opportunistic as well as deliberate, strategic initiatives would involve the constant vigilance and effort of a small planning group and the most senior team.

Of critical ongoing importance and involving a far greater number of managers would be the breakthrough projects, the aim of which would be to create SB's core capabilities. These core capabilities would be the result of reengineering and redesigning existing business and management processes into processes that were radically different and improved, or were unique to SB, and would enable it to reach the strategic intent in ten years' time.

In the case of the business sectors these capabilities would include all the major processes critical to achieving competitive advantage: sales and marketing, global manufacturing, and—most critical—life-cycle management, planning a new product from its time in development to its launch as a prescription medicine and its eventual transition to an over-the-counter medication. Capabilities identified by the corporate functions would be those such as strategic planning and training and development that crossed the businesses and supported an integrated company. These would be designated as management processes.

Once again the managers were trying to strike a balance between centralized and decentralized: placing responsibility for the business processes and their development at the operating level, and placing the management processes representing standardization, consolidation, and alignment at the center. Later a list of potential core business and management capabilities was identified by each sector and corporate function as part of their first effort at the 10>3/1 plan.

As EMC members considered the list, they realized each capability involved hundreds, maybe thousands, of smaller business and management processes. The actions required to develop, radically redesign, and standardize those deemed the real levers of competitive advantage would define the work priorities of the 3/1 business plans.

If 10>3/1 was "rolling the future back," what SB was now doing was even more specific. It was designing a detailed game plan that would focus the energy and activities of the entire company for a very long time.

The Role of the Improvement Theme

The power of the architecture was the importance it placed on the role of every single employee in helping achieve the strategic intent through incremental improvement. So even as senior and middle managers focused on defining major strategic initiatives and developing core capabilities, everyone recognized that how well they were executed and whether SB achieved its strategic intent would rely at least equally on the way employees performed their individual daily tasks, which were linked to the strategic intent through the improvement theme.

However small or fragmented, in the *Simply Better* Way every employee's task was considered important to the long-term success of the company; accordingly, each would have to be performed to the highest standard. Employees would have to learn a whole new way of thinking about how they viewed their work and be certain they were working on the right activities. Activities would no longer be directed by what the function dictated but by what the customer required. As important, employees would also have to learn how to perform their tasks differently, in ways that were consistent with the P-D-C-A cycle of continuous improvement. While *Simply Better* had identified the behaviors employees would ideally exhibit in their daily work, such as being more customer focused, the *Simply Better* Way was talking about fundamentally changing the way they worked, showing them *how* to be customer driven. It was a way of working that encouraged greater employee participation in setting goals and determining how to achieve them. They would require greater self-discipline and exactitude than they were used to, and a common language and approach that would allow them to cross the departmental borders.

For example, employees would need to spend a lot more time planning and making sure individual work processes were customer focused and made reliable—that is, capable of producing the same excellent results consistently—before actually implementing them or even trying to improve them. To an untrained observer, it would look as if an inordinate amount of time was spent thinking and analyzing rather than doing, which could cause enormous frustration in a workforce with a do-it mentality. But in the end employees had to see that their efforts paid off, that their new ideas were implemented much more smoothly and tasks often completed much faster and error free—saving time, money, and energy. Job satisfaction and morale could actually increase as more processes became reliable, and employees enjoyed greater success in their day-to-day work. Rather than seeing reliable processes as constraining, employees would find them liberating.

But before management could get employees to welcome rather than resist the new way of working, it would need to overcome the potentially debilitating frustration of some with planning, the innate resistance of many to enforced standardization of work, and a widespread belief that good decisions relied more on intuition and gut feeling than on detailed analysis.

It would take a massive investment in training and an approach that was consistent, systematic, and even more disciplined than the merger integration process had been. It would take time, a lot of time, before these skills were instilled corporatewide and demonstrated any productivity improvements. But without them, SB would never realize the potential inherent in process management that the EMC had witnessed in Japan.

IMPLEMENTING THE ARCHITECTURE

Having defined the architecture and agreeing on each of its components, the EMC now considered how to move forward to develop the capacity to implement it. The ten building blocks to the *Simply Better* Way that had been identified at Rome were refined further and clustered into four areas, each of which would be developed and coordinated as part of the overall master plan:

❖ 10>3/1 planning, including defining strategic intent and core capabilities
❖ Education and training, including developing a common methodology
❖ Communication and recognition
❖ Measurement

As the EMC had promised, the components of the *Simply Better* Way would be developed by the organization. The design team for each of these areas would be led by a functional expert but comprised primarily of line representatives from each sector.

The goal was to involve employees and promote cross-sector thinking and working. Involving people on the design teams from both the business sectors and corporate functional groups would ensure different perspectives were brought to the task and guarantee a better result. It would also mean there was cooperation from the start in determining what was centrally designed and what was locally executed. When it came time to implement the team designs, there would be a built-in cadre of salespeople to help support it. Most important, by involving line people, it would mean that whatever recommendations emerged they would be more easily integrated into the day-to-day business. (Again, the EMC was very conscious that the *Simply Better* Way be seen as integral to, not separate from, the business.) The only problem was that they seemed to keep tapping the same people, who were often the star business performers, rather than reaching further into the organization to find the new talent.

EDUCATING AND TRAINING

With work already under way in 10>3/1 and measurement, the design team with the largest unresolved mandate was education and training, headed by Tom Kaney. It would be that team's role to instill within SB the process thinking and managing that was fundamental to achieving the breakthroughs and improvement-theme-related projects. The sooner a critical mass of managers (particularly middle managers) understood the architecture and were given skills and competency in process improvement, the sooner the majority of SB employees could become involved in the *Simply Better* Way. They needed to develop a common way of working and get it into the organization as quickly as possible. Speed and urgency were back on the table.

Still, even while Tom and his team sought speed, they also sought best practice. They were still hesitant about using anything off the shelf and did not want to diminish in any way the philosophy of starting with a clean slate to lead SB to a new standard. They studied companies renowned for their education and training efforts and examined various process-improvement and problem-solving methods and supporting analytical tools that had been proven in application. Even as they looked outside, they realized that some best practice existed within SB. The good news was that it meant there was some knowledge of training in process improvement within the company. But what started as a relatively straightforward task—introducing a common approach to working— became increasingly complex as the team now had to determine how to integrate the various sector efforts into the overall training plan. Failing to do so would not only violate the underlying principle of one common approach companywide, but also dampen enthusiasm and the good results that these other programs had been generating.

All of this was taking a lot of time. It was June, and patience was beginning to wear thin.

While developing the common methods and tools had now become a top priority with the EMC, various education and training team members were working on what they felt was an even more pressing issue: how would they deliver the training, once the content had been approved?

At the EMC *Simply Better* Way workshop in late summer, team leader Tom Kaney presented the key principles that would guide SB's education strategy. These principles had been gathered from best practice, the consultants, and the EMC's own observations in Japan. The training, they agreed, would be

1. management led;

2. done in parallel (versus cascade) to sustain enthusiasm;

3. provided just-in-time/hands-on (versus mass classroom training);

4. delivered by insiders (versus outside consultants); and

5. aligned with strategic business priorities.

Tom went on to explain that there would be five modules to SB's methods and tools:

❖ Getting started
❖ Process improvement
❖ Problem solving
❖ Team work
❖ Analytical tools

The content of these modules would

❖ teach employees how to improve processes, solve problems, and work in teams;
❖ be versatile, usable from the top floor to the shop floor, the same for reengineering as for incremental improvement;
❖ assure methodical analysis of issues and fact-based improvement, focusing on task and process rather than on people and intuition;
❖ promote cross-functional participation through encouraging process thinking;
❖ provide a simple common language, encouraging one voice, one way of working; and
❖ be unique to SB, making certain the tools were relevant to all parts of the company from manufacturing to R&D to marketing.

While the skills would draw on the best practice of others, the first module was a methodology proprietary to SB. Basically all about getting started, this module would help managers understand how to manage by process and how to select the right things to work on that were aligned with the goals of the 10>3/1 strategic plans.

Consistent with making the organization the hero, the goal was to build an internal competency within SB in individual and team process improvement and problem-solving skills that could be refined over time and ultimately used by every SB employee. Three interconnecting roles were recommended: coach/trainers, unit trainers, and facilitators. Using a cascade process, coach/trainers would be trained by Deltapoint consultants first in the methods and tools and next in how to train others. This core team of about fifty people would then be responsible for training trainers from various sites, who in turn would train facilitators to support local process improvement teams.

Remembering the merger integration experience where team leaders were assumed to have certain skills they did not, criteria to assess the level of skill and competency for each trainer group was established: every trainer at each level of the organization would have to be internally certified as competent before being put to work with the managers in the organization. The criteria for the coach/trainers, for example, would be that each was a person capable of influencing the strong-minded senior management group to make certain they were actively participating. The competency standards would require not only working knowledge of total quality principles and *Simply Better* Way methodology, but also a comfort level with change and process management. It was important that coaches come from the business rather than from the more obvious human resources function and be drawn from across the company. Regardless of where they came from, all the coach/trainers—at least for a while—would be considered a corporate resource.

It sounded reasonable, but what Tom and his team were asking for was quite extraordinary in the context of SB. They were trying to create of pool of experts who would belong to no one sector but to all sectors, who would come from the line, not HR, and who would be deployed geographically rather than by sector so that they could help out where they were needed. All of this in a company that was still boundaried by all three: sector, function, and geography. It showed once again the power of cumulative learning; as people gained an understanding of the goal and the principles, they were pushing the boundaries out. It really was *Simply Better* at work: cross-functional, cross-sector, pulling for SB as a whole.

Finally, training would be placed in the context of an individual's work, and that meant that skills would be taught but then applied immediately in the course of the training to an actual task. The benefit was real-time learning, generating concrete results. Employees would experience the process improvement steps in the context of their actual work. It was learning by doing and then winning through doing, making the lessons far more memorable.

SOME STRATEGIC INITIATIVES

Even as how to involve everyone in the *Simply Better* Way was evolving, senior managers in the businesses were busy identifying the strategic initiatives that would deliver the integrated healthcare concept.

While Consumer Brands had been less affected than the pharmaceuticals sector during the merger, once the intent to become The Leading Healthcare Company was clearly defined, the sector found itself undergoing a major restructuring. Long-standing Beecham food products such as Bovril, Marmite and Ambrosia had been sold, and others were to follow. This restructuring had been started under the sector's soon-to-retire chairman John Hunter, who had joined Beecham in 1957 and rose to head Consumer Brands first for Beecham and then for SB. John had been one of the drivers behind the sector's successful "build the brands" strategy.

The Consumer Brands restructuring was now being aggressively pursued by its incoming chairman, Harry Groome. Harry, who had been president of SB Clinical Laboratories, had been named to succeed John in May 1992. In a company where the ability to transition products from prescription medicines to OTC was to become a core capability, Harry brought ideal credentials to the task. He had experience in both pharmaceuticals and OTC, having held positions in both businesses during his 27-year career at SmithKline Beckman. Furthermore, he had a proven track record. Under his leadership, Clinical Laboratories had grown significantly and had just passed $1 billion in sales the year before. And in a company dedicated to building one corporate culture, that Harry was American and from SKB originally also meant he brought an entirely different perspective to the "very Beecham" Consumer Brands sector.

His efforts to reshape the Consumer Brands into Consumer Healthcare (the name would be officially adopted in 1993) led to SB's announcing in August 1992 that it would be pooling its OTC business in the United States with Marion Merrell Dow, strengthening both companies' positions in the growing U.S. market for self-medication. The partnership would have a combined sales of $660 million, making SB Consumer Brands the fifth largest OTC company in the United States. Most important, the deal gave SB access to two potential switch products, Marion Merrell Dow's smoking cessation aid, Nicoderm, and its antihistamine, Seldane, and provided a strong partner for the switch of Tagamet to OTC status following expiration of its U.S. patent in 1994.

The SB-Marion Merrell Dow partnership was the first of several major initiatives Harry would undertake in the redefining of the consumer brands business. He later sold Beecham's toiletry products to Sara Lee in 1993 and became one of the key drivers behind the acquisition and integration of Sterling Winthrop in 1994. That would prove to be a spectacular purchase.

Later in 1992, Harry was replaced as president of Clinical Laboratories by outsider Vick Stoughton. With more than twenty years in healthcare, Vick joined SB from Duke University Hospital where he had been chief executive officer and vice chancellor for health affairs.

Vick lost no time in getting on board with *Simply Better,* citing it as an opportunity to improve every aspect of the business. "But," as he put it, "we ought to be smart about change. Let's not change for the sake of change, but for the *benefit* of change."

THE EMC TESTS PROCESS IMPROVEMENT

By late September 1992 much of the work on the training modules had been done. One exception was the process improvement methodology, the final draft of which now appeared between two white glossy covers with *Simply Better* Way stamped on the front. Again reflecting a key education principle—it would be management led—EMC members had agreed they would test the book and its methodology at their next off-site *Simply Better* Way Workshop, scheduled for mid-October. This would give them a firsthand working knowledge of improvement activities and was entirely consistent with their commitment not to introduce anything to the organization unless they had done it themselves.

When EMC members gathered in the meeting room at 8:00 A.M. that Saturday, they were not quite sure what to expect. The Deltapoint trainer started the session by reviewing the concepts that were at the heart of process improvement. So far, so good. They were entirely consistent with the nine Leadership Practices.

But the conceptual view given was at 37,000 feet. The EMC was struggling, trying to relate what it was hearing to what employees would actually be doing. Then members were told to select a current process—any process—to which they would apply the new concepts. They chose the budget review process, looking at it from the viewpoint of the country manager as the customer.

The EMC was separated into smaller groups, and when each reported its findings some hours later, all agreed that, even with minimum analysis, there were many steps that added absolutely no value when considered against the customer's needs. The number of required reviews meant the budget process was more about hierarchy than added value, and it had some troubling effects on management behavior. With so many reviews required, how much effort went into getting the budget right the first time? Furthermore, who was ultimately accountable for its achievement?

EMC members sat around the table, amazed at what they had learned that day. Their experience had given them an emotional, practical understanding of process thinking and analysis, including the need for more discipline, facts, and data than their intuitive personalities had ever allowed for. As they considered the amount of thought and the length of time it had taken them just to understand and map the existing budget process, let alone develop any recommendations, they wondered what they could expect as the entire company started to examine its work using this methodology.

Although some EMC members were impressed by what they had learned through applying the new method, the positive feeling was not universal. JP worried about making the effort too complex and wanted the methodology to embody the simplicity promoted as inherent to *Simply Better*. Some asked, incredulously if this were really the way they intended to run the company. The level of analytical detail, together with the inordinate amount of discipline it would require, could place disabling time and energy demands on the organization.

Their conclusion: the methodology appeared overly detailed and cumbersome only in contrast to the existing ways of working. The comparison illustrated clearly how little time was spent now on making data-driven, analytical decisions. To get systematic, rigorous thinking into the organization, it seemed as if they were going to have to require an excessive amount of discipline at the start.

As they departed the session, EMC members knew they had progressed one more step in their own education and understood that much better how the *Simply Better* Way would progress them toward their ultimate goal. While each step was painful, at least they knew they were going in the right direction.

COMMUNICATION AND RECOGNITION

As plans accelerated for developing the 10>3/1 process and methods and tools, working in parallel to maintain employee momentum and provide the necessary support was the communication and recognition team. This team needed to build alignment around the newly articulated strategic intent, develop understanding of the architecture and how it would affect employees' day-to-day work, and create awareness of the concepts behind process improvement that linked them clearly to the five Values and nine Leadership Practices. To help diffuse employees' concerns about the new way of thinking and working, team members needed to show it as empowering rather than constraining, and ease the inevitable included/ excluded feeling that would arise as time lapsed between training different parts of the organization. Finally, the team was asked to help maintain employee motivation and enthusiasm by recognizing role models, inspiring all employees to keep striving to be *Simply Better.*

As a first step, communication and recognition team members needed to build greater awareness and understanding among the company's key players of the concepts behind the *Simply Better* Way and the architecture, creating a common language and a cadre of champions. If these managers were going to help lead the *Simply Better* Way, it was important that they follow the thinking behind the architecture and know what would be required of them as the methods and tools were introduced to the organization. This was not just about disseminating information: it was about providing some strategic context for what they were about to undertake. How would managers know why SB was doing this? How would they help employees accept their involvement? And what was the benefit for them personally?

Through what managers said and the way they said it, team members hoped they would instill in everyone the sense of winning that SB needed to achieve the strategic intent and create the understanding employees needed to do their jobs the *Simply Better* Way. The problem was as much inspiration as it was information.

As the end of the year neared, all those involved felt good about what they had achieved to progress *Simply Better.* In the year since the EMC's trip to Japan, they had designed a comprehensive system for managing SB and expressed it through the architecture. They had defined their ten-year goal as strategic intent and agreed they would try to measure it through the five Values. They had also identified the ways to achieve it, namely through strategic initiatives, breakthroughs, and incremental improvement, and had set up the teams that would design the processes by which each would happen: 10>3/1, education and training, and communication and recognition, all of which would be incorporated into the master plan.

The EMC that left for the holiday break was much more confident and focused. Members knew where SB was going and how they could involve the entire organization to get there. On reflection it was P-D-C-A in practice. The year's effort they had put into planning the *Simply Better* Way reduced the likelihood of any area requiring major rework once it came to execution.

THE ROLE OF THE BOARD

As the teams worked toward completing design of the *Simply Better* Way, the board was kept informed of their progress. At its autumn meeting the presentations showed how SB had progressed from defining the strategic gap and the corporate business strategies, to developing the five Values and nine Leadership Practices, to arriving at the architecture.

EMC members took turns illustrating how the architecture came to life, explaining work under way in the top half, such as the business portfolio discussions, and how the bottom half would be brought into alignment through massive training in process management and improvement. The board listen attentively, absorbed with the absolute logic of what it was seeing but amazed at the magnitude of the task the EMC was proposing. When the presentation came to an end, discussion turned to the investment in both energy and time that instilling the *Simply Better* Way would take, and the potential rewards it would reap.

While the board had been kept informed, it had not actually been involved in helping the EMC to define the architecture. In hindsight, the board's involvement would have made these discussions easier.

At the end of that same meeting, the directors took on the discussion of Bob and Henry's retirement, which was scheduled for April 1994 and was just about 18 months away. Under Sir Robert Clark's guidance, the board's nomination and remuneration committee viewed SB's management succession as its most important responsibility. The committee had been working with Bob, Peter, and Henry since 1990, the period when questions of SB's future leadership were first raised.

Even when he first interviewed with Beecham, Bob had advocated that so long as there was continuity on the board and among management, then it was the chief executive's responsibility to instill in a company the ability to continuously change. And so now, as they discussed the succession, both Bob and Henry advised the board that they would leave the company together, and neither would stay on, even as a director. It was important that the new team be free to pursue the ongoing spirit of change, and not feel hindered that what they wanted to do was in any way offending those they had replaced.

The board turned first to deciding Henry's successor. Sir Peter Walters, former chairman of BP and Midland Bank, had been on the board since the merger. As someone who had knowledge of the company from its very beginning, his selection as a nonexecutive chairman would provide SB with the continuity it required. He would also bring to the position a breadth of experience in both U.K. and international business and government affairs, reflecting SB's deliberate effort to build a board of global stature. His appointment was readily agreed on.

Jan Leschly had joined SB in June 1990 with the hope that he would become the next chief executive. In the more than two years since, he had led SB Pharmaceuticals from strength to strength, and the sector was now achieving strong financial results. He had successfully launched a number of new products, all desperately needed to offset the declining Tagamet sales expected in 1994, and had developed a promising pipeline of future products. He had put together a world-class management team for SB Pharmaceuticals and was taking a lead in moving *Simply Better* forward. Convinced of Jan's ability to lead SB to even greater heights in the face of the demanding, rapidly changing industry, the board approved Jan Leschly as SB's next chief executive, to succeed Bob on his retirement in April 1994.

Equally important in the minds of board members was to have a strong replacement for Jan as head of SB Pharmaceuticals, someone who would also be considered a candidate to eventually succeed Jan as chief executive. In his two years as head of SB Pharmaceuticals in the United States, JP Garnier had transformed a relatively weak U.S. business into one of the industry's strongest competitors, with major successes in both marketing and sales. He and Jan had worked together closely to build SB's pharmaceuticals business into the industry leader it was becoming, and they made a very powerful combination. And so, in a move intended to help ensure the continuity of SB's management into the next century, the board confirmed JP Garnier to succeed Jan as chairman of SB Pharmaceuticals.

To eliminate any uncertainty about the succession either inside or outside the company the board also agreed that afternoon that all these appointments would be announced at the annual general meeting in April 1993, one year before the individuals actually assumed their positions. This would allow the transition of leadership to begin quietly and deliberately, assuring a smooth handover in one year's time.

WINNING ATTITUDE   Winning is further defined as strategic intent, and succeeding against each of the five Values, to which the EMC agreed to apply quantifiable measures. This was very difficult—for while there was agreement around the concept of measurement, gaining actual commitment to measures meant somewhere, someone was both accountable and responsible for achieving them. Still, "winning" from now on would be judged not only by financial results, but also by the requirements for sustaining competitive advantage as defined by the *Simply Better* Way.

ORGANIZATION AS HERO   The involvement of people from the business units and staff working together on the components of the *Simply Better* Way starts to give them some ownership and the right to become heroes if the *Simply Better* Way is successful. Further down in the organization the rollout of *Simply Better* continues, reaching more and more people, with tangible results starting to emanate from their efforts, instilling within them the feeling of being heroes of the effort.

CUMULATIVE LEARNING   Management puts what it learned in Japan against its previous mistakes, such as not training the merger teams or involving them in development of the merger integration guidelines, failing to engage managers beyond the EMC in development of the Values and Practices, and not providing a rigorous enough process in planning the implementation of *Simply Better.* The result is a massive effort in education and training, and a systematic development process involving managers from across sectors and functions. In creating a common way of working and core to making the organization the hero, they agreed the education should be company developed and delivered.

STRATEGIC COMMUNICATION   Communication assumes a primary role in introducing the *Simply Better* Way and in gaining involvement. It builds awareness of key concepts behind the training and aligns aspirations through sharing the architecture and creating a common language companywide. It starts to create a two-way system to involve employees first in the improvements, then in sharing best practices and key learnings. Finally, it helps to inspire employees through outlining a recognition program to celebrate the achievements of those who have performed according to the *Simply Better* Way.

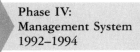

ALIGNMENT OF BEHAVIOR AND STRATEGY   This is an important chapter for illustrating this requisite of hardwiring the soft stuff. The system (architecture) has as one key goal the integration of the Values (soft stuff) with the Strategy (hard stuff). Companywide management processes (i.e., strategic planning, performance appraisal) that are normally used to align business activities need to be linked with behavioral activities. To achieve this link, skills and behaviors that are capable of delivering the strategy need to be developed. Additional management processes, such as common methods, tools, and training, should be designed to build skills throughout the company. To ensure alignment and focus, all the management processes should be standardized. Achieving standardization is always extremely difficult, as each business unit is often struggling to distinguish itself from the rest of the company. Involving businesspeople along with corporate staff to develop the management processes as well as business processes also helped the business units accept a common system and approach, and ensured that *Simply Better* Way would be integrated into the business.

Becoming The *Simply Better* Healthcare Company—A Continuing Journey

I T   W A S   A   S N O W Y   M O N D A Y morning in early January as the EMC members headed into the huge Philadelphia conference complex. Ahead of them were two and a half days to agree on the components of the *Simply Better* Way and the presentation assignments for the next management conference, which would be held in Orlando, Florida in February. Now less than one month away, the conference would be SB's largest yet, with 400 people attending from deep within the organization. It would mark the first time all parts of the Architecture would come together, and be introduced formally as the *Simply Better* Way.

As all the components were being finalized, there was one item that the EMC had not considered at all: what would be the specific objectives for the *Simply Better* Way in 1993?

Earlier that autumn, as they had struggled with developing the methods and tools, Peter could not understand why Bob had become almost fanatical about introducing them into the organization so quickly. Then it dawned on him: Bob was in his final eighteen months at SB. When asked what was the one thing Bob wanted to be certain happened before he left, Bob's response was immediate. It was for *Simply Better* to have its own momentum, for the organization itself to own and nurture it.

When finally pushed to describe what this ideal picture would look like, Bob listed ten expectations that he believed were critical to making the *Simply Better* Way a way of life throughout the organization. Most of them focused on providing the means through which the architecture's two halves—the what and the how—would be implemented. Again he was consistent in that he believed they needed to get the *process* for implementing the *Simply Better* Way right. The organization could then take responsibility for both designing and implementing the recommendations, much as they had the merger integration proposals. Organizing these expectations under four headings, and then defining some specific steps for the coming year, the EMC now saw on the screen before them:

SB Planning	Develop and implement the SB strategic planning process
Management by Process	Instill the practice of management by process in SB managers
People Development	SB managers lead and practice skilled application of the methods and tools
Support Systems	Develop the specific support systems to reinforce the *Simply Better* Way

Under each expectation, the focus was on management and designing the processes that would guide those responsible for eventually involving the entire organization in making the *Simply Better* Way endemic to SB.

EMC members agreed to formalize and broaden the principle that had been guiding their work so far and declared the 1993 improvement theme to be Learning by Doing. The theme captured their own experience: at best, the EMC was one step ahead of everyone else. Everything was new. They would benchmark and study different ideas, and then see if they enhanced or could be adapted into the SB framework. By raising the concept of learning by doing to a corporatewide theme, they had also set up the expectation that it was everyone's responsibility to learn. It became the principle that would underlie the entire training effort.

COMING TOGETHER: THE *SIMPLY BETTER* WAY

By the time the conference participants arrived in Orlando, spirits were high: 1992 had been a very good year. The company was not only making progress, it was actually achieving all the goals it had set. People were feeling good about SB, where it was going, and what part they could play in its success. Participants were also buzzing about what they would hear at the conference.

As the conference began, SB's results were positioned against those of its peer group, showing how SB had gained from the year before. Reviewed were all the 1992 business accomplishments, which included gaining marketing approvals of twelve pharmaceutical products in seventy-eight markets, signing thirty-five agreements across all four sectors to develop new medicines and services, launching several key products (the promising Relafen and Paxil in the United States, Kytril in Europe and Japan, and Havrix in Europe), and the passing of $1 billion in sales of Augmentin. All told Pharmaceuticals' sales grew 15 percent and established a new, more ambitious target: by 1996, at least 29 percent of its sales would come from new products, indications, or dosages.[1] Application for the OTC version of Tagamet had been submitted in the United States, the United Kingdom, and Japan by Consumer Brands. SB was winning, and winning against all the odds that had been set by others at the time of the merger.

"But . . ." One could almost hear the balloon pop and the audience sigh, "Here it comes!"

The audience was reminded that even heroic companies like IBM and GM lost their way from time to time, and that the growing outcry in favor of healthcare reform and predictions of further industry restructuring were presenting the company with new challenges almost daily. SB could not afford to sit still and become complacent with its success. Any pause could mean slippage—and SB would fail to create the culture it really needed to compete successfully. Real winners, after all, want to keep on winning.

Having set the stage for why they needed the *Simply Better* Way, the EMC presented SB's strategic intent and an aspirational picture of what SB could look like in ten years time against each of the Values. With that, the complete definitions of *Simply Better* and the *Simply Better* Way were shared:

❖ *Simply Better* emphasizes all that we are striving to be as a company and individually, as expressed in the Promise and by our Values and Leadership Practices. It is the way we live at SB.

❖ *Simply Better* Way defines the systems and processes by which we organize our work and the methods and tools we use to consistently achieve excellence. It is the way we work at SB.

In the sessions that followed, members of the EMC addressed all the various parts of the architecture, explaining where the company was going, how it planned to get there, and what role they hoped employees would play. The audience heard that not only did the EMC have a plan to take the company forward, but also they were making an enormous commitment in training that would enable employees to participate more fully. Having progressed from where everyone had been informed and (they hoped) inspired about becoming *Simply Better,* SB was now entering a phase wherein every employee would become involved in achieving the *Simply Better* Way through learning by doing. As if to underscore this last point, the teams that had developed the methods and tools presented them to the audience, along with actual examples of what they had learned in developing them.

The aspirational goal for human resources was to make SB "the best place to work for the best people." And the way "best" was being defined was in terms of both business performance and *Simply Better* behavior. As the four quadrants identifying where a manager fell within performance and *Simply Better* appeared on the screen, members of the audience were told that those who fell in the third quadrant—that is, who performed but who did not reflect the *Simply Better* Values—would be given a chance to change but would be asked to leave if that chance failed. This was radically different from a culture where results had been the primary focus since the day of the merger. What managers heard was that it was not results at all cost: *how* things were done to enable the company to sustain excellence for the long term would be as important as *what* was achieved to deliver results in the short term.

They were striving to create leaders, not just managers, winning teams rather than individual stars, and to encourage everyone to confront rather than avoid risk, all within a context that aligned individual aspirations with company goals. They would all be given the same opportunity but, in the end, learning to be *Simply Better* and work according to the *Simply Better* Way was a personal responsibility.

Conference participants were also reminded of their responsibility to communicate often and to be role models; to be consistent in what they said; and more important, to be credible by what they did. The Communication professionals would provide the business and behavioral context for creating strategic alignment, but only management could symbolize the reality of *Simply Better* and all it was meant to be.

The logic of the architecture and its importance as a tool that would align and focus the organization was evident as people departed the convention hall that February afternoon. Their enthusiasm was obvious as snatches of conversation were overheard: "It really could make us number one . . . it's 52,000 people acting as one. . . ." "We have the Values, now we have the methods." "It's doing everything we do better . . ."

It really had been a good meeting; the launch of the *Simply Better* Way was successful. As a communication vehicle, the Orlando conference achieved its ultimate purpose: organizational alignment, evidenced by the "one voice" tone of participants' comments. It was another step forward in promoting a two-way dialogue and making communication a true management process.

As Joanne drove away from the hotel, the self-satisfaction of past and present achievement struggled against the challenge and excitement of a new future. In October she had told Bob and Peter that she would be leaving SB to start the next phase of her career—consulting and teaching. Bob's retirement was imminent, and the design of *Simply Better* and the *Simply Better* Way was now well under way. The spirit of Now We Are One and *Simply Better* was real throughout the organization. She felt that the first steps toward her professional goal—to instill communication as a management process that would help align the organization—had been taken. But, from management's perspective, it was still in the early days of implementing the *Simply Better* Way and they wanted to keep the continuity of her strategic thinking behind marketing it to the organization. SmithKline Beecham became her first client.

Joanne's departure coincided with the start of what would be Bob's final year at SB—a year of transition when gradually but deliberately the handover to Jan and JP would take place, and their team would begin to define SB for the twenty-first century.

DEFINING THE FUTURE

While the 10>3/1 planning process was helping to bridge the identified gap between SB and its competitors in the industry today, there was not one EMC member who believed this was enough; they needed to look much further ahead to really understand where the industry would be tomorrow.

A glimpse of this future was shared while they were at Orlando. George Poste, in illustrating potential strategic initiatives and breakthroughs, presented a compelling picture of the role genetic information could play in healthcare. Through better understanding of which genes were responsible for disease, not only could disease be detected earlier, but the information could help identify people at risk before they ever became ill. Genetic information could also help determine how certain treatments were developed and targeted for greater effectiveness. The audience listened in amazed silence as George explained how gene technology could influence the way diseases were detected, treated, and cured in the future.

But the future he described was now. Following Orlando, the R&D team argued strongly for entering into an agreement with Human Genome Sciences Inc. of Rockville, Maryland, which possessed the largest data base of human-genetic information in the world. As far as George was concerned, this strategic alliance would provide the core capability that would put SB light years ahead of its rivals in new product development, making the hefty $125 million price tag (for 7 percent of the company) well worth it. The collaborative effort to identify the structure and function of genes in human health and disease could lead to pioneer drugs, vaccines, and diagnostic products and services to which SB would have exclusive worldwide rights.

In May 1993, the board finally agreed with George, and SB entered into an agreement with HGS.

Genetics had been identified as one of the clear building blocks for the future, and HGS was a both a deliberate and opportunistic move. But how would it all fit together?

In June 1993, the Vision 2000 team had been created with Jan as its EMC sponsor. With the announcement in April that Jan would succeed Bob as chief executive in one year, the serious changeover began. The two men agreed that Jan should start working with what would be Jan's team to develop the SB of the future, while Bob focused on the day-to-day operations. This was highly unusual for an outgoing chief executive; usually the roles are reversed during the last year of a chief executive's tenure.

This was the organization as the hero and the very heart of all they had been doing since day one. Whatever SB was going to be in the future was going to be driven by Jan and his team; they were the ones who needed to design the vision for the next century and outline the initiatives required to get there.

In another effort to ease the chief executive transition both inside and outside the organization, Jan began to accompany Bob to the sector and corporate staff meetings and went with him when he visited with the press and analysts. By Autumn 1993 the roles had been reversed, with Bob attending in support of Jan. Hardly a beat had been missed.

ACHIEVING THE EXPECTATIONS

Following Orlando, EMC members tackled the tasks set out against the four *Simply Better* Way expectations, assigning teams to address the management processes that would make the architecture operational.

They realized they had to run some activities sequentially (finalizing the methods and tools and training a critical mass of managers and facilitators) and do others in parallel (refining strategic intent and core capabilities at the same time they were writing the 10>3/1 planning guidelines). They needed to integrate the sector plans with all the training efforts and coordinate the many *Simply Better* Way design teams to make certain their efforts were consistent with the long term. They had to administer it all without making it bureaucratic, centralizing some aspects to ensure consistency and decentralizing others to be certain the business units felt ownership—and do it all without adding resources.

The EMC added to managers' worries by requiring that the four expectations be integrated into everyone's objectives (MBO) for 1993. They had deliberately hardwired the expectations into the bonus system to reinforce among managers the importance of the soft stuff in achieving SB's goals. But they had totally underestimated the complexity of getting the systems in place to deliver the training that managers would require to manage by process and lead the process improvement efforts. There was an enormous gap between what the managers needed to achieve the EMC-required goals and what the EMC could provide them in a reasonable time.

The First Expectation: SB Planning

The first of the 1993 expectations was to develop and implement 10> 3/1, which involved both the corporate center and the sectors. Each team was to start by defining for its function or sector an aspirational goal that was consistent with the SB strategic intent, and then identifying some potential core capabilities in terms of corporate and business sector processes. Then the team was to identify the gap between where these processes were and where they had to be, and develop some specific objectives and action plans to close it, including product plans and proposed breakthrough projects.

Where the 10>3 plan was to be done from a corporate and sector perspective, the 3/1 operating plans were to be prepared by each business and operating unit. The guidelines for the 3/1 planning process would be introduced that autumn to replace the old five-year strategic plan and one-year budget review, and the 1994 one-year plans would have to be in place by the end of the planning cycle in November. In the spirit of learning by doing, a cross-sector, cross-functional team was also established to monitor how the design and implementation of the 10>3/1 and 3/1 planning processes went in 1993. This team would integrate what it learned, along with the recommendations it received from the sectors, into the final design of the 10>3/1 strategic planning process, which would be introduced in 1994.

By year's end, while the 3/1 planning process had been received by the sectors with varying degrees of success, most agreed that for a process requiring a totally new mindset to implement, it had gone far better than anyone would have expected the first time around.

The Second Expectation: Instill Management by Process

The second expectation addressed the need to instill the practice of managing by process in SB's managers—that is, getting them to think about work as a sequence of activities performed to meet customer needs. As sector managers, they were applying this thinking to the new planning process, suggesting a number of processes as potential core capabilities and identifying them as either subjects for breakthroughs (major reengineering) or for incremental improvement. By June, close to 900 process improvement projects and over a dozen major breakthrough projects had been identified as part of 10>3/1. During the following months, these processes would be prioritized through the EMC's review of the sectors' 10>3/1 plans for improvement through 1994.

The Third Expectation: People Development

For 1993, the third expectation would focus on helping managers develop the leadership and process improvement skills necessary to lead employees in the *Simply Better* Way. The target was to train about 500 managers in the *Simply Better* Way. To illustrate how it would work in practice, each EMC member and sector manager would lead by example and sponsor at least one significant improvement process that year.

Beginning that spring and throughout the autumn, leadership workshops were held; more than 550 managers from different sectors and functions participated. Intended to make learning as personal as possible, each three-day workshop was a combination of conceptual, tactical, and emotional elements. An EMC member would open the session, sharing his personal journey of the *Simply Better* Way, including all his frustrations, successes, failures and expectations. Through illustrating his practical understanding of its principles, the EMC member showed participants that the EMC had not delegated the *Simply Better* Way; EMC members were actively involved in its design and—more important—its application. Their candidness imparted a feeling of "we're all in this together" and created a sense of us rather than you and me.

In the spirit of learning by doing, toward the conclusion of the workshop participants were asked to select a starter project to which they could immediately apply the principles they had learned. Starter projects were to be some area of their work that needed improvement in order to bring it in line with the overall corporate goals. A project had to have a clearly defined beginning and end, and be doable within a few weeks time. By providing them with a chance to see how the rigorous process outlined in the methods actually worked, and giving them an opportunity for a "quick win," the education and training team was trying to create a pool of disciples that would help to champion the new methods.

These managers identified close to 460 processes as starter projects, ranging from the prelaunch planning activity for developing the core capability of new product development to standardizing billing procedures in the twenty-four laboratories that made up the American clinical network. A number were also leading or participating in the breakthrough project, which now had been identified as part of the sectors' agreed-on 3/1 operating plans.

Following each workshop, participants reflected on what they had heard and discussed and wrote a collective letter to the EMC sharing what they viewed as the potential benefits and barriers to the *Simply Better* Way's success.

Their concern focused most frequently on resources—there just weren't enough people or funds to fulfill the ambitious targets that had been outlined at Orlando. Participants were also concerned about the apparent conflict between long-term *Simply Better* Way objectives and the immediate business goals—failing to see how *Simply Better* Way could fit within the financial targets set and the cost constraints they were experiencing. Remembering how *Simply Better* had gone deeper into some sectors than others, they were also concerned with how they could ensure a common level of readiness for implementing process improvement under the *Simply Better* Way across all the sectors.

It was a constant trade-off between time and ownership. While the *Simply Better* Way training might have gone faster if SB had used more people from outside, it would not have been done with the same degree of commitment and enthusiasm that came from SB people designing and delivering the materials and the course. For the *Simply Better* Way to be seen as intrinsic to, not separate from, the day-to day running of the business, it had to be done by people the organization knew were working alongside them—not off in a different department or firm somewhere.

Still, by year's end, almost 1,000 managers and 600 process improvement teams were involved in developing SB's future. As set out in the expectation, some of those teams were working under the direct sponsorship of a sector head or EMC member. They were finally on their way.

The Fourth Expectation: Design the Support Systems

The fourth expectation covered all those areas that would reinforce the *Simply Better* Way implementation:

- ❖ Develop corporate and sector master plans to integrate and align all activities.
- ❖ Have a managed education delivery process in place with 750 trainers and facilitators trained.
- ❖ Design and implement a measurement and feedback process for evaluating *Simply Better* Way implementation.
- ❖ Plan and implement a companywide communication plan to involve employees in *Simply Better* Way.
- ❖ Design new human resource systems such as performance and job evaluations, succession planning, and reward systems.

In many ways this was about corporate's role at the center, about defining the management processes that would be critical to holding the entire architecture together.

Of all the support systems, the one furthest along was the educational delivery system. During the last half of 1993 the five-book set of *Simply Better* Way methods and tools would be completed and printed in six languages, and training of the fifty-plus coach/trainers would begin.

During their time as a corporate resource, these coach/trainers would train more than 700 frontline facilitators worldwide, who would in turn eventually train all those employees assigned to improve the processes identified as priorities through the 10>3/1 planning process.

By far, the most difficult of these to progress were measurement and communication, and much of the reason was confusion and lack of consensus among the EMC over the role of each in the *Simply Better* Way.

The EMC knew that without a good measurement system, the likelihood of achieving any of the ambitious goals was remote. Well-defined measures would guarantee the organization's attention and direct its efforts on the right things.

They were still tussling with defining measures by Value and designing a measurement process to evaluate their progress against them when they realized that they also needed a system to monitor the effectiveness of the *Simply Better* Way. They looked to outside measurement systems such as those used for industry in Europe and the United States and agreed to adapt for SB the all-encompassing criteria that was part of the U.S. Commerce Department's Malcolm Baldrige Quality Award. Many of the standards used in the Baldrige assessment to evaluate a company's capacity for excellence were exactly those reflected in the Values and concepts underlying the *Simply Better* Way. The criteria were intended to help each unit identify where it was strong and what areas needed significant improvement, all consistent with the *Simply Better* Way.

What finally emerged from the team's work was SMARTT—an acronym for self-measurement and assessment review tool for teams. SMARTT was designed to help SB managers evaluate their overall area or function using world-class business practices as the criteria. These best practices were grouped into seven areas, including generic ones such as leadership, information, and analysis, as well as those specific to SB such as 10>3/1 planning and managing the *Simply Better* Way. The seven areas were to be measured on the basis of how they were approached: Were the *Simply Better* Way methods and tools used? How deeply and consistently had they been applied? Did they achieve the targeted results? All three approaches were fundamental to working the *Simply Better* Way.

As managers assessed their performance against these standards of world-class companies and those in their industry, they would see where their efforts differed and could be improved. While it evaluated results, SMARTT was a deliberate attempt to focus on measurement's role as a learning vehicle.

Turning to another support system, strategic communication had been one of the key support elements for *Simply Better* and the *Simply Better* Way, but it was still peripheral to the actual management of the *Simply Better* Way. Some EMC members, however, were beginning to view communication as a mainstream management process that would facilitate organizational alignment and focus and enable the architecture to work.

For the *Simply Better* Way to be effective, employees had to understand the architecture and be encouraged to share ideas, key learnings, and best practice. SB needed a reliable, two-way process that allowed for discussion and feedback between managers and employees as well as between employees of different functions and sectors.

The objective for *Simply Better* Way communications was to develop a companywide program that would involve employees in the *Simply Better* Way first by promoting consistent understanding and appreciation of its principles, and then by maintaining their enthusiasm and motivation. As a first step, the cross-sector communication team was given its own stretch goal: by 1995 all 52,000 employees had to be aware of the *Simply Better* Way, its importance to the company, and their role in achieving it. Furthermore, because communication was the most visible element of the *Simply Better* Way, it had to reflect all the principles: be customer-oriented, credible, timely, and simple in content and process.

The real objectives were alignment and a systematic dialogue between managers and employees that would keep everyone focused on SB's strategically driven goals. Communication as a reliable management process could provide the glue that intellectually held everyone together.

But creating that process was a very tall order for people who had been accustomed to viewing communication more as media than as a strategically driven management process. As time went on, however, members of the cross-sector team found a way of reconciling these views. Rather than seeing themselves as responsible for communicating, they began to focus more on supporting management as the prime communicators. (Communication was, after all, a Leadership Practice and part of every managers' annual performance appraisal.) Since evidence had always shown that direct supervisors were employees' preferred source of information, helping managers communicate better and more frequently face-to-face became a team priority. To ensure alignment, they developed the company's first truly integrated internal communications plan. Built around the premise of creating one corporatewide voice, but allowing for local accents, the cross-sector team debated and agreed on the core messages, processes, and media centrally, but then advocated and supported that all of these be delivered locally through management. Employees would then see how the *Simply Better* Way and their local business performance were inextricably linked. As important, they would see where their efforts fit within the big picture of SB. The effort created a global framework to which each sector could add the specifics that made the content and actions meaningful at the local level.

Finally, a team was established to develop more completely the institution of a corporatewide recognition program that would celebrate those who epitomized *Simply Better* at its best, creating a standard for role models and best practice that would cross all four sectors. Recognition came to the forefront of the EMC's agenda, and JP was later assigned as this team's sponsor. Its efforts led eventually to establishment of the *Simply the Best* Awards, a program that worked within each sector and culminated at an annual corporatewide recognition event. The name itself was inspirational: it came from a popular song that had been specifically rewritten for SB and had become the company's emotional and spirited expression of constantly striving for excellence.

Finally, the support systems that would actually reinforce the change in behavior that *Simply Better* Way required, the ones who would answer the simple but powerful employee question "What's in it for me?" were those relating to human resources. Employees would need to be rewarded and compensated for their efforts to further the ideas of the *Simply Better* Way, and trained and developed for the long term consistent with its principles. By year's end, proposals had been made for (1) strategic compensation/job evaluation/leadership development programs that would use the five Values as basic criteria to identify and develop *Simply Better* leaders within the company, and (2) a recruitment program to actively seek new employees who reflected behavior consistent with the kind of company SB was trying to become.

Still to be done, however, was making the *Simply Better* Way operational on a day-to-day basis.

CREATING THE DAILY INVOLVEMENT SYSTEM

Because they had approached continuous improvement as part of an entire management system, EMC members had been focusing at the top of the architecture, defining the goals and capabilities and working primarily with people at the top and middle of the organization. They had done very little with the bottom part of the architecture and employees' daily work other than to introduce a large number of employees to P-D-C-A and the concept of process improvement. But teaching people how to improve their work did not necessarily guarantee they would actively participate in achieving company strategy. SB was still a long way from genuinely involving every employee as the EMC had seen in Japan, yet it was this level of involvement the EMC was seeking. Once again it turned to benchmarking as a way to learn more.

In October 1993 the EMC visited Milliken Corporation, a South Carolina textile company that employed 14,000. Milliken had been involved with continuous improvement for over a decade and was a recent recipient of the U.S. Malcolm Baldrige Award for Quality.

Where SB had started with defining the systems at the top of the organization, Milliken had focused on the lower levels and day-to-day work. The result was a finely tuned daily management system that included day-to-day and week-to-week targets and measures as well as some systematic cross-functional management techniques, an area in which SB had barely touched the surface.

From Milliken, the EMC learned that it was on the right track with the *Simply Better* Way. All the components of the Milliken Daily Management System were consistent with SB's Leadership Practices and with the process improvement concepts underlying the methods and tools.

Where SB differed most, however, was in its lack of a Milliken-type system of working day to day that had measures, and of programs that celebrated and recognized employees' achievement of their targets. In another important step in Jan's transition to CEO, Jan would sponsor the development of an SB-equivalent of Milliken's Daily Management System.

Starting in June, Jan had begun to take on more and more of the key elements of the *Simply Better* Way management system. He was working at the top of the architecture with Vision 2000, the 10>3 and the 3/1 planning teams. He, not Bob, was setting the goals for 1994, since he would be the one accountable for the year's results. Now he was taking on development of the architecture's last piece, the one that would touch the lives of every single employee through their day-to-day work. Jan's commitment was obvious; it was he who suggested that the system be designated the Daily Involvement System (DIS) to signify his strong belief in the role of every employee.

As 1993 came to a close, there were some shifts in the management team. Fergus Balfour retired as general counsel and was replaced by James Beery, who came from outside SB. Dan Phelan, who came from within SB Pharmaceuticals, was designated to be the new head of human resources, replacing Peter, who would be stepping down at the same time as Bob. A new head of corporate affairs, James Hill, who had led SB Pharmaceuticals' strategic marketing department, was also named. Ignace Goethals was named president of SmithKline Beecham Animal Health. Ignace joined SB in 1990 as head of business development for SB Pharmaceuticals and later was given the additional responsibility for biologicals. The change from the old to the new teams was nearing completion.

COMING TOGETHER

By January 1994 many of the specific elements needed to implement the *Simply Better* Way were in place for what would be Bob's last management conference. As he and Jan developed the final agenda, they considered the questions that had been submitted by participants in advance of the meeting. Some were all too familiar, such as how to manage the day-to-day work and the long-term vision, how to balance work and personal life, what were the various outlooks and plans for the sectors, and how could they reach every employee with the *Simply Better* Way. But then sprinkled throughout the list were a number of questions with a whole different slant:

❖ Are we moving toward an integrated management structure?
❖ How do we achieve cross-sector operating efficiencies?
❖ How can we form one single, integrated company in each market, reducing duplication of effort?
❖ How can we maximize cross-sector synergies while minimizing the loss of specific competencies?

The questions reflected a level of understanding about SB's direction that was everything the EMC could have wanted. At the time of the merger, the idea of shared services was just not possible. Here it was, five years later, and the organization itself was asking for it. The questions clearly said the managers understood the Promise, and were committed to doing whatever it would take to achieve it.

The 400 participants started arriving in Philadelphia by mid-afternoon on Sunday, February 6. The atmosphere was charged with emotion from the beginning, as people recognized this would be Bob and Henry's farewell. Despite the preannounced transition and months of planning the changeover, nothing had prepared the senior team for the amount of feeling that filled the room.

As Bob recapped the journey on which SB had embarked in 1989, he noted the milestones: from the "merger of equals" and Now We Are One, through *Simply Better* and the *Simply Better* Way. He showed step by step how together they had built every one of the critical components that had made the new SmithKline Beecham, starting with *strategy* that drove the merger, to the organizational *structure* that integrated the two businesses, to the development of a unique SB *culture*, and finally the creation of an entire *management system* that would make change and continuous improvement a permanent part of the way they ran SB, achieving the ultimate goal of a sustainable competitive advantage.

Using the five Values as his framework, he went on to show the progress that had already been achieved against each one. The list was impressive and included such statistics as the U.S. pharmaceuticals sales force ranking first in the nation, achieving 15 percent sales from new products introduced within the last five years, and tripling shareholder value.

Then Jan climbed onto the stage and accepted the microphone offered by Bob. The transition that had begun a year before was complete. The audience witnessed a passage that was smooth; these were two men who liked and respected each other. The omens were good.

Jan was taking over in an industry that was growing tougher almost by the hour, bombarded daily with increasing government intervention and more intense competitive responses. He immediately brought the audience to the future and signified the start of a new era for SB, introducing the phrase that would now capture the Promise: everyone at SB, he told them, should always be "striving to make lives better." Then he presented the work of the Vision 2000 team. The integrated healthcare model, presented under the heading "SB: Beyond 2000" (see figure 10-1), reconfigured parts of the existing four sectors and added some new busi-

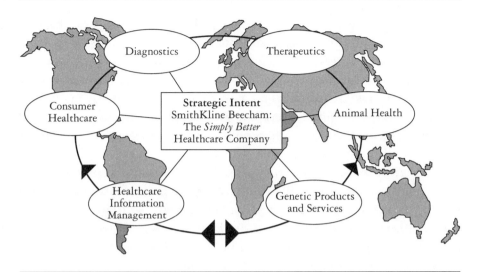

Figure 10-1   "SB: Beyond 2000" Integrated Healthcare Model

nesses that would provide the core capabilities critical to achieving SB's strategic intent: to become The *Simply Better* Healthcare Company. With its focus clearly on human healthcare, it became obvious that the Animal Health business sat uncomfortably within this model and that its future in the SB portfolio needed to be reexamined.

It was as if SB was in the middle of an open book. One chapter was ending on the left-hand page, and the reader was already looking to the right and the start of the next chapter. There was no break in the rhythm. Everything and everyone was looking forward.

As the day progressed, conference participants were introduced to the proposed Value-driven measures of strategic intent and the Daily Involvement System (DIS), including SB Ideas and The *Simply the Best* Awards as part of the suggestion and recognition elements. Several of the first teams to win the awards shared their accomplishments with the audience that afternoon, emphasizing their key learnings. It proved to be very powerful as the audience related first to the teams' frustrations, then experienced their learnings (vicariously) against their own background and experience with process improvement. The audience's respect for the teams' accomplishments was genuine.

That evening, following the presentation of the awards to the winners, Bob and Henry presented a special award. It was to Peter, in recognition of the unique role he had played and the support he had given to both. In his remarks, Henry cited the sense of fairness that Peter always exhibited on issues affecting people, especially during those early days of the merger when trust was so fragile. Bob acknowledged Peter's role as both counselor and colleague—someone who was totally integrated into the strategic business issues, but who also was never afraid to challenge the chief executive or others on the implications arising from their business policy decisions.

The next morning, the four *Simply Better* Way expectations for 1994 were presented along with the financial targets for the company. As the meeting neared its end, Henry, who had not actually addressed this group since Eastbourne four years earlier, and Bob were asked to say the closing remarks. As Henry shared what he saw as the vision for healthcare over the next decade, he urged them to take a lead in helping to shape its destiny. "SB is a *great* company," he emphasized, adding that it was capable of strongly influencing the industry's future.

When Bob's turn came, he shared some of his feelings about what the experience at SB had meant to him and how proud they should all be of the company's accomplishments. "SB will go on to achieve great things," he told them, "of that I am certain. I feel privileged to have a played a role in making that possible."

In the end, with its enthusiastic participants, targeted accomplishments, and unabashed emotional pride in SB, the 1994 conference epitomized everything *Simply Better* was meant to be.

THE TRANSITION IS COMPLETE

In the three months following the management conference, the transition became complete as Bob stayed in the background and Jan assumed the center stage.

On April 26, 1994, at the Barbican Centre in the City of London, Bob and Henry ran their last annual meeting. This final official act as the heads of SmithKline Beecham was somewhat anti-climactic after the high of the management conference, but the response of the shareholders was genuinely appreciative. The two men had, after all, delivered on all their merger promises: for each of the last five years, SmithKline Beecham had performed better than either Beecham or SmithKline had been projected in 1989 to perform alone.

At their final shareholders meeting, Henry and Bob announced pretax profits of £1.3/$1.9 billion on sales of over £6/$9.3 billion. In the five years since the merger SmithKline Beecham had met or exceeded all of its business and financial targets, achieving 11 percent compound annual sales growth and 13 percent compound annual growth in both pre-tax profit and earnings per share. New products launched since the merger accounted for nearly 15 percent of 1993 total sales and that percentage was confidently expected to grow. SB's gross margin had increased by nearly six points to 67 percent, and trading profit per employee had nearly doubled. Sales and marketing investment had shown 11 percent compound annual growth since the merger, and R&D 12 percent growth, reaching £575/$862 million in 1993.[2]

In the course of that shareholders meeting, Sir Peter Walters assumed the chairmanship of SmithKline Beecham, Jan Leschly the chief executive role, and JP Garnier the chairmanship of Pharmaceuticals. Figure 10-2 depicts their new management team. Of the nonexecutive (outside) board members, only Sir Robert Clark and Sir Peter Walters remained from the Beecham Board. (As of 1996, Hugh Collum was the last remaining executive board member from Beecham.)

The board, through its direct involvement in the leadership selection process and understanding of the strategy and *Simply Better* culture, would ensure SB's continuity; it had contributed significantly to the successful management transition now unfolding.

One of the original objectives for Beecham, and later for SmithKline Beecham, was to be the "best managed company in the industry." As Bob was leaving, not only had SB undergone the smoothest management transitions seen in recent times, but the company also had managed to keep a top team composed of some of the best talent in the industry intact. The "aggressive management team"[3] was an impressive collection of bright, successful, experienced people, more international and global in their outlook than either Bob or Henry would have dreamed possible in 1989.

CHANGE AS A LEGACY

As the attendees milled about following the meeting, the board and EMC members dispersed to different meetings, except for Bob. For the first time in years, there was nothing pressing that day he had to get to. He

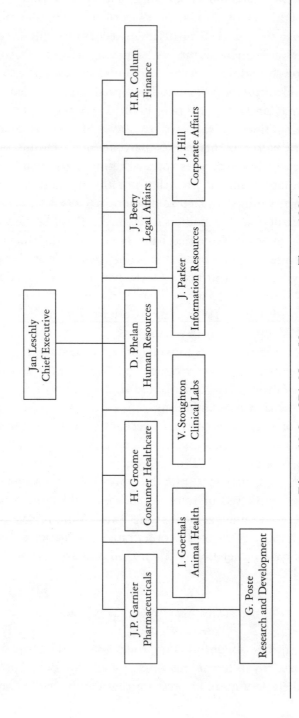

Figure 10-2 SB's New Management Team, 1994

gathered his papers and left the meeting center, walking alone through the long, empty corridor.

For SB it was once again business as usual—but now *much more* according to the *Simply Better* Way. There was still more to learn and more work to be done before 50,000 people would really be working as one. But now it would be up to the new management team to move the *Simply Better* Way forward and SB on to even greater heights.

For Bob, the journey that had begun in London at Beecham House a little more than seven years earlier had ended.

SB's journey to become **The** *Simply Better* Healthcare Company would continue: a constant search to reach a destination that could never be reached. With each milestone met, each goal achieved, a new and higher one would be set. But that was the way it was intended to be.

That was the ever-striving spirit of the *Simply Better* Way.

WINNING ATTITUDE   Defining strategic intent as becoming **The** *Simply Better* Healthcare Company established once and for all what SB meant by winning in the long-run; it was a goalpost that would keep moving. In using measures that were set against each of the five Values, SB created a clear picture of what winning actually looked like in terms the organization could understand. More important, they were measures the organization could influence and use to judge its progress toward becoming the best. The company knows what winning looks like and how it will keep score. It also has some very tangible evidence of business success, including outside recognition. It is beginning to feel like a truly winning organization and, like any winner, wants to keep on winning, going from strength to strength.

ORGANIZATION AS HERO   The management conference gave managers an opportunity to see what had been accomplished over the five years since the merger. In addition to the overall company's achievements, the success ran throughout the company, and was well down into the individual units. In seeing that success, the managers now realized that they and their teams were the real heroes of the company's achievement, not the senior management. A justifiable pride was beginning to develop.

CUMULATIVE LEARNING   This was an important period for management's continued learning. Milliken was important to the EMC's cumulative knowledge on how to involve everyone in the organization in change, while the leadership forums were a major step forward in involving and training a significant number of managers to lead the *Simply Better* Way. Everything they did at this time tried to include and encourage more learning, all in the spirit of continuously improving. When it came to evaluating how well they had implemented the *Simply Better* Way, the SMARTT self-measurement was developed as a tool for the organization to judge its progress and take corrective action.

STRATEGIC COMMUNICATION   In developing the plan for communicating the *Simply Better* Way more focus was spent on integrating communication into the fundamental work of both the *Simply Better* Way and the business planning. Key messages were identified and aligned with the training effort and 10>3/1 planning, and some effort was made to create a reliable, management-led two-way communicatino process. The corporate team also involved more of the units in planning the communication strategy. Having people from the sectors work alongside those in the corporate function ensured one voice and greater consistency in delivering the messages corporatewide. At the same time, there was more responsibility and accountability taken for implmenting of those messages through local management and media.

ALIGNMENT OF BEHAVIOR AND STRATEGY By using the Values as measures to assess SB's progress on being the *Simply Better* Healthcare Company, SB was essentially hardwiring the soft stuff. Requiring that all core business and management processes be developed against each Value provided a single direction for both the sectors and the corporate center. The management processes provided the standardization that assured "one company" and the glue that held the architecture together. The businesses were responsible for the processes that would achieve competitive advantage within their respective industries. Through measuring the Values, every effort companywide was aligned with SB's strategic intent and with achieving SB's ultimate purpose, its Promise.

CHAPTER ELEVEN

Last Thoughts

W<small>E WOULD LIKE TO REFLECT</small> back on the story of SB and our own experiences both before and since, and try to identify what we think were the key learnings that transformed Beecham Group, a large British consumer goods company with strong pharmaceutical interests, into SmithKline Beecham, one of the world's top integrated healthcare companies.

SEVEN FUNDAMENTAL LEARNINGS

Having defined and illustrated in Chapter 1 the Five Requisites we believe essential to a culture dedicated to continuous self-renewal, we would now like to focus on the learnings we consider fundamental to the actual implementation of change.

❖ Change requires a holistic approach.
❖ Change must be planned.
❖ Change requires dedicated leadership.
❖ Change requires the development of internal competencies.
❖ Change takes time, perseverance, and hard work.
❖ Change requires balancing complexity.
❖ Change is an iterative process.

Each of these fundamentals deserves a few words.

Change Requires a Holistic Approach   The most important learning we offer those about to embark on this journey is that right from the start the organization must be viewed as an entire management system—that means as a network of interconnecting, mutually reinforcing management and business processes, rather than a collection of separate corporate and business activities.

Rather than consider factions such as strategic planning or human resources as separate and discrete management areas, it is important to see them as part of a much bigger picture, so that in the end every process reinforces every other process and every work initiative adds value in support of the company's strategic goals.

Given this holistic perspective, management must first analyze the organization's current business and industry environment and revisit its purpose, assessing whether there is a need for change in the business strategy and the organizational behavior required to deliver it.

Unless the case for change is clear, can be made convincingly, and its objectives agreed on by the senior team, an effort of this magnitude is doomed to fail as the work accumulates and the months (sometimes even years!) pass before any substantial benefits are realized.

In SB's effort, the Burke-Litwin model helped our thinking at the beginning to determine what levers had to be addressed in the change effort, and the *Simply Better* Way architecture became the visualization of how strategy and behavior could be integrated into the way the company was managed.

Change Must Be Planned   In most cases of change initiatives that fail, what was missing was a comprehensive plan for how to implement the desired changes. Just as business planning helps an organization to achieve its business strategies, there must be a road map for implementing organizational change. Management needs to start with where it wants to go and determine what is the best route to get there from both a business and a behavioral perspective. Once all these factors are determined, their development must be mapped out in a way that phases them into the organization. For example, in looking back over our experience we found the actions fell into four distinct phases: strategy/structure/culture/management system. At each point developing one or more of the Requisites was dominant, until the last phase, when they were all equally integral to creating the management system.

Recognizing that there are distinct phases can help the organization sustain momentum over the period of time required to ensure lasting change. Time estimates to pace the efforts and signposts to say when they have arrived need to be provided all along the way. The plan should focus on the steps required to develop the principles and process for change, especially how to involve people. Getting the principles right ensures strategic and cultural alignment: getting the process right guarantees organizational ownership.

This need to plan cannot be emphasized enough. Our natural tendency is to want to *do;* we are primarily action-oriented. But that is another reason why many initiatives fail. In our anxiety for action we move too quickly, without thinking through all the ramifications of what we are about to do. We usually stumble on the next step as we find some actions are inconsistent at best, or contradictory at worst, when we try to integrate them into the overall way we manage. We create enormous frustration and delays as we find ourselves having to rework much of what we have done before. We often end up losing more time than we would have lost if we had taken the time to plan properly right from the start.

Change Requires Dedicated Leadership　Management needs to agree on the reason for change, set objectives at the outset, and be absolutely committed to their achievement. It is this commitment that will carry you through when time gets tough. Content with defining the ideas, even adapting them to their own organizations, most senior managers walk away at that point, feeling that implementation is the responsibility of others—or worse, assuming it will just happen if they write about it in the company newsletter. But change cannot be delegated. Senior management must devote itself wholeheartedly to implementing these important concepts at every level and into the very depths of the organization. Managers must recognize their responsibility as champions of change and actual symbols of the culture they are trying to create. Change must start with and be consistently modeled by them.

Furthermore, effective transformation needs a critical mass of leaders who are directly involved right from the start. The chief executive must know which senior team members are skeptical about the need for change and which ones can become real champions, and not limit himself or herself to the current core management group. Because change takes time, it will most likely be the next generation of management that will implement the change and live with its consequences. Representatives of that group should become involved as quickly as possible, as should those ultimately responsible for the company, members of the Board. In seeking these leaders of change, look for these characteristics:

❖ Predisposed and open to change and to learning
❖ Strategic thinkers
❖ Have an organizational rather than a divisional viewpoint
❖ Respected by the organization

Building groups of individuals into teams is hard work and perhaps hardest at the most senior levels. Senior managers' loyalties are usually to the area they run, not to the operation as a whole. To shift their allegiance, it is important that they work through something together that is meaningful and important for the whole organization, perhaps defining the purpose or a new strategy. As time passes and the work around change and the business grows more difficult, the behavior of leaders around the new values may become an issue. There must be enough mutual respect and resiliency of spirit within the team to withstand these tough times.

In the end, where members of the top team do not meet the criteria and cannot make the shift, it is important to address the differences sooner rather than later. It is a balance between maintaining stability and sustaining momentum for change. Bringing in new people with fresh insights means the company can focus all its energy on changing rather than managing personal differences.

Change Requires Development of Internal Competencies   While strategy is the domain of the few, culture is the responsibility of many. Success requires the involvement of everyone, all working in the same direction. To create this alignment requires more than a common purpose: it requires a common language and a common way of working.

Involving the organization is a sound principle. It allows an organization to accomplish a lot in a short period of time and to use the knowledge of those closest to the work to improve what must be done. It also creates enthusiasm and motivation as managers are given an opportunity to truly contribute to the company's success. But frustration can result from assuming a level of competence that does not exist. For the organization to become the hero, both managers and employees need to be equipped with the skills that will enable them to achieve the company's goals.

This is another critical juncture in implementing the change effort and one we realized almost too late. For example, if the strategy requires greater cooperation between businesses and functions and more of a process orientation, do managers know how to manage by process? Do employees know how to think about their work as a series of steps that run across rather than down the company? If employees are being asked to work in teams and be more customer focused, do they know how?

If these skills are not apparent in the company, the next step must be to identify, develop, and then introduce them, and ideally do all three through the company's own workforce so that it is developing a competency that contributes to its own cumulative learning. This may require a significant investment in developing carefully directed communication and training programs.

Communication needs to be seen as an enabling process for change rather than an afterthought, and a responsibility of management rather than the communication department. To gain commitment to the change effort, a reliable, systematic two-way process to engage others in what the company is trying to achieve needs to be part of the implementation plan right from the start. Rather than big one-off events, communication is thought of as building a consistent open dialogue between managers and employees, a dialogue that encourages listening, reflection, and thoughtful debate, building credibility and trust. Managers are kept informed and help influence the information they are expected to share, and employees know their ideas are heard and acted upon. Messages are kept simple, focused, and always placed in the same context, creating one voice, one language, and one frame of mind, helping employees understand how everything fits together. The importance of symbolism and visibility, recognized and seized upon, is used extensively to reinforce key concepts. Tools such as newsletters and videotapes are developed to support the process, not to replace it. As a required management competency, communication is hardwired into the leadership training, performance appraisal, and employee survey systems.

Communication and education and training work hand in hand. Education and training must be totally focused around the core skills that are needed to create a common way of working companywide. Through similar standards and consistency in how work is approached, these working disciplines (or methods and tools) will reinforce teamwork and enable cross-functional exchanges. This training must then be organized and delivered systematically rather than randomly. Ideally it is conducted alongside the actual work to be done rather than in a classroom. Employees learn by doing and see the learning as relevant as they generate results directly using their newly acquired skills. They are encouraged to add to, not replace or eliminate, knowledge they have gained from their own experience.

While the pace at which individual parts of the company learn may vary, *what* they learn—the content—is the same companywide. The organization is moving en masse.

Finally, senior management must pilot and model the new skills so that learning is perceived as something done *by* and *with* versus done *to* everyone in the organization. Senior managers see themselves as educators and coaches. Learning actually occurs by *everyone* doing, thereby accelerating movement along the entire organization's experience curve.

Change Takes Time, Perseverance, and Hard Work   Most companies that have been successful at transformation have devoted more than ten years to the task and have been led by senior management willing to commit an enormous amount of its own time to the initiative. These are leaders who recognize that to change an organization's collective behavior requires focus and determination for a sustained period. (Today, where employees have been more preconditioned to expect change, this timescale may be already shrinking.)

Along the way there will be high points and low points; times when you feel you're winning, and other times that are fraught with frustration, confusion, and doubt. As implementing change becomes more complex, few companies are prepared to stay the course, especially if they are unable to maintain their business momentum at the same time. It is far easier to revert back to old behavior than to continue to define a new way of working when worried about next month's financial results. This is when the leadership must be not just persevering, but relentless in its pursuit of the longer-term vision. Consistency and continuity are key.

Change Requires Balancing Complexity   Actually implementing the plan to change is done against a backdrop of enormous complexity. The managers who initiate this major effort are those who are seeking to be the best—it means that they are also driven by the need to maintain business momentum. They end up trying to manage through a maze of paradoxes and dilemmas that are difficult in normal times but seem impossible when undertaking an initiative of this magnitude. These dilemmas—real and apparent, organizational and personal, strategic and tactical—can create ambiguous environments almost to the point of chaos.

Organizational dilemmas such as how to balance short-term performance and long-term investment, which activities should be centralized or decentralized, and what should be done in-house or outsourced constantly confound management. In planning how to approach the change effort, should the method be one that has been taken off the shelf, reinvented, or tailor made?

Personal dilemmas also multiply during periods of change. The questions of how to balance home life versus work and how much risk to take versus when to play it safe; the pressure to do what is right versus what is easy; the constant, consistent dilemma as to whether one is moving too fast or too slow—these things come to dominate everyone's daily conversation. Most critical of all: how to manage positive stress versus negative stress. The adrenaline that fuels energy and impetus in some parts of an organization can literally be counterbalanced by personal, physical, and emotional costs that are just too much to pay in other parts.

But by acknowledging that these contradicting views exist, and by allowing them to be legitimately aired and not immediately judged, you can make them opportunities to learn. Their resolution through respectful debate can be highly symbolic of management's attitude towards creating a risk-free environment. When managed openly, these paradoxes can help to build the trust that is fundamental to any transformation effort.

Change Is An Iterative Process   We believe that the truly successful companies never stop changing but repeat the cycle again and again. They have found a way to systematize change and make it integral to their business strategy.

This brings us back to where we began this book, and seems an appropriate place to end.

IN CLOSING

Our belief has been, and remains, that truly sustainable success depends on the competitive advantage a company creates through its own unique combination of business strategy and employee behavior.

Beginning with Beecham's strategy to become an integrated health-care company, the merger provided an opportunity to totally redefine what were two second-tier healthcare companies into an industry leader. To deliver the Promise of the new company to customers, shareholders, and employees required a different culture from either of the previous companies. The company needed to have a single mindset—SB—and one set of behaviors—*Simply Better*—that transcended business sectors or national perspectives to actually become SmithKline Beecham. Finally, for SB to truly realize its newly defined strategic intent required making continuous change an integral part of managing the company and the *Simply Better* Way a way of working companywide. (For a summary, see table 11-1).

In trying to accomplish this complex task, we learned that there is no magic formula. So, while we offer our learnings as a guidepost for those about to embark on their own journey, we would still argue with anyone who professes that there is one best way of transforming an organization into one that can sustain success over the long term.

We do believe, however, that there is one best way for *each* organization to create its own sense of purpose and pride and transform its potential into the performance of a world class winner.

Through sharing our experiences, we hope we have helped others to find their own best way.

Table 11–1. Five Requisites as Illustrated through the SmithKline Beecham Transformation

Five Requisites	Phase I: Strategy 1988–1989	Phase II: Structure (Integration) 1990–1991	Phase III: Culture (Behavior) 1991–1993	Phase IV: Management System 1993–1994
WINNING ATTITUDE	Greater than either alone	Leader in its peer group	Leading healthcare company	The *Simply Better* healthcare company
ORGANIZATION AS HERO	Basement planning team	Integration teams	Sector-led implementation teams	Design teams, SB methods and tools
CUMULATIVE LEARNING	Study of best practice mergers	Burke-Litwin model	Japan mission study	Milliken visit
STRATEGIC COMMUNICATION	New and Better Healthcare Company	Now We Are One	*Simply Better*	*Simply Better* Way
ALIGNMENT OF BEHAVIOR AND STRATEGY	Strategy of leadership	SB-wide support systems (e.g., IT)	Five Values/nine Leadership Practices in HR systems	The *Simply Better* Way architecture designed and introduced

Epilogue

During his first twelve months as chief executive, Jan Leschly and his team continued to progress SB's strategic intent to become The *Simply Better* Healthcare Company. They implemented many of the strategic initiatives identified as part of SB: Beyond 2000, which was intended to combine a unique set of technical competencies and core capabilities into an integrated healthcare company.

The company they had envisioned would set the pace in an industry that they now knew would be fundamentally different. Every country was becoming increasingly concerned with rising healthcare costs, with the changes in the world's largest market for healthcare products and services, the United States, the most dramatic. Payers sought ways to limit increasing costs, and began to demand that healthcare companies provide better product support and services. It was no longer enough to convince physicians and patients of a product's therapeutic benefit and safety; it was now as important to convince those who paid the patient's healthcare bills of its value. A new discipline—pharmacoeconomics—had been growing rapidly as healthcare companies learned to articulate their products' effectiveness in terms of overall benefits, including less need for surgery and hospitalization. Increasingly, patients were being pressed to take greater responsibility for their own well being and treatment, with growing implications for self-medication and over-the-counter medicines. Every person touched by the healthcare system—from doctors to patients to pharmacies to payers—was involved, while each link in the healthcare chain—from developing the product to delivering it to the patient—was being affected.

SB's Promise had long before defined "healthcare—prevention, diagnosis, treatment and cure" as SB's purpose (see exhibit E-1). As the members of the new management team reassessed that definition against the changing marketplace, they began to shape SB: Beyond 2000 and make the transition of the company's focus from "selling pills" to "developing healthcare solutions." Integral to delivering this strategy was the concept of "disease management"—a means of linking SB's pharmaceutical products and diagnostics services that would cross present sector boundaries.

SB's management recognized that it was no longer enough to introduce "me-too" products: the costs were too high and the returns too questionable. Its research efforts would have to be more targeted, more innovative. SB scientists began to do more in genome science and work more closely with HGS to identify specific human genes and pinpoint their role in disease. Through understanding a gene's structure, they would be able to focus their research on compounds that could inhibit or destroy the gene's disease-creating potential. The genetic data would be transmitted by computer from HGS to SB research laboratories, where it would provide critical clues on how to combat many diseases such as cancer and osteoporosis for which treatment remains inadequate. SB's goal: use the data to produce pioneer products and reduce their develop-

---

Exhibit E-I. The Promise of SmithKline Beecham

At SmithKline Beecham healthcare—prevention, diagnosis, treatment and cure—is our purpose. Through scientific excellence and commercial expertise we provide products and services throughout the world that promote health and well-being.

The source of our competitive advantage is the energy and ideas of our people. Our strength lies in what we value: CUSTOMER, INNOVATION, INTEGRITY, PEOPLE, PERFORMANCE.

At SmithKline Beecham, we are people with purpose, working together to make the lives of people everywhere better, striving in everything we do to become The *Simply Better* healthcare company, as judged by all those we serve: customers, shareholders, employees and the global community.

ment time to under five and one-half years (versus ten to twelve years at the time of the merger).

SB would also focus more on managing a product's complete life cycle, from its development in the laboratory through its transition to an over-the-counter medicine after its patent expiration a decade or more later, and become more adept at making prescription to OTC switches. Recognizing that not all core capabilities had to be inside the company, SB also intended to continue to be "the partner of choice" to literally hundreds of external scientific communities working on new disease mechanisms.

To realize SB: Beyond 2000, Jan and the new management team made a number of significant changes to SB's portfolio of businesses in 1994. The first major move came in May when SB acquired Diversified Pharmaceutical Services (DPS), one of the largest and fastest-growing U.S. pharmaceuticals benefits managers, and entered into a strategic alliance with DPS's former parent, United Healthcare, to gain exclusive access to data from the six million patients covered by its health mainte- nance organization (HMO). The information would give SB a deeper understanding of the longer-term effectiveness of medications and medical treatment as well as provide greater insight into more innovative ways to treat and possibly prevent illnesses. Together with the information being generated through SB's alliance with HGS, SB now had access to clinical patient data that would help it better target its development of prescription medicines as well as assess the true cost of healthcare.

At the same time, OTC medicines received increasing attention as a cost-effective alternative to prescription-only medicines, and SB sought to add to its global presence and portfolio of products. In October 1994 it achieved both by acquiring Sterling Winthrop—a company that had been on Beecham's original list of "doable" acquisitions in 1988. With the Sterling acquisition, SB Consumer HealthCare became the world's third largest OTC drug company (and the leader in all major markets outside the United States and Japan). The acquisition enhanced SB's ability to switch prescription drugs like Tagamet to over-the-counter status and thus extend their product life cycle. It also added new products in countries where SB had previously lacked infrastructure or critical mass. For example, Sterling's primary product category, analgesics (pain relievers) added product offerings where SB had none, including Panadol, the world's most widely available nonaspirin analgesic. Sterling's market penetration was far greater in emerging international markets such as South America, Eastern Europe and Africa, where SB had little, if any, presence. It was a combination that was as complementary in products and geographic scope as the one which had occurred between the pharmaceuticals businesses of Beecham and SmithKline five years earlier.

While Sterling was an acquisition, not a merger, the principles that guided its coming together with SB were similar to those that guided the SKB/Beecham merger five years earlier: whatever was best for the combined company would drive the decisions. The integration process followed a familiar pattern: a team of seven members, known as the integration management committee (IMC), was established to coordinate the consolidation of Sterling and SB Consumer Healthcare and to establish the longer-term strategies that would make the newly combined SB Consumer Healthcare the best in each market. An IMC support team was also nominated to assist in the areas of communications, human resources, and finance.

The standard of "the best"—so ingrained in SB at this point—prevailed as the IMC evoked the same principle of fairness and equality of opportunity that had governed the management selection process during the merger. The end result: a mixture of SB and Sterling people at the helm of the new sector.

In the merger of SmithKline Beckman and Beecham, the consumer business had been less affected because SmithKline Beckman had not had a large consumer products business. With the integration of Sterling, it now meant that every part of the old Beecham had been transformed.

The integration process, however, went beyond restructuring Sterling into SB. SB's top management team used the Sterling integration as an opportunity to reassess many of its staff functions at both the sector and corporate level. The prospect of sharing services between sectors located in the same geographic markets—an idea that had been considered but deemed too controversial and complicated at the time of the merger—was now thoroughly reviewed. Country by country, market by market, the information resources, human resources, purchasing, and finance functions of Consumer Healthcare and Pharmaceuticals were merged. The corporate center, with offices in both the United Kingdom and United States, came under similar scrutiny as efforts focused on streamlining management and administrative processes to achieve greater effectiveness and efficiency. By year's end, both redesign efforts not only promised improved service quality, but also forecast savings of close to £50/$80 million by 1996.

Finally, to ensure delivery of the highest-quality, lowest-cost products and services, SB's immense manufacturing and supply operations were brought together under the designation Worldwide Supply Operations. The move would allow SB to better coordinate across all sectors the process of turning raw materials into finished products and distributing them globally.

Perhaps the greatest achievement of Jan and his team, however, was the company's ability to overcome the dreaded effects of Tagamet's patent expiration in the United States (which accounted for two-thirds of Tagamet sales). The sword of Damocles that had threatened SmithKline Beckman before the merger and SB thereafter, and had been a source of constant concern for the financial markets, dropped as predicted on May 17, 1994. Having consistently exceeded the FTSE 100 Index since 1993, that day SB's share price tumbled as the financial markets expressed their concern over the patent expiration as well as healthcare reform.

But while 1994 sales of Tagamet did drop significantly (28 percent, to £484 million), it was still a far less dramatic fall than had been predicted by many market analysts.[1] By 1995 Tagamet would account for less than 7 percent of SB Pharmaceuticals' sales, compared to nearly 30 percent at the time of the merger.[2] The hard work and consistent drive to develop new products and move them into the marketplace more quickly had enabled SB to introduce an impressive number of successful new products throughout 1994 and 1995. Combined sales of these new medicines, including Seroxat/Paxil (an antidepressant) and Relafen/Relifex (antiarthritic treatment), were rising rapidly and by the end of 1995 would account for more than 29 percent of Pharmaceuticals' £4.2/$6.6 billion sales—well in excess of the 15 percent target that had been set in 1989, and the 25 percent stretch goal set in 1992.

Outside recognition of the company's achievements began to build, reinforcing the sense of winning. SmithKline Beecham was named 1994 Company of the Year by both *PharmaBusiness,* an international marketing magazine, and *Medical Advertising News,* a widely read U.S. publication. The criteria used by the latter to judge the fifty companies included sustained revenue growth, solid research and development investment, a healthy product pipeline and strong prospects for currently marketed products, the company's image with investors, a strong international presence, and aggressive, cost-conscious management.[3] In December 1994 SmithKline Beecham was ranked fourth out of 260 quoted U.K. companies as "most admired by other firms."[4] Its products and people were also singled out: the company was awarded the 1994 European Prix Galien for Havrix, the world's first hepatitis-A vaccine, while the U.S. Pharmaceuticals sales force was rated number one in a survey of U.S. physicians by Scott-Levin for the third straight year.[5] (In 1995 the Canadian and U.K. sales forces would receive similar accolades from physicians in those countries.)

By early 1995 SB's share price had rebounded to again match the FT-SE 100 Index, as the market finally accepted what SB had been saying all along: new product sales would more than offset the drop in Tagamet sales. Another merger promise had been successfully delivered.

THE EMPLOYEE VIEW

In 1994 the second SB employee survey was conducted. As well as evaluating progress against the Values and Leadership Practices as had been done in the 1991 management survey, the 1994 survey included the core concepts behind the methods and goals of working in the *Simply Better* Way. This survey's scope was broader: where the first survey reflected the views of 3,650 managers, the 1994 survey incorporated those of 13,600 managers and employees from around the world.

The results showed that SB was making significant progress in accomplishing what it had set out to do: create a culture dedicated to continuous improvement through a motivated and accountable workforce. According to the survey responses, management had become better at rewarding employees, using people's skills and abilities more effectively and creating a customer-driven company. Like the first survey, its highest-ranked items showed that employees liked their jobs and felt that SB was a good place to work. They believed SB to be performance and customer driven and to have high integrity.

One significant difference marked a major step forward: since the first survey, employees had become more aligned with SB's overall goals, acknowledging that they now understood how their work contributed to meeting external customer requirements and where they fit in achieving

SB's strategic goals and objectives. The communication efforts, it appeared, had at last made some tangible headway.

All was not perfect: the survey also highlighted some worrisome areas. In a company striving for innovation, employees still believed that taking risks was not rewarded and that people were not likely to be open about failures. Bureaucracy and waste reduction were also still seen as problems.

But there was another important difference between this and the first survey: where the first survey had provided few guidelines on how to use the data it generated, this survey provided managers with a systematic plan for sharing the data with employees, and specific recommendations on how managers could engage employees in dialogue that would involve them in solving the issues it raised. This time the survey would be used to get behind the results; it would be integral to progressing the *Simply Better* Way rather than simply reporting on its progress.

SMITHKLINE BEECHAM: STRIVING TO MAKE PEOPLE'S LIVES BETTER

During 1995, Jan and his team focused their efforts on integrating all the initiatives of the previous year—no small task considering the number of people involved, the global scale of the acquisitions, and the scope and complexity of the internal re-design projects. But where the challenge at the time of the merger had been to become "new and better," the goal now was much higher. To become **The** *Simply Better* Healthcare Company meant a single-minded focus on ensuring that all the Values were reflected in the integrated structure. The new team emphasized becoming more customer driven, creating pioneer rather than me-too products and services, and better aligning its cost structure with the competitive environment.

By the end of the year, the company's enormous efforts had not gone unrecognized. As one example, in *Business Week* magazine's annual review of the twenty-five top managers of the year, the commentary for 1995 noted:

Why SmithKline Feels So Good

Jan Leschly . . . spent 1995 digesting $5 billion in acquisitions of managed-care and consumer-medicine markets, then turned

his attention to . . . managing the transition of ulcer drug Tagamet, once the world's largest-selling drug, to over-the-counter:
SB's sales could hit $10 billion in '95.[6]

For the year ended December 31, 1995, SB's trading profits had
increased 7 percent over 1994, to £1.4/$2.2 billion on sales that had
grown 16 percent, to over £7.0/$11.1 billion. The company employed
more than 52,000 people worldwide—the target number it had set at
the time of the merger in 1989. Geographically, its businesses were spread
over 100 countries, with 34 percent in Europe, 48 percent in the United
States, and 18 percent in the rest of the world.[7] It was growing its global
presence, exemplified by its effort in China, where SB was now that
country's second largest foreign pharmaceutical company, and its initiation
of a pioneering community healthcare partnership in Eastern Europe. Its
total investment in research & development had increased to £653 million/
$1.03 billion, which was double what it had been at the time of the
merger and nearly eight times what Beecham Group's had been ten years
earlier.

In commenting on SB's future, the Lex columnist in the *Financial
Times* wrote: "SmithKline Beecham's combination of strong sales growth,
aggressive management, and a full drugs pipeline looks hard to beat at
the moment."[8]

Among the new product filings made in 1995 were Kredex/Coreg
for congestive heart failure, Hycamtin for ovarian cancer, and Requip
Ropinirole for Parkinson's disease, plus a number of others in all the
major markets. Over the next three years the company announced that
it expected to make filings for fifty new pharmaceutical products around
the world.

Adding to its efforts to create truly innovative products, SB had
become a clear leader in DNA research and had aggressively pursued
becoming the industry's "partner of choice." In the past three years it
had signed more than 130 collaborative agreements to provide it with
global access to the latest technology and development ideas.

The switches from prescription medicines to OTC status had also
accelerated: in addition to the successful launch of Tagamet HB (for
heartburn) in the United States and the United Kingdom in 1995, soon
to follow were Nicoderm and Nicorette (smoking cessation aids) from
the Sterling acquisition. Offering further OTC potential were Bactroban

(antibiotic ointment for wounds), Vectavir (for cold sores), and Relifex/ Relafen (for inflammation).

In January 1996 the company took further steps toward implementing its Beyond 2000 healthcare strategy and realizing its Promise of "striving to make people's lives better." With the 1995 sale of the Animal Health business to Pfizer, a U.S.-based pharmaceuticals firm, all SB's businesses were now focused on human healthcare. The three remaining successful but separate business sectors—Pharmaceuticals, Consumer Healthcare and Clinical Laboratories—could now be redefined, creating a structure that would be better able to deliver the innovative, cost-effective products and services that could come from being a truly integrated healthcare company. Healthcare Services was introduced as a new sector, bringing together under one management SB Clinical Laboratories, the Diversified Pharmaceuticals business, the recently acquired Diversified Prescription Delivery (SB's pharmaceutical mail-order business) as well as SB's new business group, Disease Management. The businesses would report directly to Dr. Tadataka (Tachi) Yamada, a respected leader in academic medicine in the United States who had been a nonexecutive board member of SB since February 1994. Dr. Yamada was chairman of the Department of Internal Medicine at the University of Michigan Medical Center and president-elect of the American Gastroenterological Association. He brought both academic and management achievement to his new role, and was highly regarded in both medical and business communities. Tachi would be reporting to JP Garnier, who had been named president and chief operating officer of SB in early 1996. With all these changes, every circle in the chart that Jan had introduced two years earlier under the banner "Beyond 2000" had been addressed, and the integrated healthcare strategy was clearly evident. (see figure E-1.)

During the summer of 1996, SB's share price reached a high of 757 and, for a while, its shares were trading at a higher multiple than its industry competitor, Glaxo. SB's market capitalization stood at £19/$30 billion, compared to £3.5/$5.6 billion for Beecham and £7/$12 billion for the combined company at the time of the merger (see table E-1). In commenting on SB's performance for the first six months of 1996, the Lex columnist for the *Financial Times* wrote: "Yesterday's half year results from SmithKline Beecham put it on par with the best U.S. drug groups. Driven by newer products . . . SB's Pharmaceuticals division is increasing sales and profits at a very healthy 15 percent. SmithKline's premium to

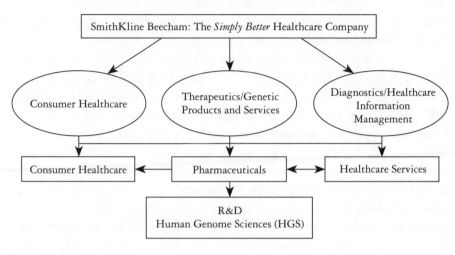

Business Description:

Product Categories:	Therapeutic Categories:	Service Categories:
Analgesics	Anti-infectives	SB Clinical Laboratories
Respiratory Tract	Vaccines	Diversified Pharmaceuticals
Gastrointestinal	Gastrointestinal	Diversified Prescription
Vitamins and Tonics	Cardiopulmonary	Delivery
Oral Care	Neurosciences	Disease Management
Dermatological	Inflammation and Tissue	Business Strategy
Nutritional	Repair	
	Allergy/Cough/Cold	

Employees:	13,000	26,000	13,000

Major Strategic Alliances	Major Strategic Alliances	Major Strategic Alliances

Figure E-1   SB: Beyond 2000, 1996

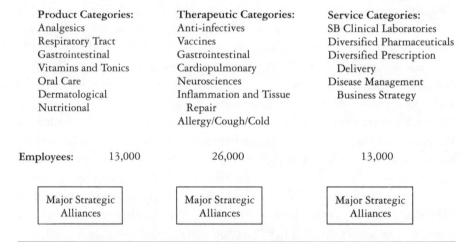

Table E-1. SmithKline Beecham—Then and Now		
	1989	*1995*
Sales	£4.3/$6.9 billion	£7.0/$11 billion
Profits before taxes	£724 million/$1.7 billion	£1.4/$2.2 billion
Market Capitalization	£7/$12 billion	£19/$30 billion
Employees	67,300	52,400

Glaxo Wellcome, a company which is growing much more slowly, has almost disappeared. . . . Given compound earnings growth of 12–15 percent over the next five years, the shares look cheap."[9] By that August, SB's share price reached 765.

Market sentiment appeared to finally (at least for the time being) favor SB over its old rival.

MOVING ON

Between 1994 and 1996, the pharmaceutical/healthcare industry responded to the changing environment by continuing to consolidate and redefine itself. Some firms—Glaxo, for example—decided to remain pure pharmaceutical companies and focused on building their research and development capability. They increased R&D budgets and sought partners that would give them added scale. Rhone-Poulenc Roher bought the U.K.-based pharmaceutical company Fisons, while Glaxo acquired Wellcome. Others, like SB, considered more seriously the integrated healthcare strategy and made stronger alliances with OTC companies, or sought outright acquisitions. Merck had already linked up with Johnson & Johnson and, in 1993, acquired Medco.

The trend toward friendly mergers accelerated, with Pharmacia & Upjohn consummating a "merger of equals" in late 1995. In early 1996 Sandoz and Ciba-Geigy announced a merger to create Novartis. If approved by the European Commission, Novartis, with prescription medicines revenues of close to $11 billion, would rank third in sales (behind Merck and Glaxo Wellcome) and second to Merck in terms of market share, with 4.4 percent of the now $150 billion global market for pharmaceuticals.[10] With a combined market capitalization of £53/$80 billion, it would be one of the world's biggest corporate deals ever.[11]

As the industry consolidation continued and competitors grew larger in terms of global sales, SB found its rank in the world league tables slipping. But SB knew that size alone was not enough to achieve true competitive advantage.

In 1989 SB had been the first in the industry to recognize that rising healthcare costs would become an issue, and greater scale would be required to achieve efficiencies in R&D and marketing. But, as JP reminded present managers at a conference in February 1996, SB had also pioneered the concept of blending its different healthcare components into a truly integrated healthcare company.

SB knew what hard work it was to make two plus two equal five. The business they were in also meant there were no shortcuts. It was not enough to sell pills; now they had to deliver healthcare solutions that met the needs of both the patient and the healthcare payer. But even as the environment for winning was getting tougher, SB's targets in terms of its own performance were growing bolder. To realize its Promise—striving to make people's lives better—SB's journey would have to take it to new and even greater heights.

And so the journey continues. . . .

The Chronology of the
SmithKline Beecham Transformation

1986

September	Robert P. Bauman becomes executive chairman of Beecham.
December	Booz•Allen hired; strategy study begins. Concept of integrated healthcare (Rx and OTC medicines) begins to emerge.

1987

January	Hugh Collum joins Beecham as new finance director.
July	Peter Jackson joins as new personnel director.
December	Beecham agrees to pursue potential partners for a merger of equals focusing on the United States.

1988

January	Visits begins with potential U.S. pharmaceutical candidate companies.
April	Joanne Lawrence joins as head of Beecham's communications.
June	Discussions initiated between Robert P. Bauman and Henry Wendt, CEO of SmithKline Beckman (SKB).
November	Joint task force creates first business plan; each company calls in external legal and financial advisers.
November 4	SmithKline Beckman and Beecham enter confidentiality agreement.
December	Rumors begin; discussions terminate as SKB share price rises.

1989

January	Discussions reconvene by telephone between Henry Wendt and Robert P. Bauman.
April 1	Approvals from both companies' boards to go ahead with merger of equals.
April 2	Beecham and SmithKline jointly announce they are in discussions.
April 12	Merger announcement detailing shareholder terms; U.K. and U.S. "close" periods begin.
April 17	First meeting of Merger Management Committee (MMC).

May 24	Merger documents sent to Beecham shareholders. Preliminary proxy materials sent to U.S. shareholders.
June 20	Beecham shareholders approve merger.

Phase II: Structure (Integration) 1989–1990

July 26	SmithKline Beckman shareholders approve merger. Merger effective, 4:26 p.m. (U.K. shares start trading).
July 27	"Now We Are One" and new visual identity welcome employees to new company around the world.
July 29	Merger integration charters approved for eight planning teams; initial project task forces created.
September	Integration work plans approved for development.
October	First Management Conference, Grosvenor House; "Strategy for Leadership" outlined; global compensation plan to reinforce SB as one company introduced to top 80 managers.
December 31	Majority of integration recommendations completed; most top jobs posted; first phase completed.

1990

January	Major implementation of integration recommendations begins.
February	Global employee road show begins; 80 sites eventually visited.
March 7	Burke-Litwin model selected as template for culture change effort.
March 14	SB's first year-end results (for 1989) announced, including £500/$803 million restructuring provision.
April 4/5	Company's first R&D Pipeline Presentations in London and New York.

Phase III: Culture (Behavior) 1990–1991

May	Company's first annual general meetings held in London and Philadelphia.
June 7	Jan Leschly announced as chairman of SB Pharmaceuticals.
July	Cosmetics business sold for half of original expectation. Debt and interest payments finally start to decline.
July 17	EMC begins Value and Leadership Practices discussions.
August	EMC agrees on final five Values, nine Leadership Practices; agree EMC will pilot everything related to culture change effort.

	Jean-Pierre Garnier agrees to join SB as head of U.S. Pharmaceuticals.
September	SB Pharmaceuticals begins rebuilding senior team under Jan Leschly.
November	Introduction of *Simply Better* to top 150 at Eastbourne conference.
	Agree to introduce Performance Appraisal against Leadership Practices for attendees in 1991.

1991

June	First employee survey conducted (5,000 random); *Simply Better* begins losing momentum.
August	EMC starts Japan mission study; agrees to dedicate a minimum of one day a month to workshops on *Simply Better.*
October	EMC defines "Leading Healthcare Company" as goal and quantifies it by shareholder value; establishes £3/$5.6 billion gap.
November	George Poste succeeds Keith Mansford as Chairman of R&D.
December	Henry Wendt becomes more of a nonexecutive chairman.
	SB passed £1 billion in pre-tax profits.

Phase IV: Management System 1992–1994

1992

January	EMC learns in Japan from direct observation; reaches consensus on moving *Simply Better* together as *one* company. Agrees on need for a massive training effort.
February	Concept of *Simply Better* Way introduced to top 250 at senior management conference in Rome; 35,000 employees now involved in *Simply Better.*
May	*Simply Better* Way architecture as management system agreed by EMC.
	Harry Groome named chairman of Consumer Brands.
September	Board selects Jan Leschly as next Chief Executive, Sir Peter Walters as next nonexecutive chairman.
October	EMC pilots Process Improvement Methodology on budget process before rolling out to employees.

1993

January	EMC agrees on *Simply Better* Way Expectations for 1993, requiring them as one of management's MBOs.
February	The *Simply Better* Way launched in Orlando, Florida, to 400 managers.
March	*Simply Better* Way Leadership workshops to introduce methods and tools; training of 650 in-house trainers begins.
May	EMC workshop to define Strategic Intent/Core Capabilities. SB enters agreement with Human Genome Sciences (HGS).
June	Methods and tools books go into publication in six languages; Vision 2000 team established under Jan Leschly; 10>3/1 planning process introduced.
October	EMC visits Milliken to learn its Daily Management System is part of its effort to implement bottom half of architecture.

1994

January	Training tied to actual processes begins.
February	Last pieces of *Simply Better* Way fall into place; Daily Involvement System introduced, including SB Ideas, "Simply the Best" awards program, and SMARTT measurement system.
April	Robert P. Bauman and Henry Wendt retire. Sir Peter Walter becomes Chairman and Jan Leschly CEO. JP Garnier becomes head of Pharmaceuticals. Company announces results. "Now We Are Five" review reveals all merger promises fulfilled and some surpassed.

Notes

INTRODUCTION

1. Smith Newcourt, *Broker Report on SmithKline Beecham plc,* September 18, 1989.
2. Lex Comment, *Financial Times,* February 24, 1995.
3. Comment at portfolio managers meeting, Scotland, April 1989.
4. James C. Collins and Jerry I. Porras, *Built to Last: Successful Habits of Visionary Companies* (London: Century-Random House, 1994): p. 9.

CHAPTER 1

1. Gary Hamel and C. K. Prahalad, "Strategic Intent," *Harvard Business Review* (May–June 1989): p. 67.

CHAPTER 2

1. Morgan Stanley, *U.S. Investment Research,* January 12, 1993.
2. Booz•Allen & Hamilton, *Corporate Strategy Study,* December 1986, p. 18.
3. Ibid.
4. Philippe Haspeslagh and Dana Hyde, "The Making of the *Simply Better* Healthcare Company: SmithKline Beecham (A)" (Fountainebleau, France: INSEAD, 1994): p. 3.
5. Ibid., p.11.
6. Ibid., p. 3.
7. Ibid., p. 2.
8. Booz•Allen & Hamilton, *Corporate Strategy Study,* December 1986, p. 9.
9. Beecham, *Annual Report,* 1986–1987, p. 39.
10. Booz•Allen & Hamilton, *Corporate Strategy Study,* December 1986, p. 9.
11. Kleinwort Benson, *Corporate Finance Report,* 1996.
12. Beecham, *Annual Report,* 1986–1987, p. 28.

13. Ibid., p. 61.

14. Ibid., p. 5.

15. Booz•Allen & Hamilton, *Current Pharmaceutical Strategy Assessment*, November 1987.

16. Beecham, *Annual Report*, 1986–1987, p. 25.

17. Booz•Allen & Hamilton, *Current Pharmaceutical Strategy Assessment*, November 1987.

18. Ibid., p. 44.

19. Ibid., p. 45, and Booz•Allen & Hamilton, Corporate Strategy Options review session, December 17, 1987.

CHAPTER 3

1. Booz•Allen & Hamilton, Corporate Strategy Options review session, December 17, 1987.

2. John Francis Marion, *The Fine Old House: SmithKline Corporation's First 150 Years* (USA: SmithKline Corporation, 1980).

3. Robert Teitelman, "Oh, Henry!" *Financial World*, March 7, 1989, p. 30.

4. Kleinwort Benson, *Corporate Finance Report*, 1996.

5. SmithKline Beckman, *Annual Report*, 1988, p. 39.

6. Ibid., p. 22.

7. Ibid., p. 39.

8. Beecham, *Annual Report*, 1987–1988, p. 2.

9. Booz•Allen & Hamilton, *Corporate Portfolio Study*, October 14, 1987.

10. Excerpt from Beecham Executive Management Committee meeting minutes, August 15, 1988.

11. SmithKline Beecham, Listing Particulars from merger documents, 1989, p. 9.

12. Kleinwort Benson, *Corporate Finance Report*, 1996.

13. Marion Ullman, "A Source Tells of SmithKline Merger Talks," *Philadelphia Inquirer*, March 29, 1989.

CHAPTER 4

1. Excerpt from Beecham and SmithKline Beckman joint press release, April 2, 1989.

2. Analyst comments, *Financial Times*, April 4, 1989.

3. Excerpt from the Merger Management Committee minutes, April 17, 1989.

4. Quotes from the original draft of the Promise written in 1989. It was condensed into its present version in 1993 to make it more memorable for employees.

5. These are excerpts from the Management Merger Committee guidelines, May 4, 1989.

6. From interviews conducted as part of Philippe Haspeslagh and Dana Hyde, "The Making of the *Simply Better* Healthcare Company: SmithKline Beecham (A)" (Fountainebleau, France: INSEAD, 1994).

CHAPTER 5

1. From interviews conducted as part of Philippe Haspeslagh and Dana Hyde, "The Making of the *Simply Better* Healthcare Company: SmithKline Beecham (A)" (Fountainebleau, France: INSEAD, 1994).
2. Philippe Haspeslagh and Dana Hyde, "The Making of the *Simply Better* Healthcare Company: SmithKline Beecham (A)" (Fountainebleau: INSEAD, 1994): p. 16.
3. Ibid.
4. Ibid.
5. Karl L. Habermas, "SmithKline Beecham," *Berstein Research Notes* (New York: Sanford C. Berstein & Co., September 28, 1989).
6. Kent Blair, "SmithKline Beecham plc (SBE)," *DLJ Securities* (New York: DLJ Securities, October 23, 1989).

CHAPTER 6

1. SmithKline Beecham, *Annual Report*, 1989, p. 7.
2. Interview with Jan Leschly from *Special News* (SmithKline Beecham news insert, Summer 1990).
3. SmithKline Beecham, *Annual Report and Accounts*, 1990, p. 10.

CHAPTER 7

1. *Simply Better* is a registered trademark of SmithKline Beecham.
2. Philippe Haspeslagh and Dana Hyde, "The Making of the *Simply Better* Healthcare Company: SmithKline Beecham (A)" (Fountainebleau, France: INSEAD, 1994): p. 22.
3. SmithKline Beecham, *Annual Review and Summary*, 1991, p. 9.

CHAPTER 8

1. SmithKline Beecham, *Annual Review and Summary*, 1991, p. 18.
2. Ibid., p. 23.
3. Ibid., p. ii, 6..

CHAPTER 9

1. "Success Everywhere," *Communiqué* (SmithKline Beecham employee magazine, Winter 1992): p. 14–15.

CHAPTER 10

1. SmithKline Beecham, *Annual Review and Summary*, 1992, p. 7.
2. SmithKline Beecham, *Annual Review and Summary*, 1993, p. 1, 5; and 1993 results presentation to shareholders.
3. The Lex Column, *Financial Times*, February 21, 1996, p. 18.

EPILOGUE

1. SmithKline Beecham, *Annual Report and Accounts*, 1995, p. 9.
2. SmithKline Beecham, Listing Particulars in merger documents, 1989, p. 26, 27, and 42; and "Bear Sterns Equity Research," *Pharmaceutical Industry*, August 26, 1991, p. 98.
3. "Company of the Year," *Pharma Business*, January–February, 1995, p. 123–129.
4. "Britain's Most Admired Companies," *Management Today*, December 1994, p. 41.
5. SmithKline Beecham, *Annual Report and Accounts*, 1994, p. 17, 20.
6. "The 25 Top Managers of the Year," *Business Week*, January 8, 1996, p. 30.
7. SmithKline Beecham, *Annual Report and Accounts*, 1995, p. 2.
8. The Lex Column, *Financial Times*, February 6, 1996, p. 18.
9. The Lex Column, *Financial Times*, July 24, 1996.
10. "Novartis is Full of Promise—and Dangers," *Wall Street Journal* (Europe), March 8–9, 1996, p. 6.
11. "Triumph of an Innocent," *Financial Times*, March 9–10, 1996, p. 11.

Index

About the Authors

ROBERT P. BAUMAN is the nonexecutive chairman of British Aerospace. He was the CEO of SmithKline Beecham for five years. His earlier positions include executive chairman of Beecham Group, president of the International Division of General Foods, chairman and chief executive of Avco Corporation, and vice chairman of Textron. In recognition of his leadership ability, the Robert P. Bauman Chair in Strategic Leadership was established by SmithKline Beecham at the London Business School in 1994. Bauman is a board member of Morgan Stanley Group Inc., Union Pacific, Russell Reynolds, CIGNA, and Reuter Holdings. On a personal note, he wrote *Plants as Pets,* reflecting a lifelong hobby of raising orchids. An American citizen, Bauman lives in both the United Kingdom and the United States.

PETER JACKSON is the managing director of PJ Corporate Consultants (International) Ltd. He was head of human resources initially at Beecham and then SmithKline Beecham during the "merger of equals." Prior to that he was the human resources director at the British Oxygen Company Ltd and was closely involved in the acquisition of Airco Inc., one of the largest transatlantic deals of the late 1970s and early 1980s. Jackson is researching and consulting on world-class organizational performance issues, concentrating on strategic HR policies that have proven to make a difference. A citizen of the

United Kingdom, Jackson splits his time between the United Kingdom and the United States.

JOANNE T. LAWRENCE is the managing director of JT Lawrence & Company, an international consultancy that specializes in project managing and communicating change. She was the vice president of strategic coordination of SmithKline Beecham's *Simply Better* program and was vice president and director of communications and investor relations first at Beecham, then SmithKline Beecham. Previously, she worked for IBM and Avco. Lawrence has twenty-five years of experience in developing communication as a strategic management process, specializing in the support of major strategic initiatives, such as mergers and acquisitions, restructurings, and process reengineering. Lawrence frequently speaks on how to support strategic and cultural change and is a regular guest lecturer at INSEAD. An American citizen, Lawrence has homes in London and Massachusetts and divides her time between Europe and the United States.